Christian Grube

Measuring the Immeasurable

GABLER EDITION WISSENSCHAFT

Christian Grube

Measuring the Immeasurable

Valuing Patent Protection of Knowledge-Based Competitive Advantages

GABLER EDITION WISSENSCHAFT

Bibliographic information published by the Deutsche Nationalbibliothek
The Deutsche Nationalbibliothek lists this publication in the Deutsche Nationalbibliografie; detailed bibliographic data are available in the Internet at http://dnb.d-nb.de.

Dissertation Jacobs University Bremen, 2008

1st Edition 2009

Editorial Office: Frauke Schindler / Anita Wilke

Gabler is part of the specialist publishing group Springer Science+Business Media.
www.gabler.de

Cover design: Regine Zimmer, Dipl.-Designerin, Frankfurt/Main
Printed on acid-free paper
Printed in Germany

ISBN 978-3-8349-1305-0

Acknowledgements

I would like to express my deep and sincere gratitude to my supervisor and the chair of my dissertation committee, Professor Dr. Andreas Bausch, for his support, constructive comments, and excellent advice over the last three years. Furthermore, I am indebted to the members of my dissertation committee, Professor Dr. Adalbert FX Wilhelm and Professor Dr. Hans Georg Gemünden, for their valuable hints and for the time and effort they have spent on reviewing this thesis.

My research was possible thanks to Siemens AG, Munich and Berlin. I owe special gratitude to Professor Dr. Winfried Büttner, Head CT I, and Klaus Kohlmann, Head CT IP MAC, for the opportunity to work as a freelancer for the patent department in Munich over the last three years. In addition, Mr Kohlmann deserves particular credit for his elaborate explanations of the legal nature of intellectual property rights under national and international patent law. My work greatly benefited from his valuable advice and friendly help. I am grateful to Peter Berg, Head CT L&T, and my colleagues in the licensing department for introducing me to the basic principles and strategies of technology licensing.

My especial thanks are due to my colleagues at Jacobs University, Justus-Liebig-University Gießen and Friedrich-Schiller-University Jena for their comments in many fruitful discussions. In particular, I thank Thomas Fritz for his suggestions and cooperation during the last three years.

My most heartfelt acknowledgment must go to my family. I thank my sister, Dr. (iur.) Friederike Grube, for enriching the legal background of my research with economic answers to complex legal questions and my parents, Dr. (phil.) Jochen Grube and Birgit Grube, for support and encouragement – not only during this PhD project. Finally, I owe more than thanks to Jana Schwartz for being such a wonderful partner and a constant source of inspiration over the last few years.

Christian Grube

Brief contents

Contents

List of Tables

List of Figures

List of Abbreviations

Abs	Absatz (paragraph)
AIPA	American Inventors Protection Act
Al	Average life
ANBERD	Analytical Business Enterprise Research and Development database
ARIPO	African Regional Intellectual Property Organization
ArbnErfG	Gesetz über Arbeitnehmererfindungen (Employees' Invention Act)
BCE	Before the common era
BFH	Bundesfinanzhof (Federal Fiscal Court)
BGBl	Bundesgesetzblatt (Federal Law Gazette)
BilMoG	Bilanzrechtsmodernisierungsgesetz (German Accounting Law Modernisation Act)
BPatG	Bundespatentgericht (Federal Patent Court)
CF	Cash-flow
CFR	Code of Federal Regulations
COGS	Cost of goods sold
CPC	Community Patent Convention
DCF	Discounted cash-flow
DM	Deutsche Mark (Deutschmark)
DPatG	Deutsches Patentgesetz (German Patent Law)
DRS	Deutscher Rechnungslegungs Standard (German Accounting Standard)
DRSC	Deutsches Rechnungslegungs Standards Committee e.V. (Accounting Standards Committee of Germany)
e.g.	exempli gratia, for example
EAPO	Eurasian Patent Office
EBIAT	Earnings before interest, after taxes
EBIT	Earnings before interest
ECLA	European Classification System
EC	European Community
EEC	European Economy Community
EPC	Convention on the Grant of European Patents (European Patent Convention)
EPO	European Patent Office
FASB	Financial Accounting Standards Board

ff.	and the following
FCF	Free-cash-flow
FMV	Fair market value
FV	Fair value
GBP	British pound
HGB	Handelsgesetzbuch (Commercial Code)
i.e.	id est, in essence
IAS	International Accounting Standard(s)
IASB	International Accounting Standards Board
IP	Intellectual property
IPC	International Patent Classification
IPRs	Intellectual property rights
IT	Information technology
INT	international
JTB	Justified true belief
Mio.	Million
MNC	Multinational corporation
MPEP	Manual of Patent Examining Procedure
MV	Market value
n. F.	neue Fassung (new version)
No.	Number
OAIP	Organisation Africaine de la Propriété Intellectuelle (African Intellectual Property Organization)
OECD	Organization for Economic Cooperation and Development
PCT	Patent Cooperation Treaty
PPP	Purchasing power parity
PSPM	Product-Sales-Profit Matrix
PTPM	Patent-Technology-Product Matrix
RUL	Remaining useful life
RDIP	R&D intensity using production
S.	Satz (sentence)
sec.	Section
SFAC	Statement(s) of Financial Accounting Concepts
SFAS	Statement(s) of Financial Accounting Standards

SPSS	Statistical Package for the Social Sciences
SPV	Special-purpose vehicle
TAB	Tax amortization benefits
U.K.	United Kingdom
U.S.	United States
U.S.C	U.S. code
USD	U.S. dollar
USPC	U.S. Patent Classification System
USPTO	U.S. Patent and Trademark Office
VRIN	Valuable, rare, imperfectly imitable, non-substitutable
vs.	versus
wacc	Weighted average cost of capital
WIPO	World Intellectual Property Organization

Introduction

An investment in knowledge pays the best interest.
Benjamin Franklin (1706–1790)

The knowledge economy

Benjamin Franklin, scientist, publisher, founder, and first president of the American Philosophical Society is not only well known for his role as a founding father of the United States of America. He also invented products and technologies that are still used today, for example, bifocals and the lightning rod. In a world in which knowledge creation, application, and protection are essential drivers for a firm's success, his 250-year-old words of wisdom are still relevant and have not become any less important.

Today, it is widely recognized that knowledge is one source for obtaining a leading competitive position. Strategic management research tells us that such a leading market position – or even a monopoly – is a basic prerequisite for creating attractive economic rents. This first of all makes knowledge a valuable asset or resource. Additionally, empirical results and management expertise indicate that knowledge creation and accumulation through research and development expenditures are important drivers of business success. These expenditures lead to the creation of new products or more efficient production processes that in turn create higher sales volume or increase existing profit margins. In the end, higher sales and/or lower cost structures result in an increase of the overall company profit. All else being equal, rising annual earnings drive the market value of a company upward. Under the paradigm of shareholder value creation, this causal relationship justifies investments in R&D programs.

A first look at macroeconomic figures illustrates that countries differ in terms of R&D intensity. In recent years, this ratio between (business enterprise) R&D expenditures and production volume shows an upward trend in the U.S. and European countries (see Figure 1). According to most recent OECD (2007) data, more than 5.64 million researchers are employed worldwide. The share of total researchers per thousand total employment varies between 11% (Japan) and nearly 6% (EU 27) and has steadily increased since 1987. In 2006, gross domestic expenditures on R&D worldwide amounted to more than 9.4 trillion USD (ppp).

However, given the intangible and public nature of knowledge, competitive advantages created by and rooted in knowledge can quickly be eroded by competitors. In order to stop or slow down this erosive process and to temporarily secure these advantages, companies might opt for alternative strategies.

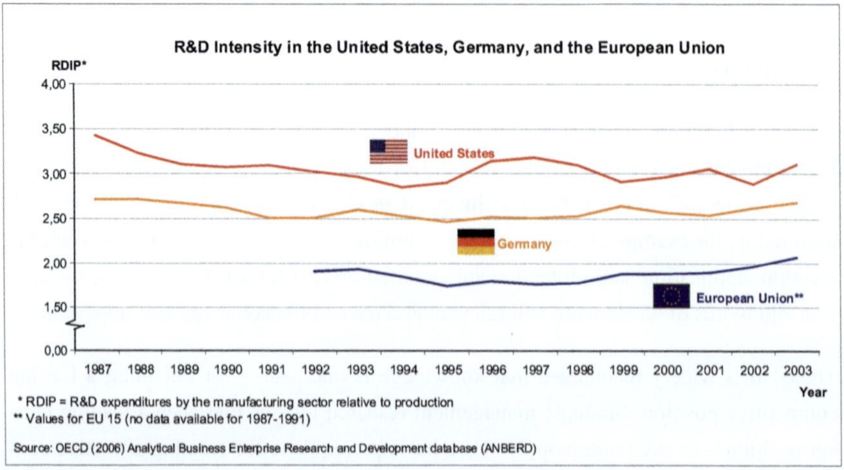

Figure 1: R&D intensity by country between 1987 and 2003

One of the oldest and most widely used strategies for protecting knowledge-based competitive advantages consists of filing patent applications and maintaining complex portfolios of patent rights. These rights are surrounded by the myth of monopolistic market positions and resulting supernormal profits. A first look at European patent statistics shows that both number of patent applications and patent grants processed by the European Patent Office have continually increased over time. Given its longer existence, data for the United States Patent Office can be collected from 1790 on; here, too, a comparable growth trend for patent applications and patent grants can be found, with a boost after the Second World War (Figure 2).

The interpretation of research and development as input and patents as output factors of the knowledge creation and application process leads to the question about measuring the interest an investment in knowledge pays. Consequently, efficient patent valuation techniques seem to be both urgently required and widely used. With regard to R&D investments and patent activity, however, academics and practitioners share the view that reliably determining patent values is a challenging and complex task.

This view is partly rooted in the complexity of patent valuation, which calls for experts with a business, legal, and engineering background. At the same time, patent valuation often takes place in the presence of a high degree of uncertainty regarding the legal validity of patent rights and economic prospects for the underlying invention. Finally, patents are heterogeneous assets. According to patent laws worldwide, each patented invention should exhibit a sufficient degree of uniqueness with regard to its technical functionality. In many cases it has been argued that this diversity hampers comparable analyses of different patent rights despite the fact that the protected inventions may create comparable economic utility.

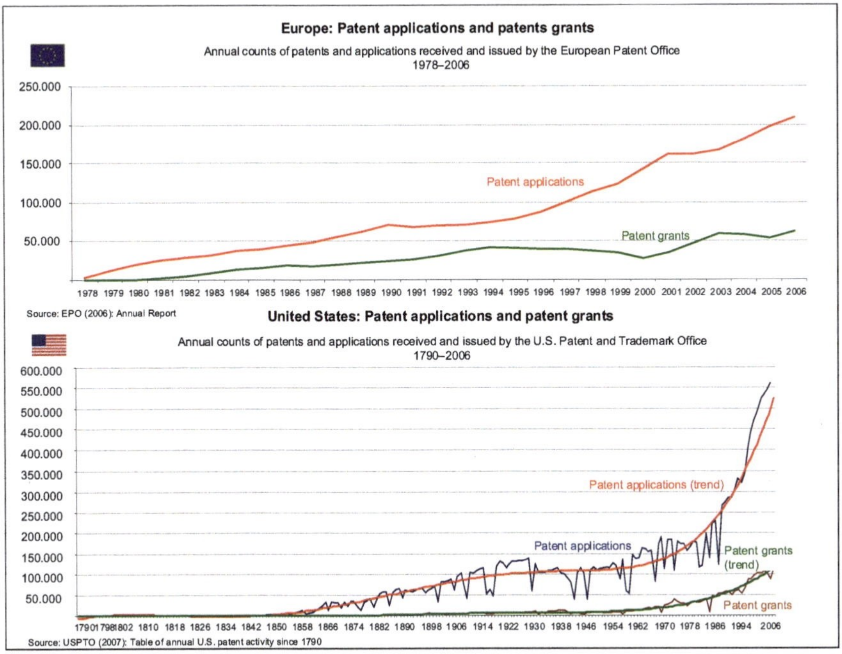

Figure 2: Patent applications and grants in Europe and the United States

With this thesis, I answer the apparent need for measuring the interest knowledge investments pay by analyzing methods and techniques that are suitable for determining the private value of patent rights. However, a thorough analysis of patent values should not focus on patents only, but must take the value of unprotected and complementary knowledge into account. In fact, patent rights are only one side of the coin. They represent one mean to ensure that any value potential of an invention can be appropriated by the inventor. Their primary advantage is concentrated in the right to exclude any third party from profiting from an invention without the consent of the patent holder. From a lawyer's perspective, a patent's value first and foremost depends on the strength of this exclusive right. The value potential of an invention, in contrast, is driven by its quality and marketability.

Thus, the unit of analysis for patent rights is a composite construct of exclusive right and the value potential of knowledge. Under a strong patent regime, patent rights are an efficient means to appropriate the economic rents from valuable knowledge. However, if knowledge is not valuable or no longer valuable – either because of the absence of a market for it or related goods and services, or because it has been replaced by new knowledge – also the exclusive right of a patent contains very little or no value. Consequently, any reasonable and reliable patent valuation requires an analysis not only of the patent right but also of the value potential of the underlying invention. Furthermore, since patents are only granted for technical inventions, additional complementary, non-technical knowledge as well as new technological insights that are intentionally kept secret by the patent holder constitute additional sources of value.

Research design

Grochla (1976) identifies three alternative research designs (Grochla, 1976, 634ff.): (1) analytical approach, (2) empirical study, and (3) model-based analysis. The analytical approach attempts to identify and deconstruct complex systems of mutually dependent relationships involving both observable and hypothetical variables. As a result of this approach, a predefined decision problem is fully described by its elements and by the connections between these elements. Based on this structured view, informative and descriptive statements can be derived.

In contrast to this, an empirical study design extends the research focus by testing descriptive statements formulated as hypotheses with a sample of observable data. Central to this approach is the wish to increase the researcher's understanding of the reliability and validity of descriptive statements. Under this approach, an evaluation of the validity of a statement is not only possible by reference to the underlying theoretical logic but also by considering the empirical results.

Model-based analysis facilitates comprehensive analyses through the formulation of abstract models. The overall aim of these models is to reduce the intricacy of a given decision problem by formulating mathematical algorithms for describing the relationship between selected variables. The main contribution of this research design is to give insights in structures that drive the complexity of a given research question or decision problem.

The complexity of the analysis and the resulting structure of the thesis could best be dealt with by choosing multiple research designs. Parts I and III, as well as the first chapter of part II, follow an analytical approach. In the second chapter of part II, I use a model-based analysis for the discussion of fundamental patent value drivers. Part IV concludes with two empirical analyses of selected research questions.

Structure of the thesis

Although the role knowledge and patents play in fostering economic progress is widely recognized and despite the fact that knowledge has been subject to philosophical analysis for more than two thousand years, no precise and commonly agreed-upon definition of knowledge exists. Part I begins with a brief introduction to various concepts of value, followed by a comprehensive summary of the philosophical and economic approaches to knowledge. Based on this analysis, I define knowledge as *interpretation of facts by the mind of a human being*.

From an economic point of view, knowledge describes two distinct goods with divergent characteristics: explicit knowledge and tacit or implicit knowledge. Each type of knowledge can be a source of value and competitive advantages, and in both cases, development and accumulation are path-dependent processes; however, explicit and tacit knowledge differ in terms of transferability. This in turn affects the degree to which they are subject to appropriability problems. Part I closes with an analysis of strategic options for overcoming these appropriability problems and the implications for patent valuation. The following three research questions define the structure of part I:

(1) What is value?

(2) What is knowledge?

(3) How is knowledge linked to patents?

Part II comprises a description of the legal and economic dimensions of patent rights. I focus on the basic legal concepts of patents and the substantial and procedural requirements under German, European and United States patent law. Although patents are first of all national rights, harmonization efforts have led to comparable patent regimes in various countries. However, certain remarkable differences do still exist. One important difference deals with the definition of the ownership of an invention (first-to-file versus first-to-invent principle). I discuss these similarities and differences with regard to their relevance for patent valuation. Needless to say, given the management focus and economic background of this thesis, my intention is not to fully describe all legal peculiarities of patent regimes that are of secondary importance from a valuation perspective.

The discussion of the economic dimension of patents begins with a short review of the main arguments for patent protection, followed by a stylized theoretical model of value constructs. The main challenge a patentee faces when deciding about filing a patent application or maintaining a patent right is comparing cost and benefits of this decision. Cost comprises more than application and renewal fees. Monopolistic rights to an invention are only granted if the invention is fully disclosed to the public. This publicity may negatively affect a company's competitive position. At the same time, the exclusive function of a patent right requires the successful detection of any infringing activity by a third party. It is only the enforcement of a patent right that leads to its value; however, enforcing rights is costly. These multiple cost considerations are complemented by a discussion of the various benefits a patent can generate. These in turn depend on the way in which a patent is used (patent functions). In addition, as shown by the model, cost and benefit analyses are influenced by the underlying value construct. Here, I extend existing theoretical research by introducing a third value construct and by explicitly modelling the degree of diffusion as value driver. Guiding research questions in Part II are:

(1) What is the nature of patent rights?

(2) How do patents create value for their owner?

(3) What are suitable value constructs for measuring a patent's value?

Part III presents reasons for patent valuation and suitable patent valuation techniques. I distinguish between direct and indirect valuation approaches. The former comprises cost-, market- and income-based approaches to value. The latter consists of econometric models analyzing the relationship between bibliographic indicators and proxy variables for the private value of patent rights. Based on this analysis and the findings of the proceeding parts, I develop a comprehensive framework for patent valuation. Part III answers the following research questions:

(1) What are reasons for patent valuation?

(2) What are suitable methods for patent valuation?

Part IV contains two empirical analyses on the value of licensing agreements and patent rights. They focus on selected research questions regarding the exploitation of knowledge assets through licensing activities and the reliability of indirect patent valuation approaches. Both papers were composed, submitted, and accepted for presentation at the annual meetings of the Academy of Management in 2006 in Atlanta, and in 2007 in Philadelphia, respectively. Hence, each includes its own separate introduction and discussion. The first paper focuses on the following two research questions:

(1) Does an effective market mechanism for technical knowledge exist?

(2) Which contractual terms drive the value of a licensing agreement?

I use a detailed and comprehensive database of licensing contracts that leads to a remarkable sample size for this field of empirical investigation. The second paper closes an existing research gap about the reliability of patent value indicators by testing their impact – not on a proxy, but by using real market values. Hence, it answers the following research questions:

(1) Do indicator-based valuation approaches represent a suitable valuation technique?

(2) What are the drivers of patent values?

This thesis closes with a review of the main findings of each part and a concluding discussion on knowledge, patents, and value.

Part I: Knowledge as a valuable resource

1 Concepts and measurement of value

Before going on to an analysis of knowledge and patent values, this chapter outlines the overall valuation process (section 1.1), alternative value definitions (section 1.2), and value dimensions (section 1.3).

1.1 Valuation process: Evaluation vs. Valuation

Each valuation is motivated by the need or the desire to determine a financial value for a predefined valuation object. Structure and borders of the content of a valuation object define its value potential. Starting with a definition of a valuation object's content, each valuation project comprises two consecutive steps. First, all variables that have an impact on any financial value of the valuation object must be identified as value drivers and implemented in a valuation model. This model describes each variable separately, as well as any observed or hypothesized interaction with other variables of the model, and the impact of each variable on the financial value of the valuation object. In this early stage, the focus is on a qualitative assessment and the complete description of all relevant value drivers. I define this first step of model building as *evaluation*.

The second step comprises the collection and analysis of numeric values for each variable. Depending on the time frame of the valuation, historical, present, and expected future values are to be taken into account. The main task here is to measure each variable, thus transforming any qualitative judgment from the evaluation stage into defined numeric values. Consequently, the valuation model is complemented by a database of precise measures for each variable. This database further allows performing sensitivity analyses. A sensitivity analysis measures the (expected) impact of modifications of variables and intervariable relationships on the numeric values of other variables and the financial value of the valuation object. The quantification of variables and their relationships in combination with the application of several valuation formulas leads to a range of financial values for the valuation object. I refer to this step as *valuation*. As a consequence of this two-step approach, each valuation is based on a given set of information and changes in this information set lead to changes in value.

1.2 Valuation content: Value definitions

Inasmuch as there are many motivations for evaluation and subsequent valuation processes (see chapter 2 in part III), the theoretical literature on valuation offers a wide variety of differing definitions for the concept of *value* (Reilly and Schweihs, 1998, 59–60).

First, economists speak of a *market value* when referring to the price at which a valuation object is actually traded in a competitive and open market with fair and reliable market participants. In the case of non-traded goods, the term *fair market value* refers to the amount of money a typical or hypothetical buyer is willing to pay to a typical or hypothetical seller. *Fair* refers to the condition under which this transaction takes place and indicates that neither buyer nor seller is under undue influence.

Apart from these two definitions of value, which are based on actual or hypothetical transactions, each valuation object can yield a different economic rent depending on how it is used by the resource owner. Therefore the *use value* describes the amount of money an owner can expect from a well-defined use of this specific resource.

The consideration of all possible values resulting from all conceivable resource deployment opportunities leads to the concept of *owner value*. This concept equals the amount of money that the owners of the valuation object can extract from its current or future use and in combination with all other current or future resources controlled by them.

If these benefits from obtaining or using a resource are infringed by an unauthorized third party, the owners have the right to expect an equal or reasonable amount of money – in legal terms, a *fair* value – for this infringement of their property rights. Although judges and juries may take market conditions into account when deciding about a fair value, the central condition of a market-based economy – the idea of independent and willing market participants – is not fulfilled.

1.3 Sources of value: Transactions and compliance with regulations

In the following, I differentiate between transaction-driven motivation and compliance with regulations-oriented motivation. The decisive criterion for this distinction is the varying degree to which a transformation of value potential into economic reality is achieved.

As already mentioned, evaluation and valuation processes lead to value ranges for the valuation object. However – particularly in case of future-oriented valuation – this value range first of all equals a certain value expectation or attitude toward the valuation object. Exploiting the expected value either requires an inflow of economic rents or the avoidance of an outflow of rents. Resource inflows imply any kind of transaction or exchange; only through such transactions do subjective value expectations transform into economic reality.

An exchange creates utility. One of the most common types of exchange is the acquisition. Assuming that two parties to a transaction exist such that one is willing to buy a well-defined valuation object from the other, the value realized depends on each party's value expectations and bargaining power. From the buyer's perspective, the value for a specific kind of knowledge or a patent equals the utility connected to the resource inflow (e.g., the acquired knowledge asset) less the loss of utility created by the outflow of resources that are given away (e.g., the amount of money paid for the purchase price). Prior to and during negotiations, both parties form and adjust their subjective expectations about these utility flows, based on their analysis of the valuation object's content. Different evaluations lead to different use or owner values and consequently result in unequal value expectations. Since a successful market transaction requires both parties to agree upon a common value or price, each serious valuation should also reflect expectations and value conclusions of the transaction partner.

Figure 3 summarizes the transactional approach. Owners' values are driven by an evaluation of content and decisions related to the valuation object and the quantification of the resulting economic consequences. Based on these owners' values, both parties form value expectations which comprise a range of different financial values (Ω_{MV} and Ω_{FMV}). As in any other market transaction, these value ranges have to overlap in order to induce a successful transaction. The size of this overlap depends on the consensus of sellers' and buyers' expectations.

In contrast to this transaction-oriented approach, utility is bound to fulfilling rules imposed by a superior authority in the case of compliance-driven regulation. Any value is a result of the regulation framework. Hence, value realization is not defined by resource inflows but by the application of rules. Value maximization requires an optimal fulfilment of the given rules.

Contrary to transaction-driven motivation, a transformation of the value potential into economic reality by an exchange of resources is not achieved. Clearly, changes to the structure of the framework or specific regulations will lead to changes in value. Regulation frameworks can be both external and internal to an organization.

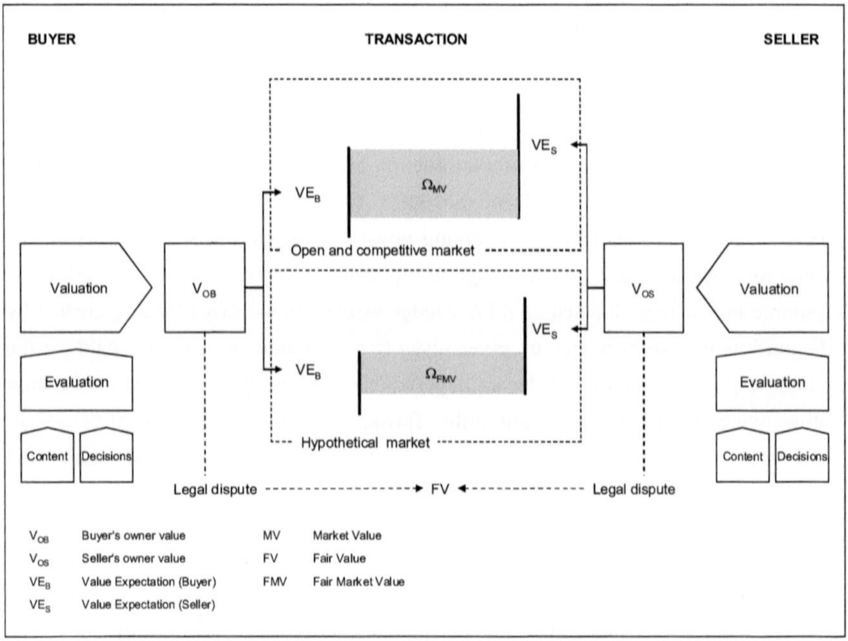

Figure 3: Definitions of value in market transactions

Examples of external frameworks include national and international tax and accounting systems; internal frameworks comprise standardized valuation processes or rules. The empirical analyses in Part IV focus on a transactional approach; however, I will discuss compliance-driven regulation in more detail in Part II.

2 Knowledge as a multifaceted concept

In order to understand the complex nature of knowledge and develop a suitable definition, I analyze two research streams: (1) epistemology (philosophical and psychological view) and (2) the knowledge-based view of the firm (economic approach). The following sections review both areas of research. Section 2.1 begins with a short description of the historical evolution of epistemology and its implications for deriving a suitable definition of knowledge. In Section 2.2, I present a summary of the knowledge-based view of the firm. This theory of the firm represents an extension of the resource-based view of the firm with a focus on knowledge as a corporate or individual asset with significant strategic relevance for firm success (Acedo et al., 2006, 628–29). Based on these two approaches, I develop the definition of knowledge for this thesis in section 2.3.

2.1 The philosophical approach to knowledge

There have been ongoing discussions about the origin and content of knowledge by various philosophers since the early days of philosophy. The branch of philosophical science dealing with the theory of knowledge is called epistemology. This term is derived from the Greek words for "science" (*episteme)* and "word" or "speech" (*logos*). Epistemology tries to shed light on content, origin, and reliability of knowledge. A commonly made distinction is the differentiation between *propositional* and *procedural (nonpropositional)* knowledge. Propositional knowledge is expressed using "that"-clauses to transport information about facts; procedural knowledge uses "how to"-clauses to illustrate the way in which an activity is performed. Epistemologists mostly concentrate on the discussion of propositional knowledge (Cruz, 2003, 24ff.).

In the following chapters I shall not discuss specific philosophical questions, such as the distinction between knowledge and truth or belief, nor will I describe in elaborate detail all the differences between the existing approaches over the last centuries. This review of alternative approaches to the concept of knowledge will, however, provide a foundation for the subsequent economic analysis.

2.1.1 Historical review from Plato to Dewey

2.1.1.1 The nature of knowledge: Justified true belief

One of the first philosophers to investigate the nature of knowledge was Plato (427–347 BCE). In his dialogues with Theaetetus and Meno (Plato, 1997), he defines knowledge as "justified true belief" (JTB). The JTB approach is characterized by the following three necessary and sufficient conditions:

Individual I_1 has knowledge of proposition *P* if and only if,

(1) *P* is true (truth condition).

(2) I1 believes that P is true (belief condition).

(3) I1 is justified in believing that *P* is true (justification condition).

According to the truth condition, I_1 can only know *P*, if *P* was true in the past, is true in the present, or will be true in the future. This condition is an objective requirement for knowledge. The second condition, the belief condition, is a subjective requirement. It says that knowledge of *P* includes a certain attitude of I_1 towards *P*: knowledge of *P* requires that I_1 truly believes in *P*. But the true belief alone is not sufficient; knowledge also needs evidence of the truthfulness of *P*. This is emphasized by the third condition (the justification condition). Belief in *P* that is not grounded on valid evidence does not constitute knowledge even if *P* might happen to be true in some circumstances (Steup, 2001).

The main contribution of this approach to knowledge is that it offers a simple logic for analyzing the nature and reliability of knowledge. However, despite the fact that some important aspects of knowledge are addressed, this definition cannot be considered to be universally applicable. Using compound sentences, Gettier (1963) demonstrates that the JTB condition is satisfied although I_1 cannot be considered to have knowledge (Gettier, 1963, 122; Cruz, 2003, 24).

2.1.1.2 The origin of knowledge: Rationalism vs. Empiricism

The discussion of the question about the origin of knowledge led to the formation of two different branches of western philosophy: rationalism and empiricism. Rationalism argues that true knowledge can be obtained solely by some ideal mental process. In contrast, the empiricists allege that the only source of knowledge is sensory experience. Rationalists opine that there exists *a priori* knowledge and that an overall truth can be developed using rational reasoning based on axioms. Empiricists, reject these central ideas by denying the existence of *a priori* knowledge and postulating the view that only experience can provide the mind with ideas.

This dualistic view is first expressed by Plato and his student Aristotle (384–322 BCE). Whereas Plato holds that the physical world is only a shadow of the perfect world of "ideas" and only knowable through pure reason, Aristotle considers perception to be the ultimate source of knowledge (Aristotle, 1928). He further emphasizes that from a scientific point of view, something is not known until its causes are recognized (Aristotle, 1998, 5).

René Descartes: The Cartesian split

With his *Discours de la méthode* and his *Méditations* Descartes (1596–1650) makes two important contributions concerning origin and reliability of knowledge. In his second *Méditation*, he analyzes the reliability of knowledge by first stating that every truth can be questioned. Descartes reasons that the only overall truth one can hold beyond all doubt is the existence of the questioner himself, the view expressed in his notable statement: *cogito ergo sum*. Descartes furthermore says that one cannot be sure about the nature of things by relying solely on one's sensory experiences. He offers the example of wax to support his ideas; depending on the temperature, wax can be perceived as either a solid or a fluid.

As representative of rationalism, Descartes strongly believes that the source of all knowledge is reason (Descartes, 1901). Based on this idea, he draws a clear distinction (the *Cartesian split*) between the mind (the knower) and the body (the known) (Descartes, 2002).

In the *Discours de la méthode*, Descartes analyses the acquisition of knowledge using four rules of method that he extrapolates from his study of mathematics. The first step for solving a problem is the identification of fundamental truths that lie beyond all doubt. The next step includes the decomposition of complex problems into simpler ones. Descartes adopts the mathematical principle of the formation of equations. He proposes, in the third step, that the single truths of the two preceding rules are to be arranged according to their degree of complexity, beginning with the simplest and ending with the most complex truth. This deductive process depends partly on memory and may be incorrect; therefore, he postulates in his fourth rule that reasoning needs to be checked (Descartes, 1968, 41).

The Cartesian dualism has mainly influenced Western philosophy and understanding of knowledge. Many attempts have been made to overcame this split, including those of philosophers such as Husserl, Heidegger, Sartre, Merleau-Ponty, Wittgenstein, James and Dewey (Nonaka and Takeuchi, 1995, 25). In contrast to this, Asian philosophers, such as Nishida Kitaro, do not distinguish between body and mind; they argue that both body and mind are places for knowledge (McCarthy, 2001, 166).

John Locke: The need for experiments

In contrast to Descartes, Locke (1632–1704) emphasizes the importance of experiments to gain scientific knowledge. As an empiricist, he also recognizes that knowledge is severely limited in its extent.

He proposes a framework with a descending order of certainty. Based on this, he distinguishes three ways in which knowledge can be gained. *Intuitive* knowledge is characterized by perfect certainty but also by its rareness. *Demonstrative* knowledge is the result of a chain of reasoning and therefore its certainty is no greater than the weakest link of the chain. Furthermore, each link must be intuitively known in order that one can be sure that the whole demonstration is certain. Finally, Locke accepts that even in the absence of evidence there can be *sensitive* knowledge resulting from a powerful feeling one cannot doubt; although the real cause is unknown, the presence of the feeling strongly supports its existence (Locke, 1975, 537ff.).

Immanuel Kant: The unification of rationalism and empiricism

Kant (1724–1804) is neither convinced of the central idea of the rationalists, that reason is the only source of knowledge, nor is he sure that knowledge could be derived solely by experience, as the empiricists assume. In his *Kritik der reinen Vernunft*, he tries to demonstrate how reason determines the conditions under which experience and knowledge are possible.

Believing that cognition exists in the form of judgments (statements, including subjects and predicates), he draws a pair of important distinctions concerning the origin of the judgments and the information transmitted by their content.

With respect to the origin, Kant distinguishes between *a priori* and *a posteriori* judgments. *A priori* judgments are based upon reason alone and therefore are characterized by universal validity. *A posteriori* judgments emerge from experience and can thus only be applicable in specific cases. With respect to informational content, Kant distinguishes between *analytic* and *synthetic* judgments. Analytic judgments are earmarked by the fact that the predicates are wholly contained in their subjects. Hence they add nothing to the concept of the subject and are merely explicative. *Synthetic* judgments include predicates that are totally different from their subject but are linked to it by a real connection outside the concepts themselves. Thus, they are genuinely informative, but also need to be justified by an outside principle (Kant, 1998).

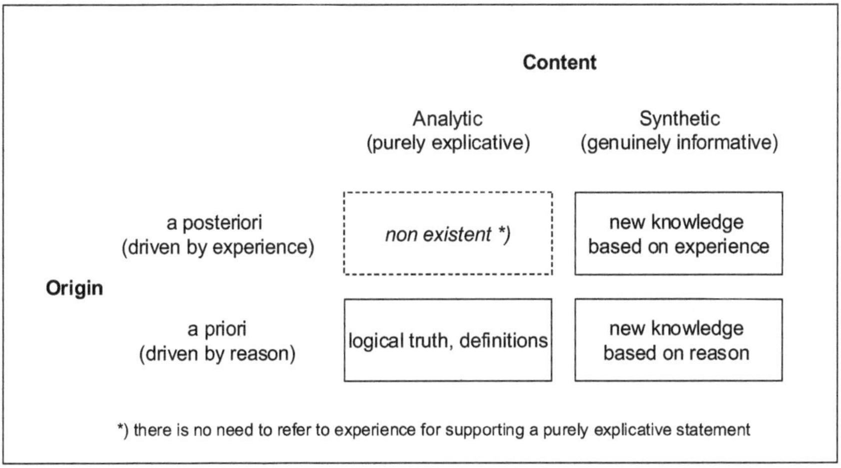

Figure 4: Content and origin of knowledge according to Immanuel Kant

Concerning the reliability of knowledge, Kant assumes that inasmuch as reality is perceived via sensory impressions, knowledge about reality is at the same time limited by the extent of these impressions. He further alleges that as knowledge is categorized based on *a priori* judgments, it is consequently limited by the existence of these judgments (Spender, 1996, 48).

John Dewey: Active perception

For Dewey (1859–1952), the explicit distinction between thoughts (or knowledge) and the world of facts that is drawn by both the empiricists and the rationalists is misleading. He assumes that the world is not known through passive perception but that knowledge results from the manipulation of the world. Therefore, the content of knowledge depends on action. The interaction of an organism with the world is produced by the coordination of sensory and motor reflexes. Dewey cites the child-candle encounter as an example of this coordination. On basis of the experience that the candle causes heat-pain, the child learns – knows – that the candle is hot. This knowledge enables the child to avoid similar experiences in the future (Dewey, 1896, 358ff.).

In one of his earlier works, Dewey already draws a distinction between pure science and applied sciences such as engineering, medicine, and the social arts, which he considers to be true science. He justifies this statement referring to the fact that applied sciences lead to the discovery of knowledge previously hidden. In contrast to this, pure science is characterized by a certain degree of abstractness and therefore comprehends parts that *qua defintionem* cannot be revealed (Dewey, 1988, 128–29).

Furthermore, Dewey favors the interpretation of human thought as steps in a practical problem-solving process. He introduces a six-step model that mainly consists of checking different opposing hypotheses against experience in order to achieve what he calls "warranted assertability" upon which conclusive actions are possible. He admits that this is the best outcome to be hoped for and therefore rejects the idea of an overall and timeless truth (Dewey, 1986, 16–17). Together with Arthur Bentley, Dewey argues that the extensive and ambiguous employment of the word "knowledge" rules out the possibility of a widely accepted notion of knowledge emerging and that other terms and definitions should be found (Dewey and Bentely, 1973, 113ff.).

Gilbert Ryle: Knowing how and knowing that

Gilbert Ryle (1900–1976) is known for his distinction between *knowing how* and *knowing that*. He highlights the fact that the performing of a skill depends on both the ability to think logically and practically as well as the capability of transforming reasoning into action (Ryle, 1949).

The quality of an action is directly linked to the efficiency with which it is conducted (Chemero, 2002). This central idea of Ryle has been further developed by David Carr (Carr, 1981) and Charlotte Katzoff (Katzoff, 1984). Carr focuses on the practical trait of knowing how by arguing that the *how* is primarily attributed to competence in execution. Charlotte Katzoff applies Carr's framework to the case of pure theoretical knowledge.

According to Carr (Carr, 1981), there are three different ways in which knowledge and *know-how* can be understood. One perspective focuses on the distinction between mental versus physical ability. In this context, the main distinguishing feature refers to the difference between being physically able to perform an activity and having the knowledge to do so. Even though an individual may be physically able to master a difficult task once, the aptitude necessary to repeat this performance may still be lacking. Therefore, the second perspective investigates whether the success in managing a task is accidental or not. Only if it is evident that the result can be repeated under the same circumstances, can one be said to have the know *how* to solve a specific problem.

The third approach examines these circumstances more closely. As Carr maintains, the content of the concept of *know-how* depends on the circumstances under which *know-how* based actions can be investigated. To be considered to know *how* to perform an activity φ, individual I_1 has to meet three basic criteria: First, I_1 carries out φ to achieve his or her target; second, I_1 is familiar with a set of methods that allow an efficient and effective way of φ-ing; and third, I_1 is successful in φ-ing.

2.1.2 Implications for knowledge definition

From the discussion of the various philosophical approaches, three main conclusions with respect to source, components, and validity of the concept knowledge can be drawn.

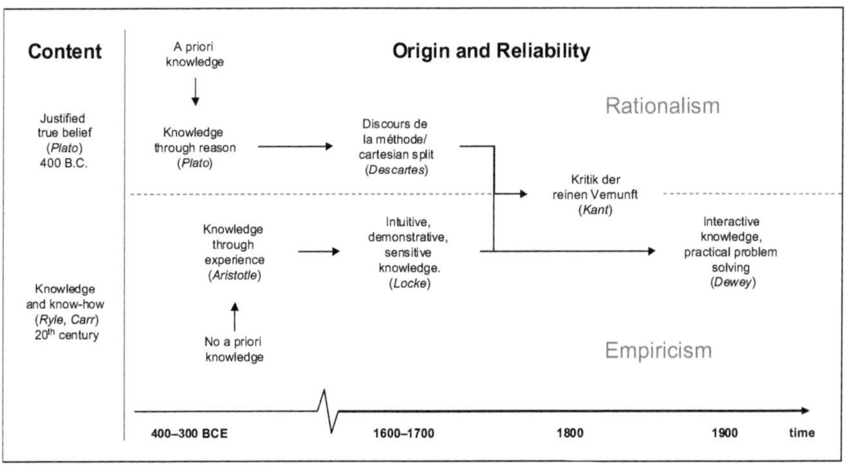

Figure 5: Philosophical approaches to knowledge

First, the persistent rivalry of rationalism and empiricism has led to the perception of two sources of knowledge obtainment: Knowledge can either be acquired *deductively* by reasoning and applying a chain of cause and effect or *inductively* from sensory experiences and learning by doing.

Second, these different origins influence the substance of knowledge. Knowledge is understood as a complex, multifaceted term, consisting of a variety of subordinate aspects. It can be characterized as being overall objectively true as well as relatively true, given certain circumstances.

Finally, to arrive at a definition of knowledge, a deconstruction (Descartes) of the overall concept seems advisable. Knowledge may contain different levels (Locke) and the content of knowledge depends on (path-dependent) experience or learning (Dewey) and on mental and physical abilities (Ryle).

2.2 The economic approach to knowledge

2.2.1 Knowledge, competitive advantages, and the resource-based view of the firm

In contrast to the epistemologists, who have focused mostly on concept, origin, and reliability of knowledge, economic theorists analyze the role of knowledge in the resource transformation process. Hence, a value-relevant taxonomy of knowledge can be developed using the resource-based view of the firm. Introduced to the field of strategic management by Penrose (1959), this theory of the firm defines a company as set of tangible and intangible resources that are combined based on a preceding decision (Penrose, 1959, 24). Resources comprise all assets which are within the range of the firm, no matter whether they are of a physical, personnel, financial, or informational nature (Bausch, 1996, 115).

In general, theories of the firm try to explain the existence of the firm, its organization, and its behavior (Grant, 1996a, 109). The analysis of the firm from alternative viewpoints can lead to differing theories of the firm. Since these theories serve different purposes, there is no theory which can be claimed to be universally applicable (Machlup, 1967, 27–28).

The resource-based view of the firm (Wernerfelt, 1984) focuses on (1) how managers can discern inputs that can be used to produce valuable goods and services (i.e., to produce an output whose value exceeds the value of the required input) and (2) the characteristics of a resource that can prevent competitors from imitating these valuable goods and services (Conner, 1991, 132ff.). The latter is essential for creating a sustained competitive advantage. In general, a competitive advantage is claimed to emerge if no *current* competitor can implement the same value-creating strategy, whereas the existence of a *sustained* competitive advantage requires that neither current nor potential competitors are able to implement or imitate this value-creating strategy (Barney, 1991, 101ff.).

Although several companies might use the same inputs to create a comparable output, every company can be characterized by a specific resource endowment. This can be defined in terms of both quantity and quality of resources that are used in a resource combination process and result in marketable goods and services. This asymmetric configuration of resources between two companies, which can be the result of the immobility of resources, imperfect factor markets, or managerial decisions, primarily influences the ability to create sustained competitive advantages (Bausch, 1996, 116).

Table 1 shows the relationship between the resource-based view and the knowledge-based view of the firm by interlinking a classification of Barney (1991), who identifies four different earmarks of resources (VRIN paradigm) that constitute a sustained competitive advantage of a company (Barney, 1991, 101ff.) with selected corresponding perspectives in the knowledge-based view of the firm. We may conclude that the knowledge-based view of the firm represents one specific branch of the resource-based view of the firm (Yli-Renko et al., 2001, 587; Acedo et al., 2006).

Knowledge is claimed to be a resource that, like other intangible resources, meets the requirements of the VRIN paradigm and therefore creates competitive advantages (Ghemawat, 1986, 55–56; Reed and DeFillippi, 1990, 90ff.; Hall, 1991, 44, 1992, 144; Quinn, 1992, 241ff.; Hall, 1993, 610ff.; Conner and Prahalad, 1996, 477; Grant, 1996b, 375–76; Tiemessen et al., 1997, 385–86; Teece, 1998, 62). Evidence can be found for the idea that intangibles, in general, positively influence sustained competitive advantages of a firm (Villalonga, 2004, 219ff.). Empirical results further show that knowledge and certain attributes of knowledge can create entry barriers and consequently create competitive advantages (McEvily and Chakravarthy, 2002).

Further support for this statement comes from the observation that knowledge can neither be purchased easily in the marketplace nor can it be acquired internally without spending a considerable amount of time (Zack, 1999, 128). In addition, sustainable advantages can emerge from knowledge, since the current stock of knowledge available to a knowing economic agent (individual or organization) supports the acquisition of new knowledge. Cohen and Levinthal (1990) introduce the term 'absorptive capacity' to emphasize that the efficiency of knowledge acquisition is driven by the current stock of knowledge (Cohen and Levinthal, 1990, 135–36).

Resource trait	**Definition**	**Selected corresponding perspectives of the knowledge based view of the firm**
Valuable (V)	Resources are valuable "*when they enable a firm to conceive of or implement strategies that improve its efficiency and effectiveness*" (Barney, 1991, 106).	The recognition of knowledge as one major main value driver in modern economics and the interpretation of explicit knowledge as a public good or a club good (see also chapter 3 in this Part).
Rare (R)	"*...Firm resources possessed by large numbers of competing or potentially competing firms cannot be sources of either a competitive advantage or sustained competitive advantage*" (Barney, 1991, 106).	The analysis of both the information paradox and strategies to reduce the public nature of explicit knowledge, as well as the investigation of tacit knowledge.
Imperfectly imitable (I)	Valuable and rare resources only originate sustained competitive advantage if those firms that do not have access to these resources cannot obtain them (Barney, 1991, 106). Resources are imperfectly imitable because of one of the following reasons: ▪ Unique historical conditions (resources are only available during a defined window of time. ▪ Causal ambiguity (neither the firm itself nor any of its competitors can reveal the connection between a firm's resources and its success). ▪ Social complexity (resources are complex social phenomena and cannot be managed or influenced systematically).	The investigation of different means to protect explicit knowledge, the recognition of path-dependency in generating and acquiring knowledge, and the analysis of organizational knowledge (see subsection 2.2.3 of this Part).
Non-substitutable (N)	This criterion focuses on the strategic equivalence of two resources. This equivalence exists if each of the two resources "*can be exploited separately to implement the same strategies*" (Barney, 1991, 106). This criterion can be met by either similar or very different resources.	The interpretation of patent protection as one way to monopolize a leading technological position and the underlying thread of inventing around activities of competitors to erode this monopolistic market position.

Table 1: Firm resources, sustained competitive advantages, and knowledge

An increased stock of knowledge allows e.g. the formulation of more reliable expectations about an uncertain future. In the specific case of patent valuation, this increased stock of knowledge e.g. leads to a better understanding of the technical and economic potential of innovations. This in turn allows the formulation of more reliable estimates.

2.2.2 Assumptions of the knowledge-based view of the firm

The theoretical foundations dealing with knowledge and its impact at the firm level are analyzed by the knowledge-based view of the firm. This approach defines the firm as a set of knowledge assets and attempts to explain how knowledge assets can be developed and applied to create value for the firm (Grant, 2002b, 176).

With regard to the general economic transformation process, we can interpret knowledge either as an input factor or as an output of corporate processes; thus, as a corporate asset (Itami and Roehl, 1987; Barney, 1991; Quinn, 1992; Teece, 1998) that exists at a specific point in time – or, applying a more dynamic view – as a facilitator in the production process emphasizing the supportive role of knowledge and its potential to increase efficiency in the process of combining different inputs (Penrose, 1959; Arrow and Hahn, 1971; Spender, 1996). In this context, knowledge is not considered to be a homogenous resource. The knowledge-based view of the firm looks at two different kinds of knowledge: tacit and explicit knowledge. Based on the distinction between these types of knowledge, scholars further extend the analysis by investigating (1) why firms exist in the presence of knowledge (subsection 2.2.5), (2) how knowledge affects the coordination within the firm (subsection 2.2.6), and (3) which impact knowledge has on the boundaries of the firm (subsection 2.2.7).

2.2.3 Units of analysis of the knowledge-based theory of the firm: Tacit and explicit knowledge

The main distinction between tacit and explicit knowledge can be traced back to epistemological approaches. The concept of tacit knowledge is derived from the reflections of Michael Polanyi (1891–1976), a Hungarian medical scientist, who coined the term *tacit knowing*.

2.2.3.1 Polanyi's concept of tacit knowing

Polanyi (1966) bases his idea of tacit knowing on the observation that human beings are unable to articulate and define all areas of their knowledge. Moreover, awareness of these inexplicable areas of knowledge emerges only in combination with other knowledge. Polanyi identifies a functional relation between two different terms of tacit knowing. One only knows of the first (proximal) term if relying on one's awareness of it for attending to the second (distal) term (Polanyi, 1966, 9–10).

For purposes of illustration, he cites several experiments conducted by Lazarus and McCleary (1949; 1951) in which a human subject was presented with a large number of nonsense syllables. After certain syllables, the subject was exposed to an electric shock. During the experiments, subjects learned to anticipate the shock (distal term) when reading the "shock-inducing" syllables (proximal term), but were unable to identify these syllables explicitly. The test subjects knew when to expect the shock, but could not define and communicate what made them expect the shock.

Polanyi argues that even though one might be unable to identify the proximal term, the recurring experience of the distal term sharpens the knowledge of the former (phenomenal aspect). In addition, he maintains that when using a tool, the feelings one experiences in applying it are interpreted by the human mind (e.g., the impact a hammer or a probe has on one's fingers, palm, and hand). This interpretation results in a certain meaning, which directs the application of the tool (semantic aspect) (Polanyi, 1966, 11ff.).

Therefore, the functional relationship as outlined above does not consist of the relation between the two terms themselves, but between the meaning one attributes to the proximal term and the distal term. Returning to the shock-syllable experiment, the test subjects did not pay attention to specific syllables but rather only to their meaning (shock-inducing or non-shock-inducing).

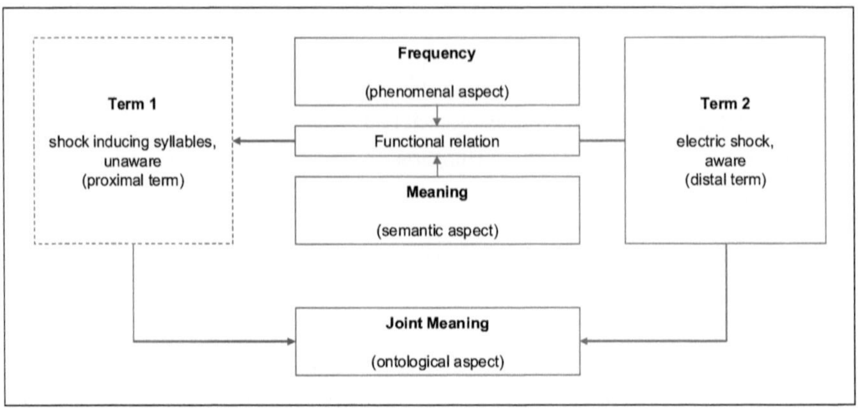

Figure 6: Polanyi's concept of tacit knowing

Finally, Polanyi combines the three preceding elements of tacit knowing and defines its very nature (ontological aspect). Since tacit knowing creates a meaningful relationship between the distal and the proximal term, it can be defined as the understanding of the entity which is constituted by both terms. The particulars of this entity create the proximal term. But one comprehends this entity only by relying on the joint meaning of both the proximal and the distal term (Polanyi, 1966, 11ff.).

2.2.3.2 Tacitness and explicitness from an economic point of view

Most economic scholars are less interested in the subtle differences between different aspects of tacit knowing. Rather are they fascinated by the quintessence of Polanyi's ideas, that individuals do in fact know more than they can tell (Polanyi, 1966, 4). Economists speak of the existence of two essential kinds of knowledge: *explicit* and *tacit* knowledge. Synonyms for this dichotomy are *codified* and *uncodified* (Choi and Lee, 1997, 36; Teece, 1998, 63–64), *objective* and *subjective*, *prepositional* and *personal*, *declarative* and *procedural* (Winter, 1987, 170ff.; Grant, 1996a, 111; Nahapiet and Ghoshal, 1998, 246; Kakabadse et al., 2001, 138ff.), *internal* and *external* (Zack, 1999, 138–39), and *alienable* and *non-alienable* (Brynjolfsson, 1994, 1649; Foss, 2002, 25).

The differences between explicit and tacit knowledge lead to two economic goods with divergent characteristics. Common to both is their intangible nature and their connection to the mind of a human being. However, they differ with respect to the degree to which they can be codified.

Explicit knowledge

Explicit knowledge can be fully codified. Here, codification refers to the possibility of compressing knowledge into a specific, standardized expression that can be understood by everyone who is acquainted with this code (Boisot and Child, 1988, 508). The degree of codification determines the definability of knowledge. This in turn is a crucial factor for transferring and valuing knowledge as well as protecting it using intellectual property rights such as patents (Nonaka and Takeuchi, 1995, 8; OECD, 1996, 13; Teece, 1998, 63; Mudambi and Navarra, 2004, 388). Facts which are expressed using language, signs, numbers, or symbols are one example of codified knowledge.

Tacit knowledge

As already discussed in 2.2.3.1 of this Part, Polanyi states that tacit knowing is destroyed by focusing one's attention on it (Polanyi, 1966, 34). Economic theorists, however, have broadened the concept of tacit knowing by introducing the term *tacit knowledge*, which they define as knowledge that is inexpressible and hence difficult to convey, either voluntarily or involuntarily. However, they do allow one to be aware of one's tacit knowledge. This difference with respect to the question of awareness and the existence of tacit knowledge distinguishes Polanyi's approach from the economic perspective.

The economic understanding of the tacit nature of knowledge has been shaped in contrast to the explicitness of codified knowledge. Nonaka and Takeuchi (1991; 1994; 1995) refer to tacit knowledge as that area of knowledge that is not easily visible or expressible and therefore only transferable to a limited extent. It is both highly subjective and deeply rooted in the personality of the individual. Furthermore, it is characterized by two aspects: (1) the technical dimension of tacit knowledge, consisting of personal skills, and (2) the cognitive dimension, comprising the mental models with which one perceives reality (Nonaka and Takeuchi, 1995, 9).

2.2.4 Sources of knowledge

2.2.4.1 Sources on the individual level

Penrose (1959) identifies two different sources of knowledge: (1) teaching or learning and (2) experience. Both can result from purposeful research or happen by pure chance without clear intention. Learning processes dealing with explicit, thus transferable, knowledge can either be the result of exchanging facts with other individuals or of studying the written word. In contrast, given its reduced communicability, experience is bound to one single human being, since it describes (implicit) learning at the personal level (Penrose, 1959, 53ff.). Figure 7 shows the interrelationships between both learning and experience. Individual I_1 gains knowledge by personal experience and learning from others (I_0) and teaches, thus transfers, (explicit) parts of his or her own knowledge to individual I_2. Both personal experience and learning increase the stock of knowledge of I_2. According to Penrose, this increased stock of knowledge facilitates either a more efficient production of an existing output or the discovery of new output possibilities (i.e., new products and services) (Penrose, 1959, 76).

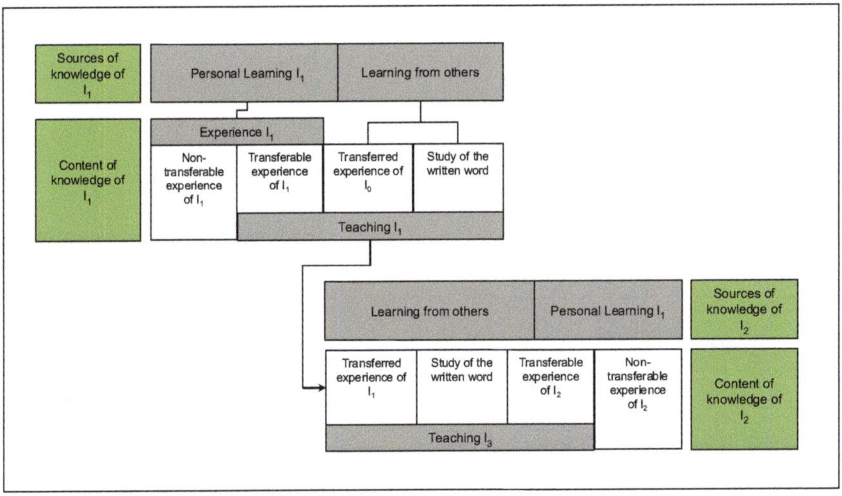

Figure 7: Teaching and experience as sources of knowledge

2.2.4.2 Sources on the firm level

Referring to Polanyi's concept of an individual skill as being a combination of muscular acts and tacit knowledge (Polanyi, 1966, 8), Nelson and Winter (1982) argue that the effectiveness and efficiency – in other words, the skillfulness – with which a task is solved on a personal level influences the capabilities of a firm (Nelson and Winter, 1982, 84ff.). They define a routine to be the predictable and customary behavior of a firm (Nelson and Winter, 1982, 14). Furthermore, they maintain that this routine at the firm level corresponds to the idea of a skill at the member level of the organization. Therefore, routines can be described as being both partially codified and tacit as well as firm-specific and of an idiosyncratic nature (Fai, 2001, 4).

Nonaka and Takeuchi (1991; 1994; 1995) identify four ways in which knowledge is created within an organization through social interaction between human beings (knowledge conversion).

They call the conversion from tacit knowledge into explicit knowledge "socialization," from tacit to explicit "externalization," from explicit to explicit "combination," and from explicit to tacit "internalization" (Nonaka and Takeuchi, 1995, 72–73). While transfers resulting in explicit knowledge (externalization and combination) are characterized by the revelation and/or creation of new facts, conversions which create tacit knowledge (internalization and socialization) either lead to changes in the combination of facts or modify the mindsets of the individuals involved.

Knowledge Conversion Matrix

FROM ↓ / TO →	Explicit	Tacit
Tacit	**Tacit → Explicit: EXTERNALIZATION** *Definition*: Articulation and systematization of tacit knowledge *Methodology*: Writing *Content*: Conceptual knowledge (e.g. metaphors, analogies)	**Tacit → Tacit: SOCIALIZATION** *Definition*: Sharing experiences among individuals and between the organization and the individual *Methodology*: Experience *Content*: Sympathized knowledge (e.g. shared mental models, technical skills)
Explicit	**Explicit → Explicit: COMBINATION** *Definition*: Combination of different bodies of explicit knowledge *Methodology*: Exchanging media (e.g. documents, conversations, IT-networks) *Content*: Systematic knowledge (e.g. prototypes, new component technologies)	**Explicit → Tacit: INTERNALIZATION** *Definition*: Conversion of instructions and principles into intuition and routines *Methodology*: Learning by doing *Content*: Operational knowledge (e.g. project management, production process)

Figure 8: The knowledge conversion matrix

Nonaka and Takeuchi further argue that an organization cannot create knowledge but has to rely on the (tacit) knowledge of its members. If the organization manages to gain access to and mobilize these individual knowledge accumulations, the different modes of conversion result in a broader and deeper stock of knowledge at different levels of the organization (ontological dimension). This "knowledge spiral" (Figure 9), however, must not stop at the boundaries of a single firm; inter-firm cooperation may further increase the stock of knowledge (Nonaka and Takeuchi, 1995, 62–70).

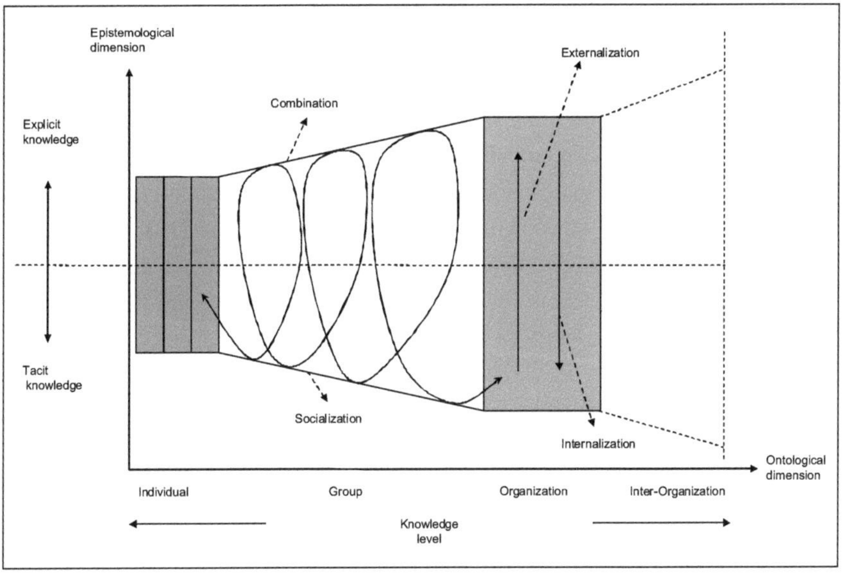

Figure 9: The knowledge spiral

2.2.4.3 On the relationship between the knowledge of a firm and the knowledge of its employees

The discussion about the relationship between the knowledge of a firm and the knowledge of its employees offers two main perspectives. Some theorists support the view that the knowledge of a firm solely rests on the knowledge of the available human resources and that a firm as organization cannot possess knowledge beyond the sum of the individual stocks of knowledge of its workforce (Penrose, 1959, 53–54; Simon, 1991, 125; Grant, 1996a, 112; Teece, 1998, 62). However, others argue that organizations themselves can create, store, and apply knowledge (Huber, 1991, 89ff.; Spender, 1996, 53ff.). This perspective assumes that the knowledge of an organization exceeds the simple aggregation of the knowledge of its members (Nelson and Winter, 1982, 63; Kogut and Zander, 1992, 383ff.; Nahapiet and Ghoshal, 1998, 246).

For valuation purposes, these different approaches matter since they examine alternative valuation objects. If the knowledge of a firm is merely the simple aggregation of its entire workforce then the main unit of analysis of the valuation is the single expert. In this case "*learning by hiring*" (Song et al., 2003) – or, more generally, changes of key personnel (see sub-subsection 3.2.1.1 in this Part) – directly affects the capabilities of the firm (Nelson and Winter, 1982, 115), especially in those cases where it relies on the tacit knowledge of single experts (Almeida and Kogut, 1999, 912ff.).

Under the assumption that firms do more than just gather and employ specialists, a firm's competencies depend on more than the private knowledge of individual workers. Their willingness to share knowledge and the degree to which this exchange is facilitated by the organization also affect the capabilities of the firm. Thus, the efficiency with which the knowledge of different specialists is combined affects the performance of the firm and can therefore be interpreted as a value-adding activity at the organizational level.

Similar to the idea of parenting advantages in strategic management, firm-specific properties can influence the quality and efficiency of knowledge utilization. During transaction negotiations these different backgrounds or properties can have an impact on the value expectations of the parties involved. Thus, these firm-specific properties, resulting from different firm histories, determine the estimated value that is attributed to the transfer object by both buyer and seller (Madhok, 1996, 584).

Additionally, since learning based on experience can be described as a process of trial, feedback, and evaluation, it is cumulative (i.e., each stage of learning lays the foundation for the subsequent learning process) at both the individual and the firm level, and therefore path-dependent. In this context path-dependency refers to the constraints in acquiring new knowledge that result from the knowledge gained in the past (Dosi et al., 1992, 191ff.; Kogut and Zander, 1992, 392; Langlois, 1992, 105). In view of the fact that knowledge of the firm rests (at least partially) on the knowledge of its employees this path-dependency and the awareness of knowledge on the personal level influence the knowledge of the firm (Penrose, 1959, 76–80). Furthermore, the concept of this idiosyncratic evolution pattern offers an explanation for different price expectations. Thus, for valuation purposes in the case of a market transaction, the guiding negotiating principle should not only focus on the value which one party assumes to be appropriate. In addition, the value expectations of the contracting party should also be taken into account.

2.2.5 Knowledge and the existence of the firm

Generally speaking, the search for the reasons for the existence of firms involves two questions. The first question focuses on reasons that explain why firms exist in a free-market economy. The second question analyzes reasons that lead to a multiplicity of firms. The knowledge-based view of the firm provides answers to both questions by referring to the special features of knowledge. In contrast to the transaction cost theory (Coase, 1937; Williamson, 1985) and the resulting contractual approach of the firm (Cheung, 1983), the knowledge-based view of the firm does not rely on the assumption of opportunistic behavior as the driving force for the creation of firms (Nickerson and Zenger, 2004, 617).

2.2.5.1 Explanations for the emergence of firms as institutions in a free-market economy

Assumptions

The view of the firm as a bundle of specialized knowledge resources (Demsetz, 1988, 157; Conner, 1991, 141ff.; Teece, 1998, 75; Osterloh et al., 2002, 64) justifies its existence by underlining the efficiency advantages of this organizational form in creating, transferring, applying, and protecting knowledge assets.

Although some representatives of the knowledge-based view of the firm explain the emergence of the firm in part by relying on transaction-cost economics (Conner and Prahalad, 1996, 478ff.; Spender, 1996, 113), the idea of opportunistically behaving agents is not considered to be a necessary condition in explaining the emergence of firms (Conner, 1991, 140; Kogut and Zander, 1992, 384, 1993, 629; Conner and Prahalad, 1996, 478; Grant, 1996a, 113; Kogut and Zander, 1996, 503; Osterloh et al., 2002, 64). The firm is not understood to be "*an avoider of a negative...* [but rather]... *a creator of a positive*" (Conner, 1991, 139). In addition, the fundamental assumption of transaction cost theory that identical output can be produced by either a firm or a group of independent contractors (Conner, 1991, 142) is rejected.

The firm as an integrator of knowledge

Since knowledge is costly to acquire (Demsetz, 1988, 157) and transfer (Teece, 1977, 247ff.), deeply influenced by the culture of the firm (Conner, 1991, 141), and subject to a high level of specialization (Demsetz, 1988, 157), it is argued that the best use of autonomous stocks of knowledge can be made within a firm. Highly specific and path-dependent knowledge can be best – or most efficiently – applied within a single integrative community such as the firm (Grant, 1996a, 114).

The added value of the firm in comparison to a set of market transactions does not simply result from the avoidance of transaction cost but from the function of endowing individuals with a corporate culture and consequently integrating the dispersed knowledge of various specialists (Grant, 1996a, 112, 2002a, 140).

In addition, organizational models such as the firm do not require contract renegotiation in the presence of changing circumstances and unforeseen developments. Market contracts are well-defined agreements on specific tasks for which the contracting parties implicitly assume a stable environment. Accounting for unpredictable changes in this environment is only possible to a limited extent and at considerable cost (see also chapter 1 of Part IV). Firms, however, do not face such problems and can therefore represent a more efficient and flexible means of organizing the cooperation of individual activities. (Conner and Prahalad, 1996, 486–87).

The firm as a creator of knowledge

As already described in sub-subsection 2.2.4.3 of this Part, some theorists, including Teece and Grant, claim that knowledge creation takes place at the level of individual human beings. The task of the firm then is to integrate (Grant, 1996a, 112, 1996b, 377, 2002a, 138) and commercialize (Teece, 1998, 63) the knowledge of various specialists. Other theorists, including Kogut and Zander (1992; 1993; 1996), Spender (1996), and Nahapiet and Ghoshal (1998), however, argue that organizations do not merely function as an integrator of dispersed knowledge held by individuals. In addition, they create knowledge by providing their members with a sense of community (Kogut and Zander, 1992, 1993, 1996; Spender, 1996, 53ff.) and a spirit of identity, resulting in shared mental models. Firms define a set of network relationships (Moran and Ghoshal, 1996; Nahapiet and Ghoshal, 1998, 243ff.) that facilitate both the exchange and development of new knowledge.

The firm as a protector of knowledge

Liebeskind (1996; 1997) offers an alternative explanation for the existence of the firm by drawing the attention to the problem of appropriating the economic benefits resulting from an application of knowledge (see also sub-subsection 3.3.1.2 of this Part). In contrast to pure market transactions, organizational arrangements within the firm reduce the incentives for opportunistic behavior. Employment contracts additionally allow for better control of employees by reducing costs related to evaluating and ensuring their performance and by reducing employee mobility (Liebeskind, 1996, 97ff.). Liebeskind identifies (1) the establishment of rules restricting a transfer of knowledge, social interaction, and physical access, (2) the design of compensation schemes, and

(3) structural isolation as three broad approaches to protecting knowledge (Liebeskind, 1997, 625ff.).

2.2.5.2 A knowledge-based explanation for the multitude of firms as institutions in a free-market economy

In connecting the efficiency perspective with the idea of path-dependency, the knowledge-based view of the firm also sheds light on the fact that more than one firm can exist within an industry. The traditional resource-based view explains the multiplicity of firms by reference to specific and idiosyncratic sets of resources (see subsection 2.2.1 of this Part). In addition, the idea of path-dependency supports the heterogeneity of existing companies, since no incumbent can be said to have incurred the same experiences and thus possess an identical stock of knowledge (Conner, 1991, 139ff.).

2.2.6 The coordination of knowledge within the firm

The analysis of the coordinating role of the firm answers two different questions, namely, (1) where the need for coordination stems from, and (2) how coordination is achieved.

2.2.6.1 The need for coordination

The knowledge-based view of the firm explains the need for coordination within the firm primarily referring to the special features of knowledge as a resource. In particular, the specialization of members of an organization and the tacit nature of knowledge drive this need for coordination.

Due to the limited capacity of the human brain, "*knowledge workers*" (Drucker, 1999, 84) specialize in certain areas of knowledge (Grant, 1996a, 111–112). The production of sophisticated goods and services involves the cooperation of these specialists (Drucker, 1988, 46–47, 1991, 75ff., 1999, 58ff.). However, achieving this cooperation requires coordination.

In addition, if tacitness of knowledge is accepted as a fundamental trait of this resource, then even goal congruence between manager and agent cannot be considered a sufficient condition for the nonnecessity of coordinating mechanisms. The inexpressibility of tacit knowledge inhibits any transfer of knowledge between manager and agent.

Due to contractual agreements, managers can prompt employees to profit from specialized tacit knowledge on the manager's side even if this knowledge is not available to employees (Demsetz, 1988, 157). By following the directions of superior managers, employees substitute the broader knowledge of the executive for their (limited) knowledge (knowledge-substitution effect). In such a case, knowledge internalization can take place at the same time as knowledge application, but this is neither a required precondition nor a certain outcome (Conner and Prahalad, 1996, 485–468). Hence, any need for coordination in a knowledge-based economy does not only stem from specialization and opportunistic behavior alone, but also from the limited transferability of tacit knowledge.

2.2.6.2 Means of coordination

The knowledge-substitution effect implicitly assumes (1) the manager to have superior knowledge and (2) that the replacement of knowledge by the manager is beneficial for achieving a defined task. However, in the presence of "hidden knowledge" on the side of employees (Minkler, 1993, 19) these may have a deeper or better understanding about the nature of an existing decision problem. In this case knowledge substitution should not take place.

This in turn draws into question the adequacy of hierarchy as primary coordination mechanism within the firm and favors direct participation and decision making by teams rather than individuals (Grant, 1996a, 117ff.). In fact, the degree to which the knowledge-substitution effect – or authority as a coordinating mechanism in general – can be considered to be beneficial or unfavorable depends on (1) the complexity of the problem and (2) the distribution of specialized tasks among a given group of experts.

Complexity refers to the limited capacity of the single human mind in solving a multifaceted problem. The decomposition of a complex problem in smaller subproblems and the assignment of experts to solve these subproblems by a superior manager is a common mean to overcome problems of complexity (Nickerson and Zenger, 2004, 619ff.). Experts (agent) and managers (principal) usually *ex ante* define the process for solving a given subproblem. They agree on a set of goals that are to be reached within a given period of time. This management by objectives calls not for the abolition of authority but for a new role and understanding of authority (Foss, 2002, 21).

This new interpretation enables intrinsic motivation of the various knowledge workers (Osterloh et al., 2002, 64ff.), and at the same time also economizes on costly and time-consuming knowledge-sharing and education processes (Nickerson and Zenger, 2004, 624).

To reduce cost of communication and learning, the following various coordination mechanisms can be implemented (Grant, 1996a, 114–115): (1) Rules and directives that standardize human interaction in general. They facilitate the conversion of tacit knowledge into explicit knowledge by defining the way in which a task has to be solved. (2) Sequencing that allows for organizing different activities as a step-by-step process in which every specialist contributes to the final product during a predefined period of time. (3) Routines that, in the absence of formal rules and directives, economize the solution of complex decision problems by supporting simultaneous and flexible interactions. If, and only if the task to be solved is too complex or unusual and important to be solved by standardized processes, group solving and decision making should be used. However, these are time-consuming and costly.

Along with the various means of coordination, there are additional factors that can influence the coordination within the firm. Kogut and Zander (1996, 505ff.) argue that coordination is improved if organizations as social entities manage to endow their members with a sense of community and identity. In addition, the existence of a "*common organizational communication code*" (Monteverde, 1995, 1629) or common knowledge, such as language, symbolic communication, commonality of specialized knowledge, shared meaning, and recognition of the different knowledge stocks available to the members of the firm, strongly increases the efficiency of managing knowledge within the firm (Grant, 2002a, 139–140). Common knowledge enables the individual to better understand firm-specific communication (Arrow, 1974, 55ff.). It allows for low-cost communication between specialists and non-specialists, which in turn supports increasing specialization (Demsetz, 1988, 157).

2.2.7 The boundaries of the firm

The framework of the knowledge-based theory of the firm answers three main questions regarding boundary-decisions: (1) Where should the boundaries generally be drawn to maximize the rents resulting from the exploitation of knowledge assets and to avoid free-rider actions by, e.g., competitors? (2) Which activities of the value chain should be undertaken within the firm and which should be acquired via market transactions (vertical boundaries)? And (3) how many different products should be produced by one company (horizontal boundaries)? While the first question analyzes the decision about where to set boundaries to enable sustained competitive advantages, the second and the third investigate the depth and breadth of the firm's value chain.

If the basic assumption of non-opportunistic behavior is abandoned, then boundaries of the firm in terms of ownership can also be explained by incomplete contracts and property-rights theory. If the contract between principal and agent does not take into account all the possible circumstances then property rights to complementary, alienable assets (e.g., physical capital or patents) should be transferred to the owner of inalienable information assets (such as tacit knowledge). This avoids hold-up situations and, consequently, increases the incentives for the party which controls the inalienable knowledge asset (Brynjolfsson, 1994, 1649ff.; Foss, 2002, 25–26).

2.2.7.1 Boundaries of the firm and competitive advantage

Due to the public nature of explicit knowledge, boundaries may be designed in order to reduce free-riding problems (arrow (1) in Figure 10) (Holström and Roberts, 1998, 90–91; Osterloh et al., 2002, 65).When used for this purpose, the boundary decision aims for the full appropriation of current and future economic rents created by the use of knowledge (Monteverde, 1995, 1632–1633) as well as for the protection of knowledge-based competitive advantages (Teece, 1998, 75).

2.2.7.2 Depth of the firm's value chain: Vertical boundaries

Static view

The number of different stages in one production process to be integrated within one firm depends on "*information cost*" (arrow (2) in Figure 10) (Demsetz, 1988, 158). These costs describe the expenditures that occur in providing users of the product with the knowledge needed to fully exploit or use a product at a given stage in the production process. They do not take into account any other transaction cost or moral hazard considerations. The more a firm has to know about a product that serves as an input factor to exploit the embedded value potential, the higher the information cost is and the more likely the firm is to internalize the preceding production stage. Stated another way, the vertical boundaries of the firm are driven by the extent to which detailed knowledge about a given factor is required and its complexity and codifiability (Kogut and Zander, 1992, 395) which affect its transfer cost.

These cost can further be increased by the lacking ability of the parties involved to communicate it (Foss, 1996b, 475).

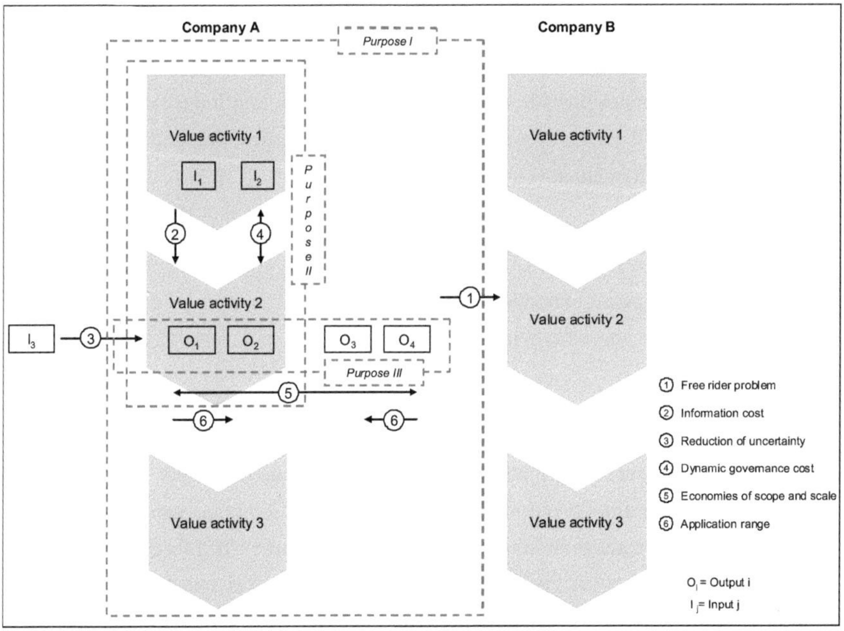

Figure 10: Boundary choices of the firm

In addition, the integration of a supplier not only results in a transfer of knowledge about the value and technical potential of an input factor, it also reduces uncertainty regarding the price of the input factor. Given a two-factor production function (e.g., factor 1 and factor 2), this reduced uncertainty has a positive impact on the entire production process. The (certain) price of factor 1 determines the amount of factor 1 to be acquired and, assuming a predetermined factor allocation, it also decides about the quantity of factor 2 to be used for the production of output (arrow (3) in Figure 10) (Arrow, 1975, 175ff.).

Dynamic view

The above arguments analyze the vertical boundaries of the firm at a given point in time; it should be noted, however, that a firm and its members' knowledge change over time. This change can be induced by learning processes, influenced by historical constraints (path-dependency), facilitated by complementary assets, and take place in the presence of technological opportunities (Dosi et al., 1992, 190ff.). Radical changes in a company can also affect its suppliers. The process of supporting important suppliers in adapting to a new situation mainly consists of teaching, persuading, and renegotiating and causes "*dynamic governance cost*" (arrow (4) in Figure 10) (Langlois, 1992, 113). If suppliers, or more generally the market, are unable to follow these changes and thus cannot provide a company with the required input factors, dynamic governance cost will raise; this in turn supports the vertical integration of various stages of the production chain (Langlois, 1992, 107ff.).

2.2.7.3 Breadth of the firm's value chain: Horizontal boundaries

Given its intangible nature, knowledge can be subject to economies of scope and scale; this in turn supports the emergence of multi-product firms (arrow (5) in Figure 10) (Grant, 1996a, 120).

However, since knowledge is also subject to high levels of specialization, the field of applications of valuable knowledge can at the same time be restricted. Thus, although knowledge might be a multi-purpose resource, its application range can comprise only a few comparable products or services (arrow (6) in Figure 10). Developing a multi-product company, however, by only relying on knowledge or capabilities that have been created internally is likely to take a considerable amount of time. It can only take place as a step-by-step process in which new ideas or capabilities are created by extending an existing stock of knowledge (Langlois, 1992, 107). Although knowledge might also be sourced externally, the availability of this option depends again on the codifiability of knowledge (Madhok, 1996, 584) or the availability of skilled knowledge workers (see sub-subsection 3.2.1.1 of this Part).

Finally it is worth mentioning that a clear distinction should be made between (1) product-related or technological knowledge and knowledge about structuring a sequence of operations, and (2) knowledge about general input factors (e.g. financial resources). In the first case, the application area might be limited to a small number of (high-tech) products. This limitation can explain single-product firms. In contrast, knowledge about general resources can be deployed in a broad set of application possibilities and therefore facilitates the existence of multi-product firms.

2.2.8 Critique and empirical tests of the knowledge-based view of the firm

2.2.8.1 Theoretical arguments

Review of assumptions

Foss (1996b) criticizes the underlying assumption of the knowledge-based view, that the existence of a firm can be explained without reference to the idea of opportunism. Contrary to Kogut and Zander (1992) and Conner (1991), he argues that neither shared culture nor higher-order principles establish a sufficient condition for the existence of the firm. In his opinion, such a coordinating mechanism results from the avoidance of opportunistic behavior and is not the reason that prevents economic agents from cheating or shirking. According to Foss, contractual agreements represent the only way to achieve cooperation between various specialists (Foss, 1996b, 473ff.).

Heiman and Nickerson (2002) attempt to reconcile these opposing views by connecting both chains of reasoning. They argue that knowledge attributes such as tacitness and problem-solving complexity determine the means by which knowledge is transferred. The transfer of knowledge in turn creates contracting hazards and opportunistic behavior which can be best dealt with within a firm. Furthermore, they recognize that firms endow their employees with a shared identity that reduces the likelihood of opportunistic behavior. But even if the organization's culture fails to converge the interests of its members, the communication channels by which information is exchanged may induce a commonality of interests. Members' positions and wealth might deteriorate if they move to another company from which access to these channels is not possible or if they were to try to acquire this information in the marketplace (Heiman and Nickerson, 2002, 109).

Review of explanations for the existence of the firm

In a following paper, Foss (1996a) expands his critique by rejecting the idea of Kogut and Zander (1996) that firms exist because they provide individuals with an identity. The desire of human beings to belong to a moral community cannot, in his opinion, explain why firms as economic institutions in particular exist (Foss, 1996a, 520). Additionally, Foss deals with the arguments brought forth by Conner and Prahalad (1996), that an employee contract can be seen as sufficient condition for the existence of the firm. They argue that it allows for a more efficient substitution of knowledge (knowledge-substitution effect) and a more flexible adaptation to changes in the economic environment (flexibility effect) (Conner and Prahalad, 1996, 484ff.). Foss maintains that both flexibility effect and knowledge-substitution effect can also be realized via a market transaction. He rejects the idea that an employee contract is a sufficient condition for the existence of the firm. In fact, in the presence of incomplete contracts, firms often emerge because they offer alternative ways to influence employees, for example, through the possession of residual rights over physical assets. These alternative ways provide a solution to incomplete contracts and define the borders of the firm (Foss, 1996a, 521–522).

Review of the explanations for coordination within the firm

Finally, Foss (2002) also discusses the argument that hierarchy is an inefficient coordination mechanism in the presence of hidden knowledge. Even if the manager is not aware of the best of all possible solutions, centralized decision-making can be an efficient tool in his opinion If the decision is urgent, the impact of the "unknown" facts on the final decision is weak and the costs for transferring these facts are high and if the manager can at least create estimates of the level of output to be expected by the agent (Foss, 2002, 20ff.), centralized decision-making is to be preferred.

2.2.8.2 Empirical results

The empirical results of an investigation of 100 major Swedish innovations conducted by Kogut and Zander (1993) suggest that knowledge attributes, namely, codifiability, teachability, and complexity, affect the way in which knowledge is transferred between and within companies. According to their findings, the likelihood of knowledge transfer increases according to the degree to which knowledge can be codified and taught. The complexity of knowledge, in turn, positively influences the decision to transfer it within the firm (Kogut and Zander, 1993, 635ff.).

Since the transfer of know-how cannot be organized at low cost due to its tacit components, specific know-how has been found to be a driver for extending the vertical boundaries of major players in the American automobile industry (Monteverde and Teece, 1982, 210ff.). Furthermore, Pisano (1990) reports for a sample of 92 the biotechnical R&D-projects that R&D internalization is driven by the concern that essential know-how would be lost if research were conducted by an external partner (Pisano, 1990, 157ff.).

Poppo and Zenger (1998) analyze surveys from the information service departments of 152 firms. They find no support for the idea that shared language and firm routines positively affect the performance of internal exchange processes (Poppo and Zenger, 1998, 872–873).

2.2.9 Implications for knowledge definition

Three main implications result from the review of the knowledge-based view of the firm. First, in economic theory, the overall concept of knowledge denominates two different economic goods, explicit and tacit knowledge. Both can be sources of competitive advantages and therefore exhibit a certain value potential.

Second, these basic types of knowledge differ with respect to codifiability and transferability. Explicit knowledge is easily articulated and therefore transferable at lower cost than inexpressible, tacit knowledge. Knowledge can, depending on its transferability, be subject to economies of scope and scale.

Third, knowledge is created, applied, and held by individuals. Sophisticated goods and services require the application of various types of knowledge and cooperation of various specialists. Firms as organizations can support these processes. However, these processes are path-dependent at both the firm and individual level. This path-dependency leads to the emergence of individual and firm-specific, complementary assets that might have a significant impact on the knowledge of an employee or an organization.

2.3 The definition of knowledge

Although many aspects of knowledge have been analyzed in the contributions mentioned above, the existing body of literature offers only a few definitions for this concept. Other than knowledge being just the "*state of knowing*" (Machlup, 1980, 56) or "*that which is known*" (Grant, 1996a, 110), it is stated that knowledge is based on information (Caldwell, 1975, 570) that is interpreted by the knowing entity (Huber, 1991, 89) and, following the JTB approach, assumed (Nonaka, 1994, 15) or proven (Liebeskind, 1996, 94) to be true.

So far, to the best of my knowledge, no consistent definition of the concept of knowledge has been introduced. I shall not try to enrich the existing body of literature with another elaborate definition that attempts to distinguish between knowledge and truth or belief; nor shall I neglect the importance of a definition for this basic concept for the following discussion.

2.3.1 Knowledge as the interpretation of facts by the mind of a human being

The development and testing of a theory requires a definition for each theoretical construct and variable. According to Wacker (2004), a definition is a clearly and precisely formulated verbal expression of a concept. Definitions are the starting point for theory building and testing and therefore have to be formulated carefully. A suitable definition for knowledge should comply with the following catalogue of requirements (Wacker, 2004, 631ff.):

(1) Definitions should be formally defined using primitive and derived terms. All definitions should follow the rule of replacement.

(2) Each concept should be uniquely defined. It should exclude as many shared terms with other definitions as possible to reduce confusion with related concepts.

(3) Definitions should only include unambiguous and non-vague terms.

(4) Definitions should use as few terms as possible to convey the essence of the concept.

(5) Definitions should be consistent within the theory domain.

(6) New formal definitions should not expand current definitions to make them less precise and broader.

(7) Formal conceptual definitions should not contain new hypotheses.

(8) Empirical tests of validity should be performed only after the formal conceptual definition passes the first seven rules.

Based on these preceding eight rules, the analysis of the philosophical approaches (see subsection 2.1.2 of this Part) and the contributions made by the knowledge-based theory of the firm (see subsection 2.2.9 of this Part), I define knowledge as *the interpretation of facts by the mind of a human being*.

2.3.1.1 The subject of interpretation: Fact

According to Cohen and Nagel (1936), a fact is "*a proposition for whose truth there is considerable evidence*" (Cohen and Nagel, 1936, 392). They furthermore stress the point that the reliability with which a fact can be identified as a fact and not as a guess or hypothesis depends on the stage of inquiry.

For valuation purposes it is useful to assume that facts upon which knowledge is based are considered to be true and reliable to a certain degree. Clearly, different evaluations of the reliability of knowledge lead to different ideas about the financial value of knowledge. These differences in estimating the financial value facilitate the trading of knowledge assets in the marketplace (see also section 1.3 of this Part).

2.3.1.2 The active interpreter: The mind

Following western philosophical approaches, knowledge is created by combining two distinct elements: mind and fact (see section 2.1 of this Part). The emergence of knowledge therefore requires both external facts *and* the intellect of an individual. Strictly speaking, facts written down in a book cannot – by this definition – be considered to be knowledge until they are read and so are known to an individual. In other words, the existence of a fact constitutes a necessary condition for knowledge, while its interpretation by the mind of a human being can be seen as sufficient condition. Consistent with this active interpretation of knowledge, I assume that the value of knowledge, in general, depends on the degree to which this knowledge supports the solving of existing and current decision problems.

2.3.2 Levels of knowledge

Based on a classification introduced by the Organization for Economic Cooperation and Development, I further distinguish four levels of knowledge (OECD, 1996, 12): (1) know-what, (2) know-why, (3) know-how, and (4) know-who. As shown in Figure 11, these different types build upon each other and can be arranged hierarchically.

2.3.2.1 Know-what

The basis of all knowledge, know-what, comprises facts e.g., the description of ingredients in a recipe or the specifications of a product on a blueprint. Generally speaking, the value of such a fact depends on the point in time one becomes acquainted with it and the degree to which this fact influences decisions of the individual knowing it.

2.3.2.2 Know-why

The connection of facts by a theory constitutes know-why. A theory is a set of statements that can be tested empirically. Theories are based on assumptions and offer explanations for fundamental connections about the principles of the economy or the laws of nature. Know-why is produced by specialized units such as research laboratories and universities. As basic research, it prepares the ground for new product or process innovations. This level of knowledge can be protected by patent rights (see also the discussion on fundamental and procedural requirements of national patent laws in Part II). Please note that facts are always an essential element of knowledge, but not every fact is linked to a theory. Therefore know-why always contains know-what, but not all parts of know-what are included in know-why.

2.3.2.3 Know-how

The application of know-why in combination with personal skills leads to know-how. Hence, know-how rests on two pillars: theoretical knowledge (know-why) and skills of the knowing individual. According to Nelson and Winter (1982), a skill is *"a capability for a smooth sequence of coordinated behavior that is ordinarily effective relative to its objectives, given the context in which it normally occurs"* (Nelson and Winter, 1982, 73). A skill can be understood as a chain of single steps that are arranged in a row and linked by (implicitly made) decisions. Thus, a skill includes a considerable amount of tacit knowledge (Polanyi, 1958, 59ff.).

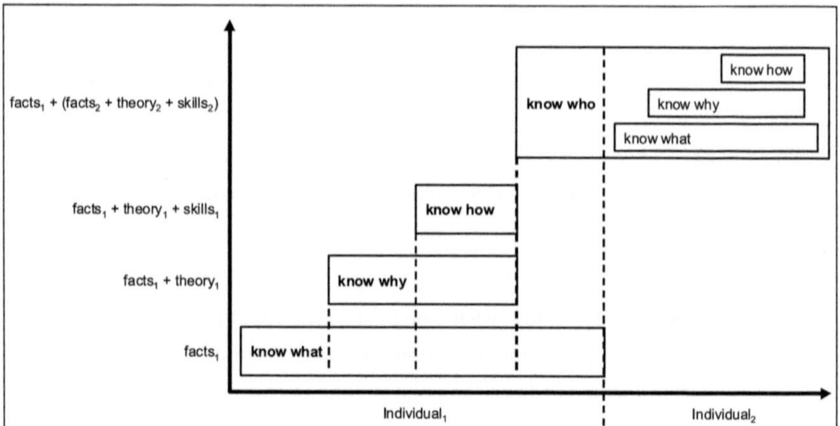

Level	Definition
Know-what	Body of facts available to the mind of a human being.
Know-why	Facts available to the mind of a human being, connected by theory.
Know-how	Facts available to the mind of a human being connected by theory and the individual skills of a human being.
Know-who	Knowing facts about other individuals.

Figure 11: Levels of knowledge

2.3.2.4 *Know-who*

The last level of knowledge, know-who, describes the knowing of facts about what others know and the extent to which their skills are useful for the solution of one's own decision problem (Cohen and Levinthal, 1990, 133). Hence, this level of knowledge could also be referred to as "knowing how to get a task accomplished" or as "knowledge substitution" (Conner and Prahalad, 1996, 484ff.). The value of know-who is mainly driven by (1) the precise idea of what skill is needed for accomplishing a desired task, (2) the word which denominates this skill, (3) the acquaintance with someone considered to be an expert in exercising this skill, and (4) the social arrangements which are used to get the task accomplished. The impact of the latter depends on the level of homogeneity of the skill needed to fulfill the task, the cost of supervising and verifying performance, the mutual trust on which the arrangement is grounded, and the enforcement of contractual rights (Nelson and Winter, 1982, 86–87).

3 The value of knowledge

Having defined knowledge as the interpretation of facts by the mind of a human being and accepting the main assumption of the knowledge-based view of the firm that knowledge is an important resource, the question still remains as to *why* knowledge is valuable. The following chapters analyze the traits that make knowledge valuable (section 3.1), review the specific characteristics that cause appropriation problems (section 3.2), and summarize suitable strategies to overcome these problems (section 3.3).

3.1 Value potential and value realization

Economic theorists usually argue that knowledge exhibits value potentials because it can be subject to economies of scale, scope, and multi-plant operations (Scherer et al., 1975, 18ff.; Markusen, 1984, 207; Foss, 2002, 13; Grant, 2002a, 136). Due to its intangible nature, explicit knowledge can be easily shared. This non-rivalry in consumption first of all enables economies of scale and scope. Clearly, the value actually realized is mainly driven by the application area of knowledge in the business process. From an economic point of view, knowledge can either be exploited indirectly through application in the production of goods and services or through the direct selling of facts. The extent to which the latter is possible depends not only on the transferability of knowledge but also on the degree to which appropriation problems can be solved. While transferability refers to the idea of leveraging the value potential of knowledge, appropriability indicates that the seller might not be able to fully appropriate the value created, due to the intangibility of both facts and mind.

Clearly, the value potential of both tacit and explicit knowledge is deeply influenced by the intellect of individuals. In combination with the path-dependent development of knowledge and the personal relatedness of tacit knowledge, this private, subjective aspect of knowledge challenges any subsequent valuation. However, please note that for valuation purposes at a firm level neither value potential nor value creation play a decisive role, but rather the degree to which the created value can be appropriated by the owner of knowledge (see also sub-subsection 1.3.2.1 in Part IV). This basic necessity is reflected in the underlying idea behind the VRIN paradigm (see subsection 2.2.1 in this Part).

3.2 Appropriating the value of knowledge

In general, appropriation problems emerge if (1) facts are transferred without the owner's clear intention and (2) if, due to this involuntary transfer, the owner is partially or fully excluded from obtaining the rents created by exploiting the economic potential of these facts. Hence, avoiding appropriation problems requires either the creation of barriers to involuntary transfer or the implementation of mechanisms that (1) either compensate the owner for the economic disadvantages following an involuntary transfer and/or (2) reduce the attractiveness to competitors of taking advantage of this involuntary transfer.

3.2.1 The publicity of facts: Transmission channels for explicit and implicit knowledge

Tacit and explicit knowledge differ with regard to transferability and consequently the degree to which they cause appropriation problems. However, prior to an analysis of these differences, I shall briefly summarize the main transmission channels for technological knowledge. I concentrate on technological knowledge as this form of knowledge can be protected by patent rights.

3.2.1.1 Mobile workforce

There are several channels by which facts can spread without the explicit intention of the fact owner. Given an open labor market, the mobility of personnel offers one pathway to involuntary transmission (Conner and Prahalad, 1996, 486ff.; Rosenkopf and Almeida, 2003, 760ff.; Møen, 2007). Almeida and Kogut (1999) investigate the extent to which knowledge localization in specific regions of the semiconductor industry is influenced by the career mobility of skilled engineers. They find support for the idea that the career paths of key patent holders affect the ability to create semiconductor design knowledge (Almeida and Kogut, 1999, 915). Song et al. (2003) analyze the conditions under which knowledge transfer via human mobility in the global semiconductor industry is most likely to happen. They look at the characteristics of both the mobile engineer and the hiring company. Their findings suggest that learning from mobile engineers is most likely to happen if these engineers have gained experience in technologies that are new to the firm or if they work in technologies that are not considered to be core technologies of the hiring company. On the firm side, success in the past negatively influences the propensity to be open to new knowledge brought in by mobile workers (Song et al., 2003, 359ff.). Recent empirical results further show the existence of a causal relationship between inventor productivity and inventor mobility. Mobile inventors (those who change employers) seem to be more productive. At the same time, increased productivity reduces the likelihood of a move to another employer (Hoisl, 2007, 634).

However, according to Phillips (2002), the consequences resulting from a shift from one company to another depend on the position of the mobile employee. His analysis of a sample of Silicon valley law firms shows that in service and knowledge-intensive industries, the transfer of key personnel, such as senior partners, from one firm to another decreases the likelihood of failure for the receiving firm and increases the likelihood of failure for the old firm (Phillips, 2002, 490ff.).

Of course, communication channels created by mobile employees do not facilitate knowledge flows in one direction only. Bidirectional relationships do in fact exist in which knowledge from the employee's new firm is also transferred to the old employer. The extent to which this happens depends on the social capital of the respective employee. Thus, not only human capital such as skills and knowledge can explain Phillip's findings but also the relationships of individuals (Corredoira and Rosenkopf, 1995; Agrawal et al., 2003).

A good relationship among experts facilitates both, the creation or discovery of new facts as well as their transfer. Garvey and Griffith (1971) find that in the field of psychology, only one research idea in seven is motivated by studying journal articles or attending presentations at meetings. They argue that scientists rely heavily on their informal network for developing new research questions. In addition, they use this network to evaluate and assess their theoretical hypotheses and empirical findings prior to publishing articles in a journal (Garvey and Griffith, 1971, 354–355).

3.2.1.2 R&D monitoring

A second way to obtain important facts is based on an in-depth analysis of any "output" a company produces. This strategy includes the monitoring of facts either published voluntarily or due to legal constraints at the product-level (e.g., product manuals and catalogues) (Zander, 1991, 51–52) or company-level (e.g., annual reports, ad hoc announcements). Empirical findings suggest that the propensity to publish R&D results in scientific papers varies by industry and country. But in some research fields, for example, the physical or chemical sciences, a third of the top-ten producers of scientific output are employees of leading companies (Hicks, 1995, 404).

In addition, Levin et al. (1987) argue that licensing agreements are considered to be a very effective way of gaining access to new technology (see also chapter 1 in Part IV). They further emphasize that independent R&D investments motivated by – but not explicitly restricted to – the desire to reveal competitors' knowledge are an effective mechanism for knowledge transfer (Levin et al., 1987, 806).

3.2.1.3 Reverse engineering

Another source of relevant facts is the close inspection of the various components of a sophisticated product, an approach commonly referred to as "reverse engineering" (Levin et al., 1987, 807). The adjective "reverse" indicates that the problem solution process does not start with an analysis of the problem itself but with the examination of the solution (i.e., the product). The primary objective of this approach is to reveal and understand the way in which a problem can be solved (the product can be produced), rather than just to imitate the solution. The success in imitating the product of a competitor by reverse engineering depends on the impact of know-why and skills in constituting know-how (Nelson and Winter, 1982, 123–124). In general, the gains from reverse engineering or imitation are influenced by the observability of products or production processes. The lower the degree of observability, the more causal ambiguity is created which in turn increases the cost of imitation (Liebeskind, 1996, 95).

3.2.1.4 Customer-specific products

The dissemination of facts is also facilitated by the specificity of a product or service a company offers. The production of tailor-made solutions requires close cooperation between market partners (supplier and customers) and the company; however, such cooperation can induce a considerable transfer of facts (Kogut and Zander, 1992, 392).

3.2.2 Implicit knowledge: Transferability and appropriation

Tacit knowledge is bound to individuals, since personal skills, or more generally know-how, cannot be transferred easily. The shift from one individual to another person is slow, costly, and uncertain (Kogut and Zander, 1992, 384; Grant, 1996a, 111).

Nelson and Winter (1982) consider reasons as to why it can be difficult to teach or imitate (i.e., transfer) tacit knowledge. They state that the transfer of tacit knowledge is constrained due to differing time needs for explaining and exercising a task and the impossibility of articulating the complete knowledge content. In addition, the serial character of communication using language prohibits a simultaneous description of both the separate aspects of tacit knowledge and the ways they are linked to each other (Nelson and Winter, 1982, 80–81).

These difficulties in transferring tacit knowledge in turn reduce problems of appropriability. However, this situation may be no more favorable than in the case of explicit knowledge. The limitations in the transfer of tacit knowledge also narrow the potential for creating value via market transactions and the realization of economies of scope or scale.

3.2.3 Explicit knowledge: Transferability and appropriation

In general, the degree to which an asset is tradable affects its ability to create sustained competitive advantages (Teece, 1998, 62). Facts, once published can be internalized by any individual who happens to become acquainted with them. The intangible nature of facts directly influences the "R-condition" of the VRIN paradigm and reduces the capability of the fact owner to fully exploit and appropriate the value potential of a fact.[1] Empirical results reveal that the degree of codification positively affects the transferability of knowledge to a third party (Kogut and Zander, 1993, 635).

Since explicit knowledge is revealed and thus transferred by communication, economic theorists consider it to be a public good (Arrow, 1962, 615; Machlup, 1980, 180; Kogut and Zander, 1993, 627ff.; Dyer and Nobeoka, 2000, 346ff.; Grant, 2002b, 177; Martin and Salomon, 2003, 298). This class of goods is characterized by the properties of non-exclusivity and non-rivalry, which in turn can lead to appropriation problems and an undersupply of the public good if consumers decide to act as free riders (Osterloh et al., 2002, 65). Non-exclusivity means that a resource owner can neither control access to nor control consumption of the resource by an unauthorized third party. A resource transfer from one party to another is possible at low or close to zero marginal cost. Non-rivalry refers to the fact that the consumption of a public resource by one subject does not reduce the overall amount available to other consumers (Arrow, 1962, 615; Grant, 1996a, 110–111; Ba et al., 2001, 1204).

It is important to note that even if fact owners can disguise important parts of information, the way in which they interpret and combine hidden facts is externally observable. Hence, the result of this interpretive combination – new facts – can be analyzed by third parties. Therefore, the examination of both result and the result-achieving-process, to the extent that this process can be broken down into new facts, supports the spread of facts and the diffusion of knowledge through organizations and economies.

The difficulties which arise when intangible goods such as facts are to be traded or transferred can be illustrated by reference to the transfer of a tangible good. During the process of transferring tangible goods via market, the sellers can influence the behavior of the buyers towards the fulfillment of the contracts by keeping the transaction objects until the stipulated prices have been paid. At the same time, any utility on the buyers' side emerges only after theses goods are within their range. Hence, utility creation sequentially follows the fulfillment of the contractual terms. This reduces the possibility and likelihood of opportunistic behavior.

Due to the intangible nature of knowledge, the transfer of facts does not imply such protection. Facts can start yielding profit for "buyers" the moment these become aware of them. In the absence of legal or contractual arrangements, a seller cannot bar poten-

[1] Clearly, the degree to which this condition is influenced by the publication of facts depends on the similarity of human minds leading to similar results and comparable actions.

tially interested buying parties from using these facts without paying for them. This problem further increases as "sellers" might often be unaware of the fact that they have just "transferred" important facts. This is due to the multitude of ways in which facts can be transmitted, ranging from the publication of new findings in articles and books to casual talks or official meetings.

At this point in the discussion, it is important to recognize the existence of mutually dependent relationships. From the point of view of company *X*, the probability of spillovers can reduce the incentive to create new facts (e.g., via R&D investment) as these new findings might be also be useful for competitors *Y* and *Z*, thus reducing the utility for the value creator (*X*) (Zander, 1991, 23). But at the same time, the competitors may also face this challenge; this may in turn lead to unintended (by *Y* and *Z*), but not undesired (by *X*), spillovers to company *X* (Nelson, 1959, 303; Arrow, 1962, 617–618; Spence, 1984, 102ff.).

3.3 Strategic options for solving appropriability problems

As described in section 3.1 of this Part, two conditions must be met in order to create appropriability problems: (1) the unintentional transfer of facts and (2) the partial or full exclusion from the obtaining of rents created by making use of this unintended transfer. Therefore, strategies for overcoming appropriability problems either avoid involuntary transfers of facts or unintentional value exploitation.

3.3.1 Strategies for avoiding involuntary transfer of facts

3.3.1.1 Secrecy

An initial strategy in avoiding involuntary transfer consists of minimizing communication of facts; the more communication is reduced, the lower the probability of an unintended transfer of facts. Empirical results indicate not only that secrecy is an effective means for appropriating economic rents (Arundel, 2001, 617–618) – especially in the case of appropriating rents from process innovations (Levin et al., 1987, 794). In addition, its use has gained in importance over the last years (Cohen et al., 2000, 13). The benefits of secrecy emerge the moment fact owners decide to apply this means and last as long as they pursue this strategy with reasonable care. Thus, it can be a quick, effective, and also comparatively inexpensive appropriating mechanism.

3.3.1.2 Organizational design

Secrecy can be an effective appropriation mechanism for a small number of individuals. However, complex problems often require the interaction and collaboration of various experts from different fields. This process can weaken the veiling nature of secrecy. By establishing and maintaining shared values and by creating social relationships among employees (Kogut and Zander, 1992, 384), firms as institutions can serve as a general means to protect firm-specific resources such as knowledge (Grant, 1996a, 110ff.). The advantage of firms in protecting knowledge derives from the fact that employers can by law impose and enforce rules on their employees (Liebeskind, 1997, 629). The most obvious way is the signing of confidentiality agreements defining an employee's duty to not transfer confidential information to a third party as well as temporary non-compete clauses that become effective should the employees leave the organization (Zander, 1991, 51–52).

Liebeskind (1996; 1997) distinguishes three classes of restrictive rules. First, rules can grant or restrict access to and the transfer of knowledge within the firm. Disaggregating a complex task into a set of simpler subtasks can not only increase efficiency of the problem-solving process by using the individual skills and strengths of different employees. It can also serve as a means to reduce the economic disadvantages resulting from a possible unintended knowledge transfer. A successful duplication of all knowledge requires (simultaneous) access to all knowledge of all subtasks. The complexity of innovative products usually leads to a modular job design with multiple teams working on specific tasks. On the one hand such a labor organization can effectively limit an undesired spread of facts and create effective barriers for knowledge transfer (Liebeskind, 1996, 99–100). On the other hand, however, the overall success of the innovative process heavily depends on an efficient coordination of the research and development efforts of all teams. This in turn requires a certain level of exchange within and between teams. For a multi-team project in the automotive industry with 39 teams and eight sub-projects, Weinkauf, Högl and Gemünden (2004) show that cooperation within and between teams is crucial for the overall success (Weinkauf et al., 2004, 425ff.).

A second class of restrictive mechanisms aims at reducing social interaction between specified employees and external parties. Whether explicitly formulated in contractual clauses or formally forbidden by senior managers, employees can be held responsible for an unauthorized transfer of knowledge to a third party.

A third option consists of selecting alternative production or research sites at which valuable knowledge in tacit or explicit form is created and applied. The geographical distance between these sites, in combination with restricted physical access and the use of security systems, can prevent any transfers of knowledge.

In addition to these restrictive rules, firms might also opt for the implementation of incentive schemes. These motivate employees and reduce moral hazard problems. This in turn has a negative impact on the likelihood of the transfer of important facts to competitors (Liebeskind, 1997, 632ff.).

3.3.2 Strategies for avoiding unintended value exploitation of facts

3.3.2.1 Costly imitation

The unintended transfer of facts does not necessarily induce appropriation problems. If competitors opt not to exploit the economic potential then the direct economic rents of the fact owner are not affected.[2] One reason might be that product complexity increases imitation cost, which in turn renders an imitation strategy unattractive from an economic point of view (Nelson, 1990, 201). Mansfield, Schwartz, and Wagner (1981) report that imitation is, on average, less expensive in terms of R&D investment and time. However, their results further indicate that there is a considerable degree of uncertainty for running imitation projects. They analyze 48 product launches in the United States that have either already been imitated or are expected to be copied in the future. They find that in 15% of the cases imitation cost exceed innovation cost (Mansfield et al., 1981, 909–910). Additional support for their analysis is also presented by Levin et al. (1987). They also find that cost and time for imitation depend on the type of innovation (major versus typical), the subject of innovation (product versus process), and the existence of valid patent claims covering the respective innovation (Levin et al., 1987, 809). Furthermore, reverse-engineering projects might fail, since the deconstruction of a complex product simultaneously destroys or damages the integrity of the entire technology (Zander, 1991, 52).

Finally, superior sales and service efforts that support product selling in the marketplace are the most effective mechanism for value exploitation in case of product innovations and are of considerable importance for capturing the value embedded in process innovations (Levin et al., 1987; Harabi, 1995). Thus, appropriation of economic

[2] Of course, there might be negative consequences that become evident only after a certain period of time.

rents resulting from exploiting knowledge can also – and sometimes only – be achieved by investing in complementary resources (Teece, 1986, 288ff.). If competitors are unable or unwilling to duplicate these complementary resources, then they may also be unable to expropriate the value of knowledge (Dosi, 1988, 1140; Teece, 1998, 72).

3.3.2.2 First-mover advantages: Increasing imitation time

In general, the value potential of facts declines over time. This value erosion is in part rooted in the specific characteristics of knowledge, such as the context- and time-specificity of facts, and also in the limited possibility of fully keeping valuable facts secret. In view of this, companies may try to extend the period over which they can keep valuable knowledge private and slow the dissemination (Zander, 1991, 23) processes that transform private knowledge into a public good. Or else they may decide to concentrate more on continuously creating new valuable facts, thus exploiting first-mover advantages. A primary source of first-mover advantages is lead time (McEvily and Chakravarthy, 2002, 288). This appropriation mechanism is the natural consequence of creating new products and processes (Levin et al., 1987, 816). However, a leading position can only be defended if inventors transform this advantage of being the first to successfully introduce new products or processes into subsequent advantages, chiefly learning curve effects and scale economies (Dosi, 1988, 1139). Empirical results show that lead time is one (Levin et al., 1987, 794) – or even the most important (Harabi, 1995, 986; Cohen et al., 2000, 10; Arundel, 2001, 616; Blind et al., 2006, 661) – appropriation means in the case of product innovations. One reason might be that being the first to introduce new products into the market not only facilitates the setting of monopolistic prices, but also establishes barriers to entry such as well-known brands and specific customer relationships. These ensure profitable business activities even after potential imitators have appeared (Mansfield et al., 1981, 910). In industries in which (product) designs or technological product standards are relevant, scale and learning become much more important as competition shifts to price after the emergence of a dominate design (Teece, 1986, 287–288.).

Needless to say that patent protection of technical standards can be very profitable should the patent holder manage to protect standard relevant inventions. Since competitors are driven by customers to offer products using this standard technology, they may be willing to enter profitable licensing agreements, otherwise they run the risk of having to invent around the existing technological standard. However, in such a case they must not only provide a better technical solution, but must also achieve a new standard.

3.3.2.3 Legal and contractual mechanisms

National and international law offer alternative legal protective means to secure specific types of knowledge. Within the group of intellectual property rights (IPRs), patents are the most prominent protective mechanism for securing technology-based competitive advantages. As I will describe in the following Parts, the basic idea of the patent system is to foster economic progress by offering temporary monopolies in exchange for revealing private facts to the general public. In addition, any contractual approach, such as a licensing contract or an employee agreement, can be a suitable means for solving appropriation problems (see also chapter 1 in Part IV).

For the following analysis, two points are worth mentioning. First, patents endow their holder with the right to exclude others from profiting from a technological invention. Thus, any value depends on the strength of this exclusivity (Teece, 1986, 287). However, the primary source of value is the value potential of the underlying technological knowledge. Clearly no value can be added by granting an exclusive right to an invention that does not lead to economic rents of any kind and thus is not profitable. Hence, a patent valuation should not be restricted to an analysis of the legal aspects, but link the exclusive function of the patent to the economic profitability of the patented invention.

Second, several studies have analyzed the effectiveness of the alternative appropriability strategies described in the preceding chapters. Levin, Klevorik, Nelson, and Winter (Levin et al., 1987) find that patents are the least effective protective mechanism for process innovations; they play a more important role, however, in case of product innovations. These general findings have been validated by Cohen, Nelson, and Walsh (Cohen et al., 2000). Please note that both studies focus on the U.S. manufacturing sector. In contrast, comparable research designs for other countries, such as Germany and Japan, show a higher effectiveness of patent protection (Cohen et al., 2002, 1354–1355; Rammer, 2002, 7; Blind et al., 2006, 660–661).

In part, these national differences result from varying degrees of exclusivity under differing patent regimes. In Part II, I therefore present the main differences between the patent regimes in the United States, Europe, and Germany. Regardless of the various patent laws, all studies find remarkable cross-industry differences. Patents are especially effective in industries with discrete technologies in which patent infringement can be easily detected and less effective in cumulative industries (see also chapter 2 in Part II).

4 Part I: Implications for patent valuation

Part I focuses on the definition of knowledge and the value potential of knowledge assets. For the discussion of patents and patent valuation methods, the following implications are to be considered:

1. *Dualism of valuation*

   A valuation rests on two pillars. First, a well-structured analysis of the underlying economic situation, the specific features of the valuation object, and the purpose of the overall valuation project should be performed (evaluation). Second, the results of this evaluation are to be transformed into comparable quantitative information. Sensitivity analyses and the application of appropriate valuation formula(s) finally lead to reasonable value ranges.

2. *Context specificity of valuation*

   Each valuation is based on a specific current data set and reflects the expectations of the parties involved. Or, put it differently, the valuation mirrors the subjective interpretations regarding the impact of a given set of data on the economic situation of each party. Hence, changes in the underlying data set or the guiding expectations can lead to changes in the conclusion of value.

3. *Dualism of knowledge and the role of organizations*

   The term *knowledge* describes two different economic goods with opposite characteristics. Given its limited codifiability, its high degree of path-dependency, and its stickiness to individuals, tacit knowledge can only be transferred to a limited extent. In contrast to this, explicit knowledge can be easily transferred. In both cases, organizations such as firms play a major role in creating, coordinating, integrating, and protecting knowledge. Alternative organizational frameworks, as well as industry-specific characteristics, establish the general surroundings of any valuation project. They influence the processes of research and development and invention and the selection of appropriate protective means. This directly affects quality and value of inventions and patents.

4. Relationship between knowledge and patent rights

As defined in subsection 2.3.2 knowledge comprises four different levels: know-what, know-why, know-how, and know-who. Patent applications are filed to protect technological inventions. One basic condition for patent protection is the disclosure of the underlying know-why by means of a detailed description of the technological features of the invention. Hence, patents are one means to protect new facts (know-what) and new technologies (know-why). However at the same time, the value of a technology and the profitability of products and services can also depend on unprotected know-how (e.g., excellent sales staff) and know-who (e.g., excellent relationships with customers or suppliers). If a joint use of several classes of knowledge is crucial for a full exploitation of valuable knowledge, the fact that patents only focus on selected aspects of knowledge (explicitly formulated, new know-why) should be reflected in any valuation.

Part II: Protecting knowledge-based competitive advantages through patents

1 The legal dimension of patents

Based on a review of the patent history (section 1.1), I present substantial (section 1.2) and procedural (section 1.3) requirements for patent protection according to the patent laws in Germany, Europe, and the United States and international patent treaties (section 1.4). After a short introduction to the main patent classification systems (section 1.5), I conclude this chapter with a discussion of the cost and benefits of patent litigation (section 1.6). The primary aim of this chapter is to introduce the basic ideas of patent protection. Understanding these basic legal features is essential for conducting a reasonable valuation since they first of all prepare the ground for any exclusive exploitation of a profitable invention. Given the management focus of this thesis, I concentrate on those peculiarities of patents and patent systems that are of major importance for patent valuation.

1.1 Roots and development of patent protection

1.1.1 The basic idea

A patent is a grant issued by the government of a country endowing the patent owner with the right to exclude others from making, using, or selling an invention within the borders of this country for a period of up to twenty years. In exchange for this grant, the patent owner agrees to the detailed disclosure of the invention, such that a person of ordinary skill could make and use it. Most important is the fact that a patent does not constitute a positive right for the inventor to profit from the invention but grants the (negative) right to exclude a third party from using, making, or selling the invention (Chisum et al., 2004, 3–4).

An invention is patentable if it meets certain substantial and procedural requirements. Central to the idea of patent protection is that the social cost linked to the creation of temporary monopolies is balanced by the benefits resulting from the diffusion of an invention (Ordover, 1991).

Due to similar historical roots and in combination with the desire to create comparable national patent regimes, there has been strong support for harmonizing the various national patent laws over the last centuries. However, there are still some differences, especially between patent law in Europe and the United States that can have a significant impact on patent valuation.

Under most patent laws worldwide, completing an invention and submitting a patent application qualifies the inventor to receive a patent. However, before the patent can be granted, the patent application must meet certain substantial and procedural requirements, which are investigated by a patent examiner of the respective patent authority following a standardized procedure. With publication in the patent gazette, the patent holder receives the rights as defined by patent law. If no written objection by a third party is submitted and in the absence of any successful nullity proceedings, the patent will expire twenty years after the application date – if the patent holder pays the required renewal fees (Wurzer and Reinhardt, 2006, 44).

1.1.2 History of patent protection

The very word "patent" is rooted in the Latin *litterae patentes*, meaning "open letter". This translation already sheds light on the core of patent protection: the granting of monopoly rights in exchange for the disclosure of an invention. Early attempts to grant exclusive rights to inventors had been made by the Republic of Venice in the 14th century. In 1421, Phillipo Brunillesci was granted a monopoly to exclusively use his invention of a floating construction crane (Hall, 1992, 137).

And it was in Venice that the first patent law was established (*parte veneziana*), on March 19, 1474. Between 1474 and 1549, 109 "patents" were granted. Most of them dealt with inventions for mills and canalization techniques. The patent terms differed, ranging from five to more than seventy years. In the case of a *perpetuum mobile*, invented by Giovanni Paolo in 1547, the patent was even granted not only for the duration of his lifetime but also for that of his heirs. The granting of such patents, however, was more a strategy to attract skilled craftsmen – for which the major cities in northern Italy were then competing – than an effort to foster economic progress through the disclosure of inventions. With the cities' decline, also these early patent laws disappeared (Mandich, 1948).

During the following centuries, patent regimes as legally defined systems to protect inventions were introduced in many European countries, including England (1623–24), France (1791), Austria (1810), Russia (1812), Prussia (1815), Belgium (1817), Sweden (1834), and Portugal (1837). However, an increase in international trade affairs and the spread of the idea of a worldwide free trading system led to a controversial and intensive debate on the cost and benefits of patent protection. This discussion resulted in a process of partial abolition and reduction of the existing patent regimes during the 18th century. In light of this, advocates of the patent system responded by launching an intense and comprehensive propaganda campaign. In particular, industries leaders such as the Siemens brothers organized pro-patent support groups to protect their leading technological position in rapidly industrializing countries such as Prussia and England. American participants in the world exhibition of 1873 in Vienna refused to present their inventions unless they were given provisional patent protection. During this world exhibition, a patent congress proposed the introduction of strict compulsory licensing principles and the establishment of national patent laws. This changed the concept of the patent system from that of pure mercantilist monopoly privileges into a system for supporting technological progress. Furthermore, rising nationalism, protectionism, and a severe economic crisis in 1873 led to a change in public opinion and reinstitution of reformed patent systems in all major countries of Europe (Machlup and Penrose, 1950, 2ff.; Kaufer, 1989, 9).

1.2 Substantial requirements according to German, European, and United States patent law

1.2.1 European and German patent law

The signing of the Convention on the Grant of European Patents (the European Patent Convention, EPC) on October, 5, 1975 laid the groundwork for the creation of the European Patent Office (EPO), which administers a centralized patent grant system for all countries party to the EPC. The EPO can grant patents for every member state that is designated by the patent applicant. However, the EPO does not replace national patent authorities but offers an alternative route to obtain patent protection in the member states. In contrast to the Patent Cooperation Treaty (PCT, see also subsection 1.4.2 of this Part), which only defines a centralized patent application system, the member states of the EPC have delegated the power to decide on the patentability of an invention to the EPO. If a patent application submitted to the EPO meets the substantial and procedural requirements of the EPC, the patent applicant will receive a collective bundle of national patents.

In the past, efforts have also been made to introduce a European patent law, offering a unitary and autonomous patent that is granted for all member states and can only be recalled or allowed to lapse equally in all member states. On December 15, 1975, the Community Patent Convention (CPC) was signed by the nine member states of the

European Community (Kraßer, 2004, 89–90). However, this treaty never went into effect. In 2000, the European Commission made a new attempt by publishing a Community Patent Regulation Proposal. Discussions of the cost and benefits of such a common patent system are still ongoing (EPO, 2006a, 21).

Due to the historical development of patent law in Europe (Beier, 1978), the substantial requirements of the EPC are in accord with the German Patent Act (DPatG). According to § 1 DPatG and article 25.1 EPC, patents are granted for inventions that (1) are new, (2) involve an inventive step, and (3) are susceptible of industrial application.

1.2.1.1 Novelty

According to § 3 DPatG and article 56.1 EPC, an invention is new if it does not form part of the state of the art. The state of the art comprises all information that has been made available to the public by oral or written description, by use, or in any other way prior to the date of filing the patent application. Patent examiners review not only scientific literature and existing patents but also product catalogues and any other kind of information that is related to the invention. In particular, pending patent applications that have not been published prior to the application date but have already been submitted can hamper a successful fulfillment of this criterion.

1.2.1.2 Inventive step

According to § 4 S. 1 DPatG and article 56.1 EPC, an invention contains an inventive step if it is not obvious at a given state of the art to a person who is skilled in the art. Evaluating the existence of the inventive step requires a review of two separate criteria: (1) the state of the art and (2) the skills of an average specialist of the respective technological field. Although assessing the state of the art might meet the criterion of objectivity, determining the skills of an average expert involves a high degree of subjectivity. This in turn affects the objectivity of the entire criterion of the inventive step.

1.2.1.3 Industrial application

According to § 5 DPatG and article 57 EPC, an invention is susceptible of industrial application if it can be made or used in any kind of industry, including agriculture.

1.2.2 United States patent law

Article 1, section 8, of the U.S. Constitution gives the Congress of the United States power to ratify a patent law. It is codified in Title 35 of the United States Code. In addition, on November 29, 1999, Congress enacted the American Inventors Protection Act of 1999 (AIPA), which further revised the existing patent law (see sub-subsection 1.3.3.1 of this Part).

During the last 20 years, the U.S. patent system has undergone four main changes. First, patent protection was extended to new subject matter by defining genetically engineered bacteria (1980: Diamond vs. Chakrabarty), software (1981: Diamond vs. Diehr), business methods, and financial service products (1998: State Street Bank and Trust vs. Signature Financial Group) as being patentable. Second, the Court of Appeals of the Federal Circuit was installed, in 1982, for cases concerning patent infringement and validity (see also section 1.6 in Part III). Third, the maximum patent term for patent protection was changed in 1995 from seventeen years (from the date of the patent grant) to twenty years (from the application date) for all patents (Mayer, 2003, 10–11)[3]. Furthermore, in an attempt to take into account the time spent on pre-market testing and the approval process of the Food and Drug Administration for new drugs, the Drug Price Competition and Patent Restoration Act (also known as the Hatch-Waxman Act) of 1984 defines an additional extension period of up to five years for new drugs (Gallini, 2002, 133–134). European and German patent law contain similar procedures (see § 16a DPatG and EC 1610/96 ECC 1768/92). The fourth major change results from the Bayh-Dole Act, which resolved the discussion about the ownership of patents and inventions resulting from public funds in favor of the recipients of these funds (Jaffe, 2000, 533–534; Goldfarb, 2008; Rafferty, 2008).

U.S. patent law defines the subject matter for which a patent can be obtained and the conditions for patentability. It is on the basis of this legal framework that the U.S. Patent and Trademark Office (USPTO) was established. The USPTO issues three different kinds of patents: utility patents, design patents, and plant patents. The criteria for the patentability of an invention are (1) novelty, (2) non-obviousness, and (3) usefulness.

[3] If the patent application was filed after June 7, 1995, then the patent expires after 20 years. All applications filed prior to this date and all patents valid as of this date expire either 17 years after the date of granting or 20 years after the patent application was filed, depending on which rule offers the longer patent protection (Mayer, 2003).

1.2.2.1 Novelty

An invention is considered as being novel if it differs from all previous inventions (so called "prior art") in one or more of its constituent elements. The USPTO takes all prior art into account that existed as of the date the inventor filed a patent application on the invention for deciding about the novelty of this invention.

In contrast to most other patent laws worldwide, the United States Patent regime is based on a first-to-invent-system. German and European patent law, for example, postulate a first-to-file-approach (Frost, 1967; Dolfsma, 2006, 941). According to German and European law, the person who is the first to file an application for a given invention has the right to the grant of the patent, regardless of the point in time when the invention was actually made. The USPTO, in contrast, divides the patent application process into two stages: the first step comprises the conception of the invention. The second stage consists of diligently reducing the invention to practice by further testing and/or filing a patent application (Frost, 1967, 936). If two inventors file patent applications for the same invention, the USPTO will institute an interference proceeding to review evidence of conception and diligence. The inventor who is found to be the first to conceive the invention will receive the patent grant even if he or she was still working on diligently reducing the invention to practice at the moment the second inventor filed an application. However, unlike German and European law, a period of grace does exist (see 35 U.S.C. 102). All publications made during the twelve months prior to the application date are not part of the prior art during the examination process. In other words, an invention will not pass the novelty test if it was described in a published document or put to public use more than one year prior to the patent application date.

The cost and benefits associated with both systems – first-to-file and first-to-invent – mainly focus on the questions of fairness and the efficiency of the patent system (Coster, 2002, 11). The first-to-invent system is said to be fairer as it takes into account that smaller companies or single inventors face competitive disadvantages in receiving patent protection. Resource constraints not only force them to follow a more focused patent application strategy but can also extend the duration of the application process. In contrast to this, large corporate inventors can afford the costs associated with early and frequent filing of patent applications.

In a first-to-invent-system, the emphasis is not on agility and speed in filing a patent application but on the inventive action (Frost, 1967, 926). In a-first-to-file-system, smaller inventors might face the risk that their inventions are granted to someone else. Furthermore, such a system might induce a patent race between competing firms (Scotchmer and Green, 1990, 133) and an increase of too many, poorly drafted, and premature patent applications that do not promote technological progress but increase transaction costs (Kieff, 2003, 96–97).

Advocates of the first-to-file-system argue that it leads to procedural certainty, which in turn increases efficiency since the filing date of an application can very rarely be challenged (Frost, 1967, 927). The first-to-invent-system induces a higher degree of uncertainty as the right to grant a patent can be challenged by a second party and can only be finally determined by extensive consideration of the making of the invention. Supporters of the first-to-file-system further argue that unfairness only exists if the costs for filing an application in a first-to-file-system are higher than the litigation costs in a first-to-invent system (Coster, 2002, 1–2).

1.2.2.2 Non-obviousness

The criterion of novelty guarantees that the prior art contains no mention of the invention. However, granting patents based only on this criterion would lead to "inventions" that would only be new in the patent sense that they had not been described prior to the application. They would not, however, necessarily follow the basic idea of technological progress. Therefore, the final criterion for patentability of an invention is the test of non-obviousness as defined by 35 U.S.C. 103 (Witherspoon, 1980). It serves as a "gate-keeping function" (Mergers, 1992, 2) by analyzing the situation of the inventor in the moment before the making of the invention and asking how non-obvious it was that the invention would work. Thus, an invention is considered as being non-obvious if someone skilled in the particular field of the invention would view it as an unexpected or surprising development. Three analytic approaches can be used in order to analyze the non-obviousness criterion: A first approach focuses on the definition of the capabilities of a person having ordinary skill in the art. In the second approach, a set of rules as defined in the manual of patent examination procedure (MPEP) can be applied. The third option is offered by secondary empirical facts dealing with the success of the invention in the market place or the question of whether it fulfils a long-felt need (Barton, 2003, 477–478).

However, since the entire patent examination process takes time, patent examiners will usually have to conduct a retroactive assessment of the non-obviousness test of an invention. Therefore, they might be unconsciously affected by technical improvements that occurred after an invention was made. Thus, the criterion for novelty as of the date of the invention must be applied in combination with the non-obviousness test.

1.2.2.3 Usefulness

In 35 U.S.C. 101 (inventions patentable) and 35 U.S.C. 112 (specification), an invention is obligated to meet the criterion of utility. The main task of the utility criterion is to prevent the patenting of inoperative devices. Following MPEP guideline 2107, this criterion is met, if a (1) person of ordinary skill in the art would immediately appreciate why the invention is useful based on the characteristics of the invention (credible utility) and (2) if the invention is useful for any particular practical purpose (specific and substantial utility).

1.3 Procedural requirements according to German, European, and United States patent law

1.3.1 German patent law

1.3.1.1 The examination process

According to § 34 Abs. 1 S. 1 DPatG, a patentee has to file a patent application with the German patent office containing (1) the name of the applicant, (2) a request for the grant of a patent that clearly and accurately describes the invention, (3) one or more claims defining the matter for which protection is sought, (4) a detailed description of the invention, and (5) any drawings that either refer to the claims or the description (§ 34 Abs. II DPatG). To determine the extent to which information about the invention must be reported, § 34 Abs. 4 DPatG says that the degree of disclosure is sufficient if a person skilled in the art can execute the invention based on the information provided by the application.

Based on this application, the patent office engages in a two-stage examination process. First, formal requirements defined by §§ 34, 36, 37, and 38 DPatG are checked. Furthermore, in accordance with § 42 Abs. 2 DPatG the patent office will investigate whether the subject of the application obviously (1) does not, by reason of its nature, constitute an invention, (2) is not susceptible of industrial application, (3) is excluded from patentability under § 2 DPatG, or (4) whether its purpose is not, in the case of the second sentence of § 16(1), an improvement or further development of the invention. The examination section of the patent office notifies applicants in the case that their application does not pass this first stage of the examination process and invites them to submit their comments within a specified period of time. If applicants do not remedy the defects mentioned by the examination section or if the examination section concludes that the invention is not patentable then the application is rejected (§ 42 Abs. 3 DPatG).

Eighteen months after the application or priority date, the patent application is published in the Patent Gazette irrespective of the current status of the application process (§ 35 Abs. 5 DPatG). If the application successfully passes the first stage in the examination process the patent office then evaluates in a second step whether the subject matter of the application meets the substantial requirements of the German Patent Act upon the request of the patentee (§ 44 1 DPatG). If the patentee does not initiate this second stage within a period of seven years after the filing date, the application is deemed not to have come into force (§ 58 2 DPatG).

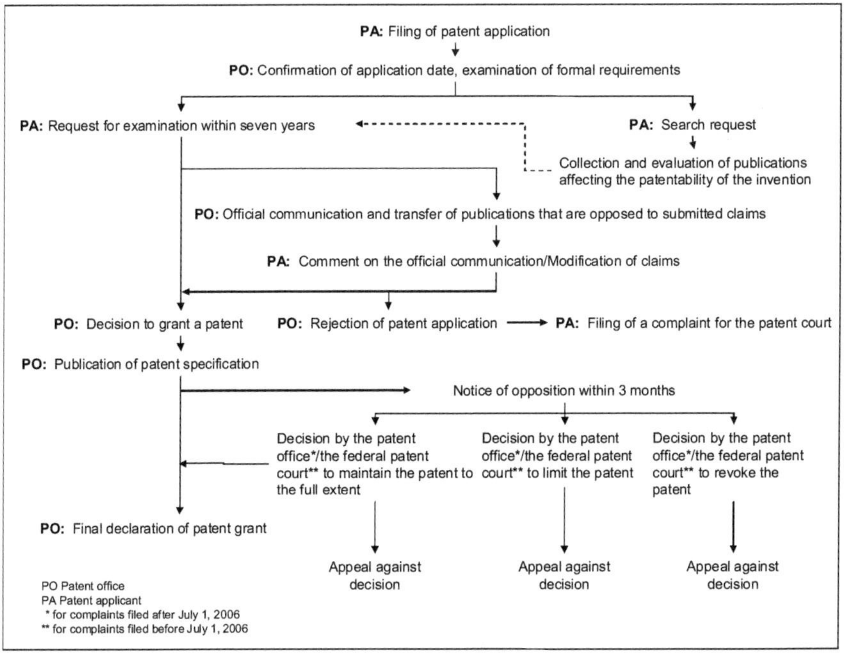

Figure 12: Patent application and patent grant procedure according to DPatG

Patentees may also request the patent office to identify those publications to be taken into consideration in assessing the patentability of an invention (§ 43 Abs. 1 DPatG). As a result, patentees receive a search report, which enables them to evaluate the patentability of their invention. This in turn might help them to avoid the cost of an unsuccessful and time-consuming examination process.

1.3.1.2 Opposition by a third party

If the application complies with the formal and substantial requirements, the patent is granted (§ 49 Abs. 1 DPatG). If the patent application is rejected then the patentee can file a complaint before the Federal Patent Court (Bundespatentgericht, BPatG). Due to recent changes, the patent office is responsible for all complaints filed after July 1, 2006.

The German Patent Act defines two legal options a third party can use in order to erode patent protection: by either giving notice of opposition to a new patent grant within three months after the publication of the grant (§ 59 Abs. 1 DPatG) or by bringing legal action for a declaration of nullity of a patent (§ 81 Abs. 1 DPatG), a third party can completely or partially reduce patent protection.

Opposition proceedings

According to § 59 Abs. 1 DPatG, a third party can only raise objections if one of the following grounds of opposition exists (§ 21 DPatG): (1) the subject matter of the patent is not patentable, (2) the degree of disclosure of the invention does not allow a person skilled in the art to carry it out, (3) the essential parts of the patent have been taken from another person without this person's consent (usurpation), or (4) the subject matter of the patent extends beyond the content of the application as originally filed with the competent authorities.

The patent division will decide whether or to what extent the patent shall be maintained or revoked (§ 61 DPatG). Up until July 1, 2006, patentees could divide their patent during the opposition proceedings (§ 60 Abs. 1 DPatG). The separated part was transformed into a patent application for which the original request for examination had been filed. Thus, the patent division only decided whether or not the remaining part of the patent should be maintained or revoked. The new law for the modification of the opposition proceedings and the law of patent fees (Gesetz zur Änderung des patentrechtlichen Einspruchverfahrens und des Patentkostengesetzes), which became law on July 1, 2006, overrules § 60 DPatG; hence, the division of the patent is no longer a feasible option.

Declaration of nullity

According to §§ 81, 82 and 83 DPatG, anyone can initiate proceedings for a declaration of nullity of a patent by bringing legal action against the patentee if one of the grounds for nullity as defined in § 21 DPatG exists or if the scope of the patent has been broadened (§ 22 DPatG). However, such an action for a declaration of nullity can not be brought as long as opposition may still be filed or opposition proceedings are pending (§ 81 Abs. 2 DPatG). The decision of the patent court is delivered in the form of a judgment (§ 84 DPatG).

1.3.2 European patent law

1.3.2.1 The examination process

As already mentioned, the substantial and procedural requirements of the European patent law, defined in articles 75–98 of the EPC resemble those of the German Patent Act. In order to obtain a European patent, a patent applicant files a patent application with the EPO and designates at least one member state. For each designation the patent applicant must pay a designation fee. However, the maximum number of payments is limited to seven. Thus by paying the designation fee for seven countries, the patent applicant can receive patent protection in all countries party to the EPC. According to article 14 EPC, the application must be submitted in one of the three official languages of the EPC (English, French, or German).

The granting procedure comprises three steps. First, the branch of the EPO at The Hague serves as receiving section and examines the requirements for the accordance of a date of filing as defined by article 80 EPC, and decides whether the filing fee and search fee have been paid in time. In the next step, the receiving section determines whether the application meets the formal requirements as defined in article 91 EPC, draws up the European Search Report, and transfers it to the patent applicant. This search report marks references to other patents or to any kind of document with an "*A*" (no threat to novelty), a "*Y*" if a referenced document in combination with one or more other documents is harmful to novelty, or an "*X*" if one document, on a stand-alone basis, negatively affects novelty or the inventive step (Harhoff and Reitzig, 2004, 448). In the third and final step, the patent applicant must file a request for examination and pay the examination fee within a period of six months after the European Patent Bulletin mentioned the publication of the European Search Report. Otherwise, the application is deemed withdrawn (article 94 EPC).

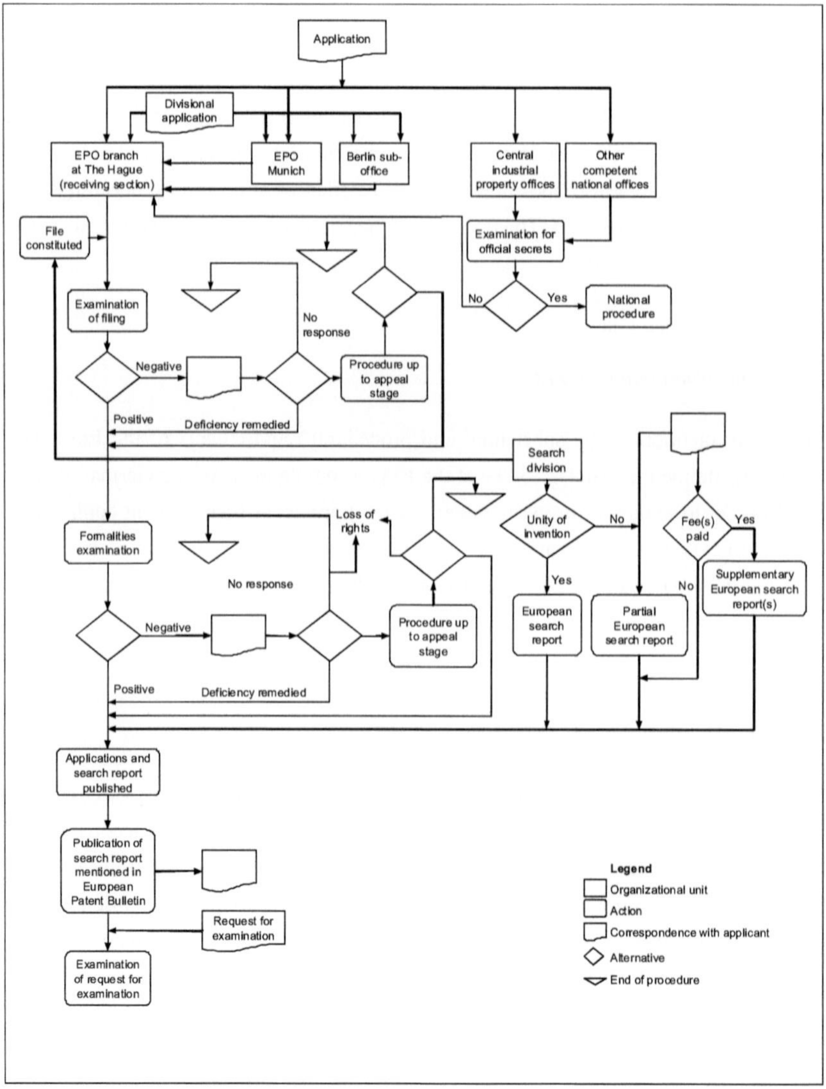

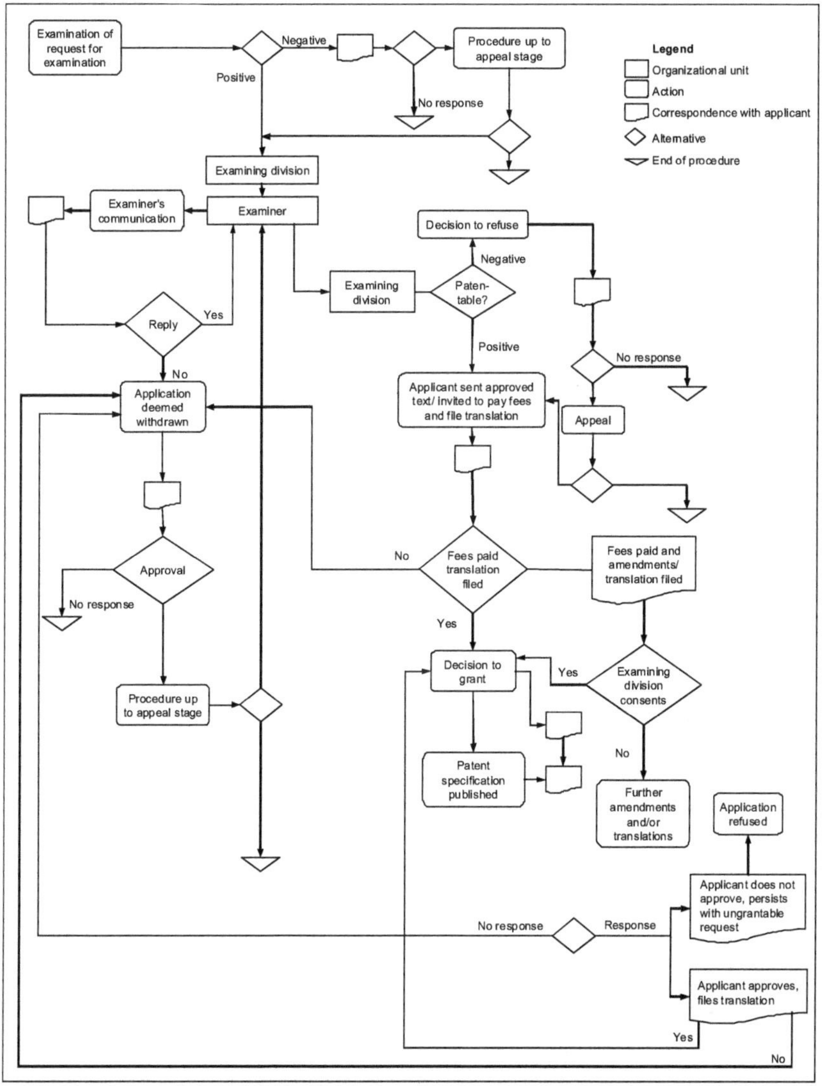

Figure 13: Patent application and patent grant procedure according to EPC (continued)

The definition of invalidity of a patent is bound to rules formulated by the EPC. Any other reason for invalidity that is based on national patent laws does not affect the validity of a European patent. However, according to the rules of the EPC, national patent authorities can decide on the validity of an existing patent. Thus, it can happen that a patent is found to be invalid in one member state whereas it is still in force in other states. Like German patent law, the EPC patent examination procedure ends with either a grant or a refusal (article 97 EPC). However, in case of a grant, the European patent disaggregates into a bundle of national patents that endow patent holders with the same rights they enjoy when holding a national patent in the respective countries (article 64 EPC). Empirical result on the duration of the patent granting process, from the filing of an application to the final grant of a European patent, show that it takes about 4.2 years on average (Harhoff and Reitzig, 2004, 449).

1.3.2.2 Opposition by a third party

An opposing party must file an opposition with the EPO and present evidence that the fundamental requirements were not fulfilled or that disclosure was insufficient. With respect to opposition procedure, two main differences exist between the German patent law and the EPC. (1) According to article 99 EPO, any person might give notice of opposition to the European Patent Office within a period of nine months after the patent grant (under German patent law: three months). (2) This opposition procedure is furthermore the only way to attack the patent in all member states with one centralized procedure. After nine months, or in case of an unsuccessful opposition, a third party can proceed with actions of nullity in each single country in which a national patent has been granted based on the European patent. However, this second strategy is more expansive and the probability of winning a national trial after an unsuccessful opposition diminishes since national authorities are likely to consider arguments brought forth during the previous hearings.

Harhoff and Reitzig (2004) analyze all oppositions filed with the EPO between 1978 and 1996 in the field of pharmaceuticals and biotechnology. They find that the likelihood of opposition positively correlates with the number of designated countries and information asymmetries between patent holder and opponent, which lead to diverging expectations regarding the outcome of an opposition (see also the discussion of the prediction-failure model in section 1.6. of Part III). Finally, recent empirical findings for biotechnology patents show that information on patentability is not identically assessed during the examination process and in the case of an opposition (Burke and Reitzig, 2007, 1415ff.).

From 1980 to 2005, patent applications as well as patents grants have shown an upward trend (see Figure 13). During this period, on average 86,914 applications were submitted to the EPO, 29,258 EPO patents were issued, and 1,840 oppositions were filed each year, which corresponds to an average opposition rate of 6.49% (EPO, 2000, 2005).

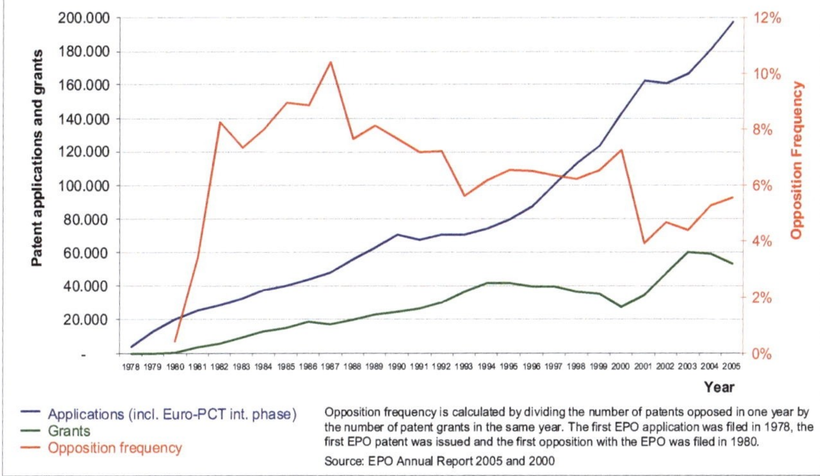

Figure 14: European patent applications, grants, and opposition frequency

1.3.3 United States patent law

1.3.3.1 The examination process

The process of obtaining a patent, the patent prosecution, begins with the filing of a patent application with the USPTO (Chisum et al., 2004, 103ff.). This application must contain a written description of the invention and the claims being made. Upon submission of the application it is assigned to a particular examiner who first ascertains that the application contains all elements necessary (written description, claims, and any required drawing) to obtain a filing date. Furthermore, the examiner analyses whether the application is formulated in a clear and understandable way and whether it is focused on one invention only. The examiner's findings are communicated to the applicant (office action). Examiners can allow, reject, and object to claims; they may also object to the written description (substantive action) or include a restriction requirement in the case that more than one invention is claimed in the application. The applicant must respond to these objections or rejection within a maximum period of six months or the application will be considered abandoned (Mayer, 2003, 236). After reconsidering the applicant's response, the examiner can inform the applicant of allowance of the application (notice of allowance). Alternatively, the examiner can issue a second office action if the response is not satisfactory or even reject the application. In the case of rejection, the applicant can: (1) abandon the application; (2) filing an appeal with the Board of Patent Appeals and Interferences; (3) take any allowed claims (if they exist) and cancel the non-allowed claims, or (4) file a continuing application, a continuation-in-part application, or a divisional application (Mayer, 2003, 175ff.; Chisum et al., 2004, 108ff.). After receiving a notice of allowance, the applicant must pay the sum specified by the notice within three months of the date of mailing to avoid abandonment of the application (MPEP § 1.311) and to finalize the issuance of the patent (MPEP § 1.314).

Despite the precisely defined examination process and the organization of the USPTO, which consists of approximately 235 specialist subgroups, examiners can exercise discretion, which in turn can lead to a considerable degree of diversity in their judgment. Cockburn, Kortum, and Stern (2002) analyze the extent to which three factors of heterogeneity between different patent examiners – (1) generosity in deciding on the scope of patent claims, (2) reliance on past experience, and (3) time spent approving an application – lead to an excess allocation of patent rights, which in turn affects litigation outcomes. They test their hypotheses using a set of 298,441 patents attributed to 196 patent examiners. Furthermore, they investigate whether these three examiner-specific aspects affect the quality of a patent. As a proxy for patent quality, they use the probability of the U.S. Court of Appeals for the Federal Circuit finding the patent assigned to a specific examiner valid if the patent is litigated. They show that no strictly homogenous patent examination process exists, since patent examiners differ with respect to generosity, reliance on past experience, and approval time. Differences in experience and workload seem to have no effect on the quality of patents. However, their results suggest that an examiner's generosity can have a negative impact on the quality of a patent – the broader the claims granted by the examiner, the more likely an invalidity ruling by the U.S. Court of Appeals for the Federal Circuit.

Prior to the American Inventors Protection Act of 1999 (AIPA), utility and plant patent applications filed in the United States were kept secret by the USPTO. A patent applicant thus had no enforceable patent rights before the issue date of a patent. The AIPA authorized the USPTO to publish applications filed on or after November 29, 2000, after a period of 18 months from the earliest domestic or foreign filing date of the application. Exceptions to this general rule are formulated in 35 U.S.C Sec. 122(b) (2) (2001). In exchange for the publication of a patent application, patentees receive the right to obtain a reasonable royalty during the period beginning on the date of publication of the application by the USPTO (likewise, the date of publication under the Patent Cooperation Treaty of an international application designating the United States) and ending on the date the patent is issued (provisional rights, 35 U.S.C. 154(d)).

1.3.3.2 Reexamination procedure

According to 35 U.S.C. 301, any person, patentee, or a third party, can request a reexamination proceeding at any time during the period of enforceability of a patent. The USPTO will then conduct a second examination of any patent claim in view of cited prior art. For a request for reexamination to be granted, the requesting party must (1) explain in written from form the substantial new question of patentability for at least one patent claim, (2) deliver all relevant documents to be considered by the USPTO in English, and (3) pay a reexamination request filing fee (37 C.F.R 1.510).

A reexamination procedure may be *ex parte* or *inter partes*. In the former, members of the public initiate the reexamination procedure, but do not actively participate in the proceedings after submitting the request. In the latter, those who file the request also continue to participate in the proceedings and may (1) file written comments, (2) appeal any decision favorable to patentability to the Board of Patent Appeals and Interferences, and (3) be a party to any appeal taken by the patent owner. The procedure ends with the issue of a Certificate of Reexamination (Chisum et al., 2004, 151–152).

The majority of reexaminations are filed by third parties already involved in a patent infringement lawsuit. Their primary goal is to reduce their legal cost by invalidating the patent rather than having to enter a time-consuming infringement trial. However, many requests for reexamination are also filed by inventors themselves, whose main goal is to ensure that the claims of their patent are still valid in light of any prior art they have discovered after the patent was issued. Additionally, a small number of reexaminations are initiated by the patent office itself (director-initiated) and might be filed in a situation where a patent of questionable validity attains a lot of publicity (see NTP, Inc. vs. Research in Motion[4]).

---

[4] NTP hold a patent portfolio of 50 patents covering inventions in the field of wireless technology and RF antenna design. In 2000, they informed a number of companies about their patent portfolio, selected one, Research in Motion (RIM), and brought a patent-infringement lawsuit against them. The NTP patents covering Blackberry technology were undergoing a number of reexaminations. Some of these reexaminations were *inter partes*, some were *ex parte*, and some were also director-initiated.

1.4 International patent treaties

1.4.1 Paris Convention for the Protection of Industrial Property

Due to the historical development, different perspectives regarding scope and breadth of patent protection emerged, leading to divergent degrees of quality of patent protection under the various national patent regimes. Along with increasing international trade relationships, the need for a harmonized system of patent regimes became evident. Thus, on March 20, 1883, the Paris Convention for the Protection of Industrial Property was signed; as of December 2007, the union includes 172 contracting parties. The most important aspects of this treaty are (1) the right of priority and (2) the national treatment for nationals of countries of the union.

1.4.1.1 Right of priority

According to article 4 of the Paris Convention, the filing of a patent application in one of the countries of the union can create the right of priority (if claimed by the applicant). If the patent applicant claims priority and files subsequent applications in other countries of the union within a period of twelve months after the initial application was submitted, then materials published between the priority date and the subsequent application filing dates are not prior art to these applications. As a consequence of the priority claim, later applications for the same invention in other member countries must be treated as if they had been filed already at the time of the filing of the first application. Any publication and exploitation of the invention within this period of twelve months is not prejudicial with respect to novelty.

1.4.1.2 National treatment for nationals of countries of the union

Based on article 2 of the Paris Convention, nationals of any country of the union enjoy in all other countries of the union the advantages national patent laws now grant or will grant in the future to natives. Thus, no distinction is made between foreigners and natives regarding their rights and duties as formulated by the national patent law. Even if the country of origin of the patent holder should offer weaker patent protection (e.g., shorter patent terms as it was the case for U.S. Patent law until 1995; see subsection 1.2.2 of this Part) to its residents, the patent holder will enjoy the stronger national patent protection in other countries of the union.

1.4.2 The Patent Cooperation Treaty

The intent of the Patent Cooperation Treaty (PCT) concluded on June 19, 1970, is to increase cooperation between the patent offices of its member states and to rationalize and simplify the process of filing, searching, and examining patent applications in more than one country. By filing only one international application, the patent applicant can create a bundle of national applications in all countries party to the PCT (Kraßer, 2004, 103).[5] However, the PCT does not lead to an "international patent" since the task and the responsibility for granting patents remains in the hands of the (national) patent offices. Thus, the PCT is not a competitor to the Paris Convention but complements it (Chisum et al., 2004, 122ff.).

1.4.2.1 Patent application and examination procedure

Patent applicants wishing to obtain international patent protection file an international application, either with the national office of their country (the receiving PCT office) or with the International Bureau of the WIPO. An applicant who is a national or resident of a contracting state which is party to the European Patent Convention, the Harare Protocol on Patents and Industrial Designs (Harare Protocol), the revised Bangui Agreement Relating to the Creation of an African Intellectual Property Organization, or the Eurasian Patent Convention may also file the application with the European Patent Office (EPO), the African Regional Industrial Property Organization (ARIPO), the African Intellectual Property Organization (OAPI), or the Eurasian Patent Office (EAPO), respectively.

When filing an application, the applicants must define the countries in which they wish to obtain patent protection (designated states). The receiving PCT office sends a copy to the International Bureau of the WIPO and another copy to a (national) patent office that has been appointed to act as international searching authority[6], which then initiates an international search. As a result, applicants receive an international search report citing documents of relevant prior art and allowing them to evaluate the chances of obtaining patent protection in the designated states (Chapter I PCT). Both the application and the search report are published eighteen months after application or priority date.

[5] As of December 2007, the PCT has 138 contracting parties.

[6] The following patent offices act as international search authorities: the Australian Patent Office, the Austrian Patent Office, the Chinese Patent Office, the European Patent Office, the Japanese Patent Office, the Russian Patent Office, the Spanish Patent and Trademark Office, the Swedish Patent Office, and the United States Patent and Trademark Office.

Additionally, patent applicants may request an international preliminary examination according to Chapter II of the PCT in order to obtain an opinion on whether the invention meets the criteria of novelty, inventive step, and industrial applicability. This opinion does not constitute the right to obtain patent protection in one of the designated states, but it assists applicants in finally deciding in which designated countries they are likely to obtain a patent. In fact, an empirical analysis of 22,911 patent applications at the EPO shows that the probability of a grant is higher if the application is filed with the EPO after passing through Chapter II of the PCT (Guellec and van Pottelsberghe de la Potterie, 2000, 112). In order to finalize the patent application process, patent applicants must enter the national phase by paying the prescribed national fees to the national patent offices in the countries in which they intend to receive a patent and, if required, translate their international application into the local languages.

1.4.2.2 Advantages of the PCT

For applicants searching for patent protection in more than one country, the main advantage of the PCT is created by the fact that they avoid the cost of filing separate national patent applications as well as translation costs and costs for national agents until they are able to evaluate the likelihood of obtaining patent protection in more than one country (Grupp and Schmoch, 1999, 387).

In addition, there is a time advantage due to the possibility of postponing decisions. Under the Paris Convention, a patent applicant must decide within one year whether to file patent applications in other countries which would claim priority from the first application. In contrast, article 22 PCT offers a way to extend the time during which a decision must be made about foreign patent filings up to thirty months[7] from the priority date (Guellec and van Pottelsberghe de la Potterie, 2000, 111; Chisum et al., 2004, 124ff.).

1.5 Patent classification systems

Patent classification systems are used to organize and index the technical content of patent specifications. They support easy and accurate identification of information on a specific topic or a given area of technology. A classification system enables patent applicants as well as patent examiners to decide on the patentability of an invention and the given state of the art.

---

[7] Until April 1, 2002, the time frame comprised twenty months.

The following sections briefly describe the two most important classification systems: the international patent classification (IPC) and the European classification (EUCLA). Please note that in addition to these two systems, alternative classification schemes exist. For instance, the USPTO uses two classification schemes in parallel – a national system (United States Patent Classification System, USPC) and the IPC. They differ in terms of quality, classification principles, and classification hierarchy (Lerner, 1994, 321).

1.5.1 International patent classification

The IPC is used by all the authorities of the major industrialized nations (and by virtually all of the active patenting authorities in the world) as a common means of classifying patent specifications. It is based on an international multi-lateral treaty administered by WIPO, the Strasbourg Agreement Concerning the International Patent Classification, which was concluded in 1971 and became law in 1975. The Agreement is open to countries that are parties to the Paris Convention for the Protection of Industrial Property (see section 1.4.1 of this Part).

The industrial property offices of more than 100 nations, four regional offices, and the international bureau of WIPO under the Patent Cooperation Treaty (PCT) actually use the IPC. The Strasbourg Agreement concerning the International Patent Classification provides for a common classification for patents for inventions including published patent applications, utility models, and utility certificates. Therefore, it is possible to carry out an international search for patents on a specific subject using the IPC as a key.

The IPC is a hierarchical system in which the whole area of technology is divided into a range of sections, classes, subclasses, and groups (Vijvers, 1990, 27). It is periodically revised in order to improve the system and to take account of technical developments (Makarov, 2006, 123ff.). This, in fact, is one of the main advantages of the IPC compared to the USPC, as the latter has not been revised since 1872 (Lerner, 1994, 321). The current, eighth, edition of the IPC, which took effect on January 1, 2006, comprises 8 sections, 120 classes, 630 subclasses, and over 10,000 subgroups (WIPO, 2006, 7ff.).

1.5.2 European classification system

The European classification system (ECLA) extends the IPC system by offering an extensive classification – currently 132,200 subdivisions or about 62,000 more than the IPC – allowing for a more precise, more homogeneous, and more systematic classification of patent applications. ECLA classifications are assigned to patent documents by EPO examiners in order to facilitate prior-art searches. The ECLA is revised continuously and applied retrospectively (Rampelmann, 1996, 150–151; Rampelmann, 1999; Stephen, 2000, 293). Hence, the entire database is modified when there is a revision of the classification schedule. As a consequence, only the latest classifications codes need to be searched to look back in time (Dickens, 1994, 28). The codes are also applied consistently by a single group of examiners, and the data goes back much further than that of the IPC – 1877 for Germany, 1909 for Britain, 1911 for France, and 1920 for the U.S. However, since the data is often only applied several months after the publication of the specifications, it is not suitable for current-awareness searching.

1.6 Patent infringement and patent litigation

Excluding third parties from a profitable technology segment for a well-defined period of time constitutes the core of patent protection (see subsection 1.1.1 of this Part). However, patents must be enforced by their holders. Hence, the strength of patent protection depends not only on the negative consequences a patent-infringing party faces in case of a litigation process, but also on the probability that the patent holders will recognize this breach of their property rights. In short, patent protection depends *ex ante* on the design of the patent claim(s) and *ex post* on the competence and resources available to enforce these claim(s). Any value conclusion, in fact, rests on the assumption that patent holders are fully aware of patent-infringing activities by third parties and also willing to defend their rights.

If a patent is found to be infringed, the patent holder must opt for one of the following strategies (Meurer, 1989, 78–79.; Crampes and Langinier, 2002, 260): (1) Reaching a settlement, (2) instituting legal proceedings, or (3) choosing neither to settle nor to sue and accepting patent-infringing actions by competitors. Since the last option is equivalent to a fully-accepted erosion of patent protection, the value of a patent in this case becomes zero.

The choice between signing a settlement and taking legal action depends not only on the cost of a trial relative to the cost of a settlement. Two other factors must be taken into account: (1) the expectations of plaintiff and defendant regarding the likelihood that the plaintiff will prevail at trial (subsection 1.6.1), and (2) the expected cost and benefits associated with the predicted outcome of such a trial (subsection 1.6.2).

1.6.1 Expectations and the prediction-failure model

As for the case of patent valuation in general, the decision to file a suit instead of signing an amicable arrangement is also strongly driven by expectations. If both patent holder and infringer have symmetric stakes (meaning that the amount the infringer avoids paying or gains equals the amount the plaintiff cannot realize) and in the absence of any external effect the decision of both parties to go to court instead of signing a mutually beneficial settlement is motivated by optimistic, but opposing, predictions regarding the probability that the plaintiff will prevail (Kobayashi and Parker, 2000, 6ff.). As only one party can win, one of the respective opponents has based his or her decision on faulty predictions (prediction-failure model).

Priest and Klein (1984) present a deeper analysis of how these mutually inconsistent, optimistic predictions emerge. They assume the existence of a decision standard that is applied by judges or juries to decide about whether a verdict will be rendered in favor of the plaintiff. Both plaintiff and defendant know this decision standard. They form expectations about how close the quality of the claim is to the quality level needed for the plaintiff to win (i.e. the decision standard*)*. Given similar expectations and equal stakes, the closer their dispute lies to the decision standard, the higher the probability of a trial will be. This is due to the fact that plaintiff and defendant are uncertain about the outcome of this trail (in contrast to clear-cut cases in which one party is likely to opt for a settlement). Furthermore, in this case of consistent expectations, the probability of winning is close to 50 percent for both (Priest and Klein, 1984, 8ff.).

In addition to these expectations with respect to the outcome of the lawsuit, the litigation rate is mainly driven by comparing cost of litigation (relative to settlement cost) and benefits resulting from winning the trial. Priest and Klein expect a lower rate of litigation if litigation cost is relatively high compared to settlement cost and the benefits are relatively low (Priest and Klein, 1984, 17ff.).

1.6.2 Cost and benefits of patent litigation

Kingston (1995) highlights the fact, that during a trial both parties must spend not only a considerable amount of money but also devote time and human resources in order to clarify their positions regarding the case and to convince the court of their point of view. This burden can, in fact, deter smaller companies from taking legal action (Kingston, 1995). Jaffe (2000) further argues that the anticipated danger of litigation costs not only influences the decision on whether to settle or not, it also has an impact on a firm's research decisions (Jaffe, 2000, 549).

In addition to assessing the direct legal cost (for the legal department and/or external lawyers as well as possible court costs) compared to the cost associated with signing an amicable agreement, cost-benefits analyses should also reflect decisions and legal measures of the opponent. By requesting a preliminary injunction, the plaintiff can increase the cost to an infringing party. The basic idea of this remedy consists of preserving the status quo during a trial and prior to a decision by the court (Cunningham, 1995, 214). The granting of a preliminary injunction changes the cost- and benefit-analyses of both parties. Prior to a preliminary injunction, the defendants may use the inventions that the plaintiffs claim to be protected by their property rights. If, and only if the court decides in favor of plaintiffs, will the defendants have to compensate them for the damages caused. Thus, a plaintiff first has to pay the legal costs and can only create expectations regarding possible compensation. In contrast, a preliminary injunction prohibits the use of the innovation by the defendant until the court comes to a decision. In this case, the infringing party bears the damages during the trial and receives compensation *ex post* only if the plaintiff is not successful. Depending on the expected duration of the trial, this change in the chronological sequence of cost and benefits can influence the defendant's propensity towards signing an agreement.

A cost-benefit analysis must furthermore take into account the external effects of the current litigation on the plaintiff's reputation as well as the competitors' perceptions of the plaintiff's willingness to pursue current or potential infringers. The existence of external effects can dominate the decision between litigation and settlement. Regardless of whether the plaintiff's and defendant's stakes differ in terms of size, litigation may even occur in the case of equal expectations regarding the final decision of the court. If a plaintiff fears that opting for a settlement might have a negative impact on public reputation, the judgment similarly expected by the plaintiff and the defendant may be less than the minimum amount postulated by the plaintiff. In this case the benefit from filing a suit consists only partly of the financial compensation defined by the judgment (Priest and Klein, 1984, 25–26; Kobayashi and Parker, 2000, 9). In fact, the majority of the benefit might result from avoiding a loss in reputation that in turn might negatively affect future economic gains in terms of sales volumes or profits.

Thus, an aggressive behavior in patent infringement cases can reduce the need to engage in future legal actions (Lanjouw and Schankerman, 1998, 232). At the same time, suing a potential infringer might also reveal information to potential imitators that can motivate additional infringing activities. Even in the case of a plaintiff's victory, not only the enforcement capabilities of the patent holder but also the probability of a plaintiff's successes can be analyzed at zero cost (negative information effect) (Choi, 1998, 1250ff.).

In the end, a trial will take place if both parties individually reach the decision that this option is more efficient or beneficial than agreeing on a settlement. In general, the higher the cost of litigation compared to settlement and/or the more pessimistic one party is about the outcome of a trial, the higher the probability of a settlement will be (Cooter and Rubinfeld, 1989, 1076).

1.6.3 Empirical results for patent litigation

1.6.3.1 Results for the failure prediction model

The theoretical model of Priest and Klein (1984), in particular the hypothesis of the 50-percent plaintiff win rate, has motivated a large number of empirical tests as reviewed by Kessler, Meites and Miller (1996). In a recent study on the impact of patent examiners on the quality of patents, Cockburn, Kortum, and Stern find support for the 50-percent rule (Cockburn et al., 2002, 22). Waldfogel (1995) analyzes the relationship between trial rates and plaintiff win rates using data relating to civil cases from the Southern District of New York filed during 1984 to 1987. For cases related to IPRs (patents, copyright, trademark) he finds that not only trial rates vary between 10 to 50 percent but also that plaintiff win rates fluctuate between 30 and 90 percent, depending on the presiding judge. On average, 71.3 percent of all filed IPR cases result in a plaintiff's victory. Furthermore, he finds support for the idea of asymmetric stakes as measured by the indicator α. The value of α for IPR cases of 1.336 indicates that the plaintiff is likely to gain 33.6 percent more than the defendant stands to lose (Waldfogel, 1995, 251).

Empirical results indicate that uncertainty about the quality of patent litigation cases is the lowest in comparison with civil right, contracts, labor, prisoner, and torts (Siegelman and Waldfogel, 1999, 126). This comparably low uncertainty regarding the outcome of trials related to IPR implies that both parties *ex ante* have a clear idea about the quality of their case. Despite the fact that each IPR case might be unique in some detail, most IPR cases bear resemblance to historical trials. Further evidence for the homogeneity of patent cases can be found by comparing plaintiff win rates prior to and after the installment of the new U.S. Court of Appeals for the Federal Circuit. One motivation for the creation of this court was to strengthen the weak and comparably ineffective U. S. patent system at that time. Handling patent trials in a more consistent and predictable way is one of its main tasks. Before this court was established, on October 1, 1982, plaintiff win rates averaged 61 percent; in 1987 they increased to 75 percent (Lanjouw and Lerner, 1998, 230), and in 1990 this percentage rose to 90 percent (Jaffe, 2000, 532–533).

However, industry effects have to be taken into account. Lanjouw and Schankerman (1998) analyze a sample of 3,887 patent cases that had been submitted to a U.S. court between 1980 and 1984. With respect to litigation rates, they find strong inter-industry differences. The different factors that drive the decision to litigate or not are not of equal importance for the industries they investigate. However, their results indicate that litigation rate increases with a raising propensity to patent and a high uncertainty connected to emerging markets. Across all the industries they investigate, one out of a hundred patents is expected to be the subject of an infringement trial, whereas in the pharmaceutical drugs and health sector this number increases to 2.1 and in the chemical industry drops to 0.54 (1998, 9ff.).

1.6.3.2 Results for the cost and benefits of litigation

A survey performed by Bouju (1988) shows that the litigation costs of patent infringement cases vary substantially in European countries. In France, a patentee's costs associated with infringement cases before the court of first instance would be about \$33,515 in 1988 U.S. dollars. However in the U.K., this would be \$164,768, nearly four times more than in France. Litigation cost in Germany is the lowest among the three countries. The average cost for a case valued at \$68,400 would be \$6,525; for a case valued at \$222,300, this would amount to \$14,095; and even for a case with a value of \$684,020, the litigation costs are \$30,074, on average – significantly lower than in France.

Lanjouw and Schankerman (1998) find that size of stakes and divergence in the stakes for the parties involved drive litigation rates, supporting the idea that external effects are taken into account. If the benefits of going to a trial consist only partly of creating a strong reputation, the cost advantage of signing a settlement might motivate corporate patent owners to opt for this strategy instead of taking court action (Lanjouw and Schankerman, 1998, 5ff.).

2 The economic dimension of patents

From a legal perspective, the key unit of analysis within a patent valuation process is the protected invention. As already described in the previous chapter, an invention is an idea that is new. For patents, decisive criteria for defining the novelty of an invention are given by substantial requirements that each new idea has to meet in order to qualify as an invention. These criteria reduce the degree of subjectivity involved in defining the novelty of an idea (Rogers, 1983, 11; Zaltman et al., 1984, 10). Even so, only those new ideas qualify as inventions that are perceived to be new by examiners of the patent office.

In contrast to the legal concept of invention, economic theory uses the concept of innovation to describe a new idea. In most cases, the novelty of this idea is defined with regard to existing products and processes in a given market and in contrast to the concept of imitation. Imitation is the absorption of knowledge from competitors. Hence, this knowledge is only new to the imitator but not to the market (Marr, 1993, 1797). In addition to new products (product innovation) or new technical knowledge used for producing goods and services (process innovation), the concept of innovation can also cover social, financial, market, and organizational innovations (Damanpour, 1991, 556). Since the latter types of innovations describe new ideas for which no patent protection can be claimed, they will not be discussed further in this thesis.

Understanding the relationship between inventions and innovations is important for patent valuation. As already described in chapter 1 of this Part, patents constitute an exclusive right. In the case of one patent that protects one innovation, the value of this exclusive right depends on the legal quality of the patent and the value potential of the underlying innovation. Hence any value of a protected invention is always linked to the economic rents that the inventor can generate from using it (Roberts, 2007, 36).

Depending on its technical complexity, one innovation can include several inventions. Consequently, several patent rights may be needed to fully protect the economic rents from one innovation. Measuring the concentration of patents per innovation facilitates the differentiation between discrete and cumulative technologies. Products or processes associated with discrete technologies contain only one or very few innovations. Given comparable patent propensity, they are characterized by a low concentration of patents per innovation, which supports both the detection of infringing activities and the enforcement of patent rights. These two factors in turn drive the effectiveness of patents as an appropriability mechanism (Levin et al., 1987, 798). In contrast to this, cumulative technologies involve strongly interconnected innovations that build on each other (Scotchmer, 1991, 29). Pioneering innovations lay the basis for further developments. Products and processes therefore consist of complex systems comprising different components. Hence, comprehensive protection calls for complex patent portfolios (Mergers and Nelson, 1990, 7–8; Hall and Ziedonis, 2001, 102). This has two main implications. First, detecting patent infringement and enforcing patent rights tends to be more difficult in contrast to discrete technologies. Second, if rights to the various components of one product belong to multiple patent holders, a mutual blockade might be a possible outcome (Grindley and Teece, 1997, 9).

The following chapters focus on the economic dimension of patents by analyzing the basic economic rationale of patent protection (section 2.1), functions of patents (section 2.2), and suitable patent value constructs (section 2.3) for measuring the value of patents.

2.1 Arguments for patent protection

Four main arguments are currently used to support the idea of creating temporary monopolies by granting patent rights. Each of them emphasizes different aspects of patent protection. Furthermore, they do not build on each other, meaning that each argument can stand alone even if the others must be rejected (Machlup and Penrose, 1950, 10ff; Machlup, 1961, 367).

2.1.1 Argument one: Natural property rights

The first argument focuses on the property-rights theory and emphasizes that inventors have a natural right in their own ideas. From a moral point of view, a society is obliged to recognize and protect these rights. The best way to enforce these property rights is by means of granting exclusivity to inventors.

2.1.2 Argument two: Inventor's reward

The second argument emphasizes that inventors must be rewarded for their service in proportion to the amount of utility that is created for society by said service. As inventions are useful to society, an appropriate way to ensure sufficient compensation to the inventor is to grant a temporary monopoly.

2.1.3 Argument three: Incentive to invent

The third argument reflects the basic necessity of industrial progress for the wealth of a society, on the one hand, and the individual risks inventors face in investing time and money for developing new products and technologies, on the other. Thus, the expectation of receiving the right to exclusively exploit the economic potential of an invention motivates inventors by increasing their future earnings, which in turn is compensation for undertaking risky research and development projects.

2.1.4 Argument four: Incentive to disclose

Finally, the fourth argument considers the risk not on the inventor's side but on the side of society. In the absence of any kind of protection, the best strategy for the inventor is either not to invent or to keep any invention secret. Once again, the basic idea behind this argument is that industrial progress is both necessary and desirable. If a society fails to provide its members with protective mechanisms for inventions, the overall technological progress will slow down and knowledge about major inventions might also die with their inventors. In exchange for the disclosure of inventions, society grants a temporary monopoly.

2.2 The use of patents in modern economies: An analysis of patent functions

2.2.1 Primary patent function: Temporary monopoly and diffusion of inventions

The grant of temporary exclusive rights to an inventor in exchange for disclosure of the details of the invention to the broad public is the primary function of the patent system (see subsection 1.1.1 of this Part). Patents are, in fact, one of few legal means to obtain a temporary monopoly in a well-specified field of technology. From a macroeconomic perspective, monopoly theory tells us that monopolies pose a threat to customers as they can lead to inefficiencies and a shift of rents from customers to producers (Leibenstein, 1966, 397ff.; Comanor and Smiley, 1975, 178ff.; Posner, 1975, 809ff.).

This thesis analyses patents from a firm's perspective (private value of patents). Thus the advantages and disadvantages of this legal means need not be analyzed with regard to the entire economy (public value of patents). In fact, I focus specifically on the owner or use value (see also section 1.2 in Part I), hence the private value of patents.

Strategic management research analyses the conditions under which companies can create competitive advantages. The VRIN paradigm highlights the importance of obtaining and securing resources that can create a (temporary) superior market position or even a monopoly. It is this ability to endow patent holders with (temporary) monopolistic market positions that makes patents particularly valuable to firms (see subsection 2.2.1 of Part I). The exploitation of superior economic benefits resulting from monopolistic advantages can traditionally be achieved by either implementing an invention in a sophisticated good or by using it to offer services. Alternative modes of exploitation include the transfer of the exclusive right through a patent sale or the granting of licenses (see also Part IV).

Clearly, the power of patents for creating such a strong position is also limited, since patent holders must not only consider antitrust regulations (Gilbert and Shapiro, 1997, 286ff.; Rubinfeld and Maness, 2005). In addition, they should also evaluate the disadvantages resulting from disclosing inventions to the public in general (Pavitt, 1984, 90ff.; Ernst, 1998, 281ff.; Granstrand, 2006, 26) and to competitors in particular (Horstman et al., 1985; Duguet and Kabla, 1998, 304; Anton et al., 2006, 12). The monitoring of patent applications supports the identification of weak signals that can help competitors in estimating how a company's competitive situation will be affected by new technological developments. The filing of a patent application may, furthermore, reduce the period of time during which an inventor is able to profit from it simply because competitors may become aware of the invention earlier and react more quickly (Horstman et al., 1985, 840ff.). Please recall that according to German and European patent law, all applications are published 18 months after the application date even if no patent will be finally granted (see chapter 1 of this Part).

Since patent applications are often filed during an early stage of product development, especially under a first-to-file regime, patent applicants will initially form rough estimates about the value potential of an innovation and a related patent rather than having a precise idea of the financial value of a patent. They will learn over time about the marketability of their inventions and how these can lead to a monopolistic market position (Lanjouw, 1998, 675). For the following analysis I assume a rational behavior of the patentees. This implies that they base their decisions regarding application and renewal of patents on the premise that patent protection will have a positive impact on their competitive position, although they might only know the probability-density function over their possible future returns.

2.2.2 Secondary patent functions

The right to exclude a third party is not bound to an active use of the patented invention. Patents allow both a passive as well as an active exploitation strategy. They can protect a competitive position (protective function) leading to superior economic benefits and an exclusion of competitors (exclusive function). In addition, from the private perspective of the patentee, there are additional secondary functions of patents that are important. These describe alternative ways to exploit the value potential of patents (Grindley and Teece, 1997, 10ff.; Duguet and Kabla, 1998, 306ff.; Cohen et al., 2000, 16ff.; Rivette and Kline, 2000, 56ff.; Harhoff and Reitzig, 2001, 513ff.; Pitkethly, 2001, 432; Cohen et al., 2002, 1358ff.; Blind et al., 2006, 657; Moser and Goddar, 2007).

Patentees might decide to apply for and maintain patent protection in order to block competitors. Depending on the purpose of this blocking function, we can differentiate between offensive and defensive blocking. In the first case, patentees create patent fences and thickets that exclude others from entering new markets (Reitzig, 2004b, 459–460) even though patentees might not be currently active in this technological field. Here, value is mainly driven by weakening competitors and equals the sum of unrealized profits on the side of competitors. This strategy is particularly useful for discrete technologies such as chemicals and pharmaceuticals. If patentees opt for a defensive blocking strategy, they try to avoid allowing the patenting activities of competitors to limit their own access to profitable technological fields. Additionally, patents might support the overcoming of entry barriers and the conquering of market shares from competitors (attack function) or the enforcement of one's own technological standards (Blind and Thumm, 2004, 1586ff.).

In case of an infringing action, benefits result from damage awards obtained in a suit for infringement. In this case, the likelihood of infringement and the industry-wide propensity to litigate are key drivers of value. Most recently, we can observe the emergence of patent sharks or patent trolls. These are patent-holding individuals who seek to generate profits only from enforcing patent rights against accused infringers. They do not manufacture products or supply services based on the patents in question. In many cases, they also do not invent or file patent applications but merely purchase patent portfolios from entities that are not actively enforcing these rights (Reitzig et al., 2007, 135). While the value of a patent is traditionally driven by the active use of the patented technology and the exploitation of the protected technological field, the most valuable patents in this case are those which are most likely to be found infringed.

In industries with cumulative technologies, such as electronics, firms amass patents to create a strong negotiation position in the patent-litigation game. Patents are used as a bargaining chip or a currency in complex licensing and cross-licensing negotiations (bargaining function). In these industries it happens that more than one of the competing companies holds patent portfolios covering essential parts of the overall technology needed for successful business operations. Since products involve many patentable elements and the firms each hold large numbers of patents, they presume that they may be infringing on someone else's patents just as others infringe on theirs. Often described as a "Mexican standoff" (Grindley and Teece, 1997, 11), this situation can lead to the paradoxical situation that patent holders renounce their rights to sue an infringing competitor to avoid being countersued for their own infringing activities with respect to the competitor's patent portfolio (Cohen et al., 2000, 19ff.). In the end, both parties agree upon a mutual, non-exclusive license to receive access to these overlapping patent portfolios. Rather than empowering the patent holder to exclusively exploit the economic potential of technological knowledge, patents serve as a means to support and maintain freedom of action, which in turn is often a precondition for successful business operations.

This bargaining function further supports the creation of complex patent portfolios with several hundred patented inventions. In general, the complexity of comprehensive patent portfolios exhibits a portfolio effect. Given overlapping patent scopes, the value of the portfolio exceeds the sum of individual patents, since any challenge of the validity of one patent can be, at least partially, compensated by neighboring patent rights (cluster function).

In the specific case of mutual infringement, the relative importance of the respective patent portfolios of each party involved is another value driver. A weak competitor only partly infringing a company's patent portfolio but without generating a considerable sales volume from this infringement is, despite its overall weakness, in a stronger position if the respective company strongly relies on the competitor's patent portfolio for generating revenues than a strong competitor with comparable infringement activities and sales volume would be. Hence, the competitor's weakness and limited sales volume turns out to be a strength since the dependency on each other's resources is not equally distributed between the competing companies.

In addition, patents can enable and support the expansion of a firm's value chain. Two strategies for this use of patents in vertical relations with suppliers and customers can be distinguished. One focuses on a negotiation of the allocation of rents between different stages in the production process. If patents are of importance for producing goods or services but not for distributing them, rents can be shifted by licensing agreements from the producer (licensee) to the patent holder (licensor). The second strategy aims not only at exploiting the economic potential of protected technology but also extending the business activities over the value chain. Companies with a strong patent-based market position on one stage of the production chain try to use their IP to enter cooperative modes such as strategic alliances with suppliers or customers who are in need of access to the protected technology.

Furthermore, from the perspective of the general public and the capital market in particular, patents promise monopoly profits and a leading technological edge. Thus, patentees can create and maintain the image and reputation of being a technology leader, which in turn facilitates access to equity or debt capital for financing growth. In this context, patents can be also interpreted as an evaluation of the quality of an invention and therefore may therefore be used to assess and reward R&D personnel.

2.3 Measuring patent values through value constructs

An economic analysis of patents from a firm's perspective must reflect the disadvantages or costs resulting from revealing inventions and the benefits associated with the grant of a temporary monopoly. However, cost, benefits, and consequently value depend on the overall valuation perspective. The question of selecting an appropriate valuation perspective is answered by value constructs. These constructs describe varying sets of benefits and costs for determining the private value of patent rights.

Harhoff, Scherer, and Vopel (2003a) define two different constructs for the private value of patents. They compare the situation of a company having a valid patent with the situation of the same company having no valid patent (renewal value). From this point of view, the private value of the patent equals the (discounted) sum of differences in the firm's return that could be generated from this innovation with and without patent protection. Furthermore, they analyze the value of a patent when the firm is the patent holder as compared to the situation in which the strongest competitor enjoys the property right to this patent (asset value). Again, the private value equals the (discounted) sum of profits a firm generates from a protected invention less the stream of returns in the case of no patent protection.

For reasons of simplicity, value constructs usually focus on the exclusive function of a patent. Additional patent functions as described in section 2.2 of this Part are not included in the analysis. In this section, I extend the model of Harhoff, Scherer, and Vopel (2003a) by (1) explicitly modeling the degree of diffusion as value driver and (2) by adding a third value concept (competition value).

2.3.1 A stylized theoretical model of value constructs

2.3.1.1 Model assumptions

In their model, Harhoff et al. (2003a) analyze a symmetric oligopoly in which all firms offer a product with a quality q. They introduce a patent-protecting a technology that allows the patent holder to increase the product quality (q_1). The patent holder can thus produce a superior product quality ($q+q_1>q$). Furthermore, they allow patent protection λ to be less than perfect. This induces costless learning processes on the side of the competitors and leads to an improved quality of their own products by $(1-\lambda)q_1$ (with $0 \leq \lambda \leq 1$). If $\lambda = 1$, then patent protection is perfect, whereas in the case of $\lambda = 0$ patent protection is totally ineffective. Harhoff et al. (2003a) then define $\prod_1(a,b)$ to be the profits the patent holder generates by offering a product quality a when all other N+1 firms in the industry produce and sell goods of quality b. Thus, the profits of each of the N competitors are defined by $\prod_N(b,a)$. Due to the assumption of a symmetric oligopoly, the following relationship holds: $\prod_1(a,a) = \prod_N(a,a) = \prod_{N+1}(a,a)$. Finally, they assume that $\prod_1(a,b)$ and $\prod_N(b,a)$ are monotonically increasing in b and a, respectively (Harhoff et al., 2003a, 1345–1346). Based on these model specifications they analyze the value of renewed patent protection (renewal value) and the asset value of a patent right in the case of (1) no cumulative invention and no blocking patents (standard case), (2) cumulative inventions (blocking power), and (3) substitute technology (sleeping patent).

2.3.1.2 Basic prerequisites for effective patent protection

Effective patent protection requires more than just a valid patent. In fact, four essential conditions for effective patent protection must be fulfilled simultaneously. First, patent holders must actively guard against and intensively monitor potential patent-infringing activities of third parties. Only if they detect an infringing action, be it willful or unintentional, can they decide whether to initiate legal proceedings. Second, although the usual reaction might well be to sue an infringer (or at least threaten to do so), other strategic considerations might lead to an opposite decision. If the infringing party is at the same time an important partner in other business areas, patent litigation could negatively affect the relationship between both parties. Under these circumstances patent protection is (at least partially) ineffective (Lanjouw, 1998). Third, if patents are infringed by third parties and patentees decide to defend their rights, they must file a complaint with the respective court and allocate the resources necessary for litigation trials. If they cannot successfully conclude these lawsuits, the patents' values will decrease or fall to zero. Finally, the quality of a patent is driven by the strength of the entire patent system and the degree to which knowing and willing patentees with enough resources can enforce their rights. If the patent system fails to provide patentees with the exclusive right for which they ask when they apply for a patent, a patent's value is again equal to zero.

For the following analysis of value constructs, I assume that all conditions for effective patent protection are present: After detecting an infringing action, patentees are willing to file a lawsuit against the infringing party; given a strong patent regime, patentees can successfully defend their property rights.

2.3.1.3 An extended model of value constructs for the private value of patents

The following analyses build on the assumptions of Harhoff et al. (2003a) as described in sub-subsection 2.3.1.1 of this Part. However, I extend their model by adding two additional features. First, I introduce a dimension of diffusion, μ (with $0 \leq \mu \leq 1$), and directly analyze the cost connected with the publicity of inventions. Second, I present the competition value as a third value concept.

The degree of diffusion is driven by the learning skills of competitors. The shorter the period they need to understand the novelty of the invention, the higher the rate of diffusion will be. Empirical results show high but also industry-specific degrees of diffusion (Lanjouw, 1998, 692). In addition, Mansfield, Schwartz, and Wagner (Mansfield et al., 913) report that the majority of successful innovations is imitated or invented around within roughly four years after introduction. Schankermann and Pakes (1986, 1065) further show that the rate of decay in returns from holding patents is higher than the rate usually assumed for tangible goods and that this rate varies over time and also depends on the underlying patent regime.

A rapid spread of new technological ideas is one of the benefits advocates of the patent system expect and the rationale upon which temporary monopolies rests (see section 2.1 of this Part). However, this implicitly requires that competitors are fully aware of new technological developments and that the patent document fully discloses all information and related know-how needed for an immediate use of the innovation.

In the presence of complex and cumulative technologies that require a deeper understanding of the relationships between multiple inventions, values of $\mu < 1$ are plausible. In addition, lower values for μ can also result from strategically acting patent applicants trying to satisfy the fundamental information requirements of the patent system without disclosing too much information.

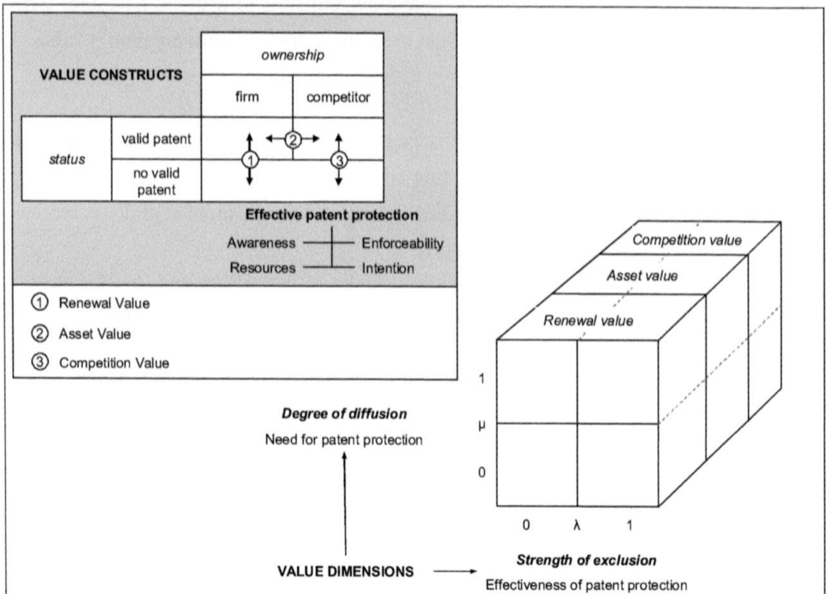

Figure 15: Value constructs and value dimension for patents

Harhoff et al. (2003a) define value by comparing the profits a firm can generate in two alternative situations. The concept of renewal value V_R (arrow 1 in Figure 15) calculates the value of a patent by subtracting the profits a firm enjoys under patent protection from the profits it can realize if the patent is not renewed. Asset value V_A (arrow 2 in Figure 15) equals the difference in profits given the case that the patent belongs to the company and the situation that the strongest competitor is the patent holder.

Empirical results show that a firm's value is not only affected by its own patent portfolio (Lerner, 1994, 327ff.) but also by the patent portfolio of its rivals (Menga and Klock, 1993, 368–369). One motivation for applying for and maintaining patent protection over the years is that it can be used as a means to deter entry of competitors into or block their access to a technology field. In this case, value potential is given by the economic disadvantage competitors face due to patent protection (see subsection 2.2.2 of this Part). Hence, I define the competition value V_C (arrow 3 in Figure 15) as being the absolute value of the differences in profits a firm realizes in the presence of a competitor having a patent and the profits the same firm can generate if the competitor's patent lapses.

2.3.1.4 Standard case

In the standard case one patent protects one independent invention. This invention enables the patent holder to produce goods of superior quality ($q+q_1>q$). The value of a patent is driven by (1) competitors' awareness of the invention and their willingness to copy or use it without the patent holder's approval (degree of diffusion, μ) and (2) by the strength of the patent system (λ).

Renewal value

Based on the value concept of renewal, value is calculated by comparing the situation of having a patent $\Pi_1(q+q_1,q+(1-\lambda)\mu q_1)$ with the situation of not renewing patent protection $\Pi_1(q+q_1,q+\mu q_1)$. Of course, in case of a low degree of diffusion ($\mu \rightarrow 0$), patent protection is simply not required as the invention may not be attractive for competitors. A comparably unattractive invention is given if one or more alternative solutions for a technical problem exist that provide customers with comparable utility. This reduces the uniqueness of the patented invention. In case of low values for μ, obtaining patent protection might even have a controversial effect on the competitive position as it increases competitor's awareness about a firm's R&D efforts.

In an oligopolistic industry, however, competitors might have a more precise idea of each others' qualities and competencies. Thus, higher values for the degree of diffusion seem to be plausible ($\mu \to 1$). The better an invention is known and the higher its potential to increase product quality and consequently company profits, the more important patent protection will be. Under a weak patent regime ($\lambda \to 0$), however, patent holders only have limited possibilities to defend their property rights. Table 2 summarizes these reflections by combining alternative values for λ and μ.

Each cell shows the different relevant value formulas for specific values for μ and λ. Applying for and maintaining a patent pays off in the presence of a high degree of diffusion and under a strong patent regime. For reasons of simplicity, costs for obtaining and maintaining patent protection are not included here, but even for high values of λ and μ, standard cost-benefit analyses should also be conducted to evaluate the advantages of patent protection.

Renewal		$\Pi_I(q+q_I,q+(1-\lambda)\mu q_I)-\Pi_I(q+q_I,q+\mu q_I)$	
		λ	
		0	1
	0	$\Pi_I(q+q_I,q)-\Pi_I(q+q_I,q)=0$	$\Pi_I(q+q_I,q)-\Pi_I(q+q_I,q)=0$
μ	*1*	$\Pi_I(q+q_I,q+q_I)-\Pi_I(q+q_I,q+q_I)=0$ or* $\Pi_I(q+q_I,q+q_I)-\Pi_N(q+q_I)=0$	$\Pi_I(q+q_I,q)-\Pi_I(q+q_I,q+q_I)>0$ or* $\Pi_I(q+q_I,q)-\Pi_N(q+q_I)>0$
* $\Pi_I(q+q_I,q+q_I)=\Pi_N(q+q_I)$ if $\mu=1$			

Table 2: Renewal value construct (standard case)

Asset value

Calculating the asset value of a patent requires a comparison of the profits a firm generates having a patent with the situation in which the strongest competitor has property rights to this patent. The profits of the firm prior to and after the sale of the patent are given by $\Pi_I(q+q_I,q+(1-\lambda)\mu q_I)$ and $\Pi_N(q+(1-\lambda)\mu q_I,q+q_I)$, respectively.

A sale of an important patent not only changes the profit structures of both contracting parties, it also increases the degree of disclosure. In fact, given a duopoly, both players in the market will *ex post* have a precise idea about the characteristics of the invention

($\mu \approx 1$). This finding is based on the assumption that patent holders will create comparable stocks of *know how* and supporting *know why* through the use of the patented invention.

Asset		$\Pi_I(q+q_I,q+(1-\lambda)\mu q_I)-\Pi_N(q+(1-\lambda)\mu q_I,q+q_I)$	
		λ	
		0	1
μ	*0*	---*	---*
	1	$\Pi_I(q+q_I,q+q_I)-\Pi_N(q+q_I,q+q_I)=0$	$\Pi_I(q+q_I,q)-\Pi_N(q,q+q_I)>0$
		* In the case of a duopoly, patent holders will be fully aware of their inventions after the patent has been sold thus $\mu = 1$.	

Table 3: Asset value construct (standard case)

Again, much like the concept of renewal value, patent values above zero only exist in the case of a strong regime. However, V_R and V_A differ regarding the quality offered in the counterfactual situation. If a patent lapses, the quality-improving invention is taken up by every market participant, yielding average profits in the industry of $\Pi_I(q+q_I,q+q_I)=\Pi_N(q+q_I)$. In contrast, under the asset-value concept the patent is still in force, which leads, given a duopoly, to an *ex post* profit for the seller of $\Pi_N(q,q+q_I)$. Since $\Pi_N(q,q+q_I)<\Pi_N(q+q_I)$, the asset value is higher than the renewal value.

Competition value

The third value concept judges the profit situation of a firm facing a competitor having a patent on a quality-increasing invention with the situation in which this patent lapses. Given a high degree of disclosure and a strong patent regime, the firm will be able to increase profits if the patent lapses to the public. However, this implies a passive strategy under which the firm waits until the patent term expires.

In contrast, the firm could also choose to actively attack the competitor's patent or to get around it. Thus, differences in value of $|\Pi_N(q,q+q_I)-\Pi_N(q+q_I,q+q_I)|>0$ equal the sum that could be used either to circumvent the patent or to invest in nullity proceedings (see section 1.3 and 1.6 of this Part).

Competition	$\left|\Pi_N(q+(1-\lambda)\mu q_1, q+q_1)-\Pi_N(q+\mu q_1, q+q_1)\right|$	
	λ	
	0	1
μ 0	$\left|\Pi_N(q, q+q_1)-\Pi_N(q_1, q+q_1)\right|=0$	$\left|\Pi_N(q, q+q_1)-\Pi_N(q, q+q_1)\right|=0$
μ 1	$\left|\Pi_N(q+q_1, q+q_1)-\Pi_N(q+q_1, q+q_1)\right|=0$	$\left|\Pi_N(q, q+q_1)-\Pi_N(q+q_1, q+q_1)\right|>0$

Table 4: Competition value construct (standard case)

2.3.1.5 Case of blocking patents

In a second step, Harhoff et al. (2003a) extend the unit of analysis by introducing cumulative patent protection. They assume the patent holder to have made two inventions leading to two quality improvements q_1 and q_2. Both inventions are under patent protection. However, the second invention was made after the first; thus, the second patent cumulatively builds on the first patent and can only be fully exercised if the patent holder also has property rights to the first patent. In this situation, the patent holder of the first patent has blocking power over the second, even when this second patent does not belong to him. Of course, if the first patent lapses into the public domain, problems of blocking power no longer exist and this case transmutes into the standard case. However, if both patents are valid and belong to one firm, this firm will generate profits of $\Pi_1(q+q_1+q_2, q+(1-\lambda)\mu(q_1+q_2))$, whereas profits for all other players in the market are given by $\Pi_N(q+(1-\lambda)\mu(q_1+q_2), q+q_1+q_2)$.

Renewal value

Table 5 shows no differences to the standard case (except for the number of quality improvements). The concept of renewal value does not reflect the blocking power of the first patent. In fact, renewal values implicitly assume that no relationships between the different members of a patent portfolio exist.

However, in many technological fields such as semiconductors and electronics (Grindley and Teece, 1997, 9) not only are the most important inventions patented, so are minor inventions. This leads to complex portfolios of connected patent rights that create substantial blocking power for the patent holder.

Renewal	$\Pi_1(q+q_1+q_2,q+(1-\lambda)\mu(q_1+q_2))-\Pi_1(q+q_1+q_2,q+\mu(q_1+q_2))$	
	λ	
	0	1
μ 0	$\Pi_1(q+q_1+q_2,q)-\Pi_1(q+q_1+q_2,q)=0$	$\Pi_1(q+q_1+q_2,q)-\Pi_1(q+q_1+q_2,q)=0$
1	$\Pi_1(q+q_1+q_2,q+q_1+q_2)$ $-\Pi_1(q+q_1+q_2,q+q_1+q_2)$ $=0$	$\Pi_1(q+q_1+q_2,q)$ $-\Pi_1(q+q_1+q_2,q+q_1+q_2)$ >0

Table 5: Renewal value construct (case of blocking patents)

Asset value

As already outlined above, blocking power emerges in the situation where the patent holders of the first and the second patent differ. For the following analysis, I assume that the first patent is sold by the inventor to a rival firm. This transaction not only transfers property rights to the first patent, it also limits the use of the second patent. Prior to the transaction, the selling party receives profits of $\Pi_1(q+q_1+q_2,q+(1-\lambda)\mu(q_1+q_2))$. After the first patent has been sold, the profits of the firm are given by $\Pi_N(q+(1-\lambda)\mu(q_1+q_2),q+q_1+(1-\lambda)q_2)$.

Asset	$\Pi_1(q+q_1+q_2,q+(1-\lambda)\mu(q_1+q_2))-\Pi_N(q+(1-\lambda)\mu(q_1+q_2),q+q_1+(1-\lambda)q_2)$	
	λ	
	0	1
μ 0	---*	---*
1	$\Pi_1(q+q_1+q_2,q+q_1+q_2)$ $-\Pi_N(q+q_1+q_2,q+q_1+q_2)$ $=0$	$\Pi_1(q+q_1+q_2,q)-\Pi_N(q,q+q_1)>0$
	* In case of a duopoly, patent holders will be fully aware of their inventions after the patent has been sold thus $\mu = 1$.	

Table 6: Asset value construct (case of blocking patents)

Since $\Pi_1(q+q_1+q_2,q+q_1+q_2)$ is smaller than $\Pi_1(q+q_1+q_2,q)$ and due to the fact that $\Pi_1(q+q_1+q_2,q+q_1+q_2)$ exceed $\Pi_N(q,q+q_1)$, it follows that the asset value always exceeds the renewal value. And of course, the lower the value for λ, the weaker the patent regime, and the lower the blocking power and patent values become.

Competition value

Much as in the standard case, a lapse of a competitor's patent has a favorable effect on the profits of the firm. However, a comparison of the profit situation in the standard case with the profits in the blocking case shows that competition value increases with the size of the competitor's patent portfolio for $\mu = \lambda = 1$. In fact, the profits the company generates in the case of blocking patents held by competitors $\Pi_N(q, q+q_1+q_2)$ are lower than the profits in the standard case given by $\Pi_N(q, q+q_1)$.

Competition		$\left\|\Pi_N(q+(1-\lambda)\mu(q_1+q_2), q+q_1+q_2) - \Pi_N(q+\mu(q_1+q_2), q+q_1+q_2)\right\|$	
		λ	
		0	1
μ	*0*	$\left\|\Pi_N(q, q+q_1+q_2) - \Pi_N(q+, q+q_1+q_2) = 0\right\|$	$\left\|\Pi_N(q, q+q_1+q_2) - \Pi_N(q, q+q_1+q_2) = 0\right\|$
	1	$\left\|\Pi_N(q+q_1+q_2, q+q_1+q_2) - \Pi_N(q+q_1+q_2, q+q_1+q_2)\right\| = 0$	$\left\|\Pi_N(q, q+q_1+q_2) - \Pi_N(q+q_1+q_2, q+q_1+q_2)\right\| > 0$

Table 7: Competition value construct (case of blocking patents)

This results from the basic assumption that higher quality allows a higher price premium to be set. The sales volume in the counterfactual situation of the standard case is described by $\Pi_N(q+q_1, q+q_1)$ and for the case of blocking patents given by $\Pi_N(q+q_1+q_2, q+q_1+q_2)$. If patent protection ceases, the increase in profits for the company is higher than the comparable increase in the standard case, hence $\Pi_N(q+q_1+q_2, q+q_1+q_2)$ exceed $\Pi_N(q+q_1, q+q_1)$. Thus, the absolute amount of the differences in sales is higher in the case of blocking power, which in turn leads to a higher competition value.

2.3.2 Theoretical implications for patent valuation

Table 8 summarizes the results of this stylized model. First of all, patent values are driven by two dimensions: the quality of patent protection and the degree of diffusion.

If no diffusion takes place then there is no need for patent protection and consequently patent values are zero. Of course, this leads to the question of whether such a low degree of diffusion seems plausible. One possible situation in which low values for μ are likely is the case of process inventions. Levin et al. (1987) find that patents protecting process inventions are considered to be less effective than patents covering product inventions. Clearly, if competitors are unable to copy or imitate the protected invention, as is often the case for process inventions, inventors simply do not need patent protection. In fact, they are likely not to patent because they want to avoid the disclosure of details of the invention. In this case, a patent might even have a controversial effect on the competitive position as it increases competitors' awareness of the patentee's research efforts (Horstman et al., 1985; Duguet and Kabla, 1998, 304; Anton et al., 2006, 12).

Furthermore, low values for μ are likely if the protected invention is unattractive from a competitors' perspective. A comparatively unattractive invention is given if one or more alternative solutions for a technical problem exist, since competitors have already successfully invented around the patented invention. Such a substitutive technology reduces the uniqueness and the value of the patented invention.

Clearly, if a patent covers a unique product invention, higher values for the degree of diffusion seem to be plausible ($\mu \rightarrow 1$). The wider an invention is known and the higher its potential to increase product quality and, consequently, a company's profits, the more important patent protection will become. However, under a weak patent regime ($\lambda \rightarrow 0$), patent holders have only limited possibilities to defend their property rights. In fact, for $\lambda = 0$ and $\mu = 1$, the model describes the information paradox (Arrow, 1962).

Please recall that low values for λ depend not only on the legal options offered by the patent system, but also on the patentees' wish to actively defend their rights by taking infringers to court. Lanjouw (1998) shows in a two-stage game of litigation and settlement that patent protection is meaningless if patentees are not willing or able to enforce their property rights. In contrast, if patents are used as a means to overcome the disadvantages described by the information paradox, then (1) the ability of the patentee to credibly threaten potential infringing parties with legal proceedings, as well as (2) the strength of the patent in particular and, of course, (3) the patent regime in general are important drivers of patent values (Lanjouw, 1998, 674). A valuation technique therefore should take the (legal) quality of a patent into account. Of course, this model focuses only on the exclusive function of the patent system. In addition to excluding competitors from profitable technological fields, other patent functions exist that create (financial) value for the patent holder (see patent functions in section 2.2 of this Part).

Under a strong patent regime, different value concepts lead to different values. As shown in Table 8, the asset-value concept (VA) always dominates renewal value and competition value. This is not surprising since a strong patent effectively protects a leading technological position, which in turn induces higher profits. Thus, under a strong patent regime, patent holders can generate monopoly profits. However, as discussed in chapter 1 of this Part, the exclusive effect of a patent requires patent holders to actively manage their patents in order to achieve a sufficient degree of exclusion. This active patent management comprises an intensive monitoring of competitors to successfully detect infringing activities. The competition value, in turn, describes how a company is affected by the competitor's patent management.

Given a high degree of disclosure and a strong patent regime, the firm will be able to increase profits if the competitor's patent lapses and enters the public domain. However, this implies a passive strategy under which the firm waits until the patent term expires. The firm could also choose to actively attack a competitor's patent or to get around it. Based on the standard case of the model, we can calculate the competition value (V_C) for $\mu = \lambda = 1$ as $V_C = |\Pi_I(q, q+q_I) - \Pi_I(q+q_I, q+q_I)|$. Thus, V_C equals the maximum amount of resources that should be devoted either to circumventing the patent or attacking it in nullity proceedings. However, if competitors fail to enforce their property rights ($\lambda = 0$), then the model correctly defines the patent value to be zero, since the patent holder does not exclude a third party from using the patented invention. The renewal value concept does not explicitly consider this blocking mechanism of a patent. Thus, it defines the maximum cost a patent holder might be willing to accept for the prolongation of patent protection.

The analysis of the second case further reveals that portfolio size does matter. Protecting a technology covered by various different patents can create a value for the entire patent portfolio exceeding the sum of the individual values. Let V_A^S denote the asset value in the standard case and V_A^B the asset value in the case of blocking patents. Based on the assumption that higher quality results in higher profits, it follows that the values in the case of a blocking patent exceed the values of a single patent, thus $V_A^B > V_A^S$, $V_R^B > V_R^S$, and $V_C^B > V_C^S$.

Hence, protecting a technology field by various different patents can lead to a value for the entire patent portfolio that exceeds the sum of all stand-alone patent values. Finally, we may conclude that the value of patents is driven by external factors such as the strength of the patent regime and the attractiveness of the invention and by the underlying value construct.

Summary			λ	
			0	1
μ	0	*Standard case*	$V_A = V_R = V_C = 0$ *	$V_A = V_R = V_C = 0$ *
		Blocking power		
	1	*Standard case*	$V_A = V_R = V_C = 0$	$V_A^S > V_R^S > V_C^S > 0$ **
		Blocking power		$V_A^B > V_R^B > V_C^B > 0$ ***

* In case of a duopoly V_A does not exist

** $V_A = \Pi_1(q+q_1,q) - \Pi_N(q,q+q_1)$

$V_R = \Pi_1(q+q_1,q) - \Pi_1(q+q_1,q+q_1)$ with $(q+q_1,q) > (q+q_1,q+q_1) > (q,q+q_1)$

$V_C = \left|\Pi_N(q,q+q_1) - \Pi_N(q+q_1,q+q_1)\right|$

*** $V_A = \Pi_1(q+q_1+q_2,q) - \Pi_N(q,q+q_1)$

$V_R = \Pi_1(q+q_1+q_2,q) - \Pi_1(q+q_1+q_2,q+q_1+q_2)$ with $(q+q_1+q_2,q) > (q+q_1+q_2,q+q_1+q_2) > (q,q+q_1) > (q,q+q_1+q_2)$

$V_C = \left|\Pi_N(q,q+q_1+q_2) - \Pi_N(q+q_1+q_2,q+q_1+q_2)\right|$

S – Standard case

B – Case of blocking patents

A – Asset value

R – Renewal value

C – Competition value

Table 8: Summary of value constructs

3 Part II: Implications for patent valuation

Patents are a legal means to secure technological inventions and the value potential of innovations. The size of this value potential, in combination with the strength of the patent right, are important value drivers. In addition, valuation should also reflect the following findings:

1. *Legal dimension of patents*

Despite the fact that patents are national rights, a strong degree of harmonization has led to comparable patent systems. However, some differences between United States and European patent law exist that are noteworthy in valuation projects. A first-to-file-system can lead to a prevalence of poorly drafted patent applications. A first-to-invent system creates uncertainty about the creator of an invention. In addition, patent protection in the United States can be obtained for a broader set of inventions, for example, new business methods and financial products. With regard to the patent examination and granting procedure remarkable differences exist between the EPO and the USPTO (Harhoff et al., 2007):

Patent office	Examination procedure	Probability of a patent grant	Duration of proceedings
EPO	State of the art primarily defined by patent examiner	67%	On average: approximately 4 years
USPTO	State of the art mainly described by applicant, Inflationary use of citations	>90%	On average: approximately 2 to 2.5 years

Table 9: Major differences between EPO and USPTO

Furthermore, patent documents and examination reports present information in a qualitative but standardized way which can be used for transforming qualitative statements into quantitative variables (e.g., the *X*, *Y*, and *Z* typology of citations). The procedure choice for obtaining patent protection can itself carry option values that in turn can impact patent values. Finally, the decision about the patentability of an invention depends, on the one hand, on legally defined criteria. However, these substantial requirements are reviewed by patent examiners; this introduces a certain degree of subjectivity in the patent-granting procedure.

2. *Economic dimension of patents*

The primary function of the patent system, the disclosure of inventions in exchange for a temporary exclusive use, is more and more frequently accompanied by alternative uses of patent rights that try to create additional value out of this primary function. Needless to say, for a specific valuation project, the specific underlying patent function is a main value driver.

3. *Valuation perspective and value constructs*

Based on the exclusive function of a patent, three alternative valuation perspectives are possible and lead to three alternative value constructs: renewal, value, asset value, and competition value. Each focuses on alternative sets of costs and benefits and will therefore result in different value conclusions. Multiple patents taken together can exhibit a portfolio effect.

4. *Patents and knowledge*

In combination with the implications from Part I, the stand-alone value of a patent is driven by the amount of explicit and implicit knowledge needed to exploit the full potential of a technological field. If most of the value rests on sticky, implicit knowledge and/or if this patent belongs to a well-populated portfolio of patents that are not subject to valuation, then the stand-alone value of one patent is lower than it would be if it granted full access to a technological field and protected all the explicit knowledge necessary to successfully operate in this field.

At the same time, however, the strength of the exclusive right is the second main value driver of the stand-alone value of a patent right. If the patent cannot be enforced, it is of course of very little value. Thus, valuation should reflect varying degrees of implicit and explicit knowledge and the strength of the exclusive function of the patent right

Part III: Patent valuation

1 Valuation background

In the following chapters, I further refine the general valuation process (section 1.1) as described in Part I and review the main functions of patent valuation projects (section 1.2).

1.1 Process of valuation

As defined in Part I, a quantitative assessment of any valuation object comprises two main stages, evaluation, and valuation. Based on this general structure, the specific case of patent valuation can be further subdivided into four main steps (Reilly and Schweihs, 1998, 88ff.). First, the motivation behind a valuation of a selected patent portfolio must be thoroughly analyzed. In a second step, qualitative and quantitative data on these patents is collected and reviewed. Based on this information set, different approaches to value can then be used in order to arrive at a conclusion of value. This final result is then further tested using sensitivity and scenario analyses as well as simulation techniques. The valuation process concludes with a comprehensive valuation report describing the underlying economic rationale of the valuation.

1.1.1 Step one: Motivation for valuation

Posing the right questions is the key to successful patent valuation. First, both client (recipient of the valuation report) and analyst (author of the valuation report) must fully understand the economic situation and motivation behind the need for the following valuation. This serves (1) to create a common understanding of the number and type of patents and patent families subject to valuation, the objective and purpose of the overall valuation project, and the valuation date, and (2) allows the derivation of the most suitable value definition (see section 1.2 in Part I).

1.1.2 Step two: Data collection and analysis

A valuation, in principle, focuses on collecting, evaluating, and adjusting qualitative and quantitative data in order to arrive at a quantitative result. Clearly, this process of transforming qualitative information into financial values usually requires the making of reasonable assumptions, especially in the case of valuation approaches based on future events. Each assumption must be clearly communicated, discussed with the client, and if necessary, adjusted. Since patents protect technological inventions, in addition to the historical and future costs and benefits relating to any products under patent protection, the legal quality, and thus the exclusive character of patent rights should also be carefully determined and considered. Making reasonable assumptions also calls for a deeper understanding of the nature of and surrounding conditions in the overall economy, relevant industries, and strategic groups. The complexity of any valuation process usually requires the expertise of various specialists from patent department and business units. Again, a policy of clear and transparent communication is necessary for an efficient valuation process.

1.1.3 Step three: Application of three approaches to value

Based on the information databases provided by various sources and compiled by the analyst, three direct approaches to value can be used in order to arrive at a well-supported estimate for a patent's value. I describe these basic approaches in more detail in the section 3.1 of this Part.

1.1.4 Step four: Conclusion of value

At the end of the valuation process, all qualitative and quantitative information is condensed into a final numeric value conclusion. This is derived from the overall valuation model (steps one to three) and therefore is heavily dependent on the underlying assumptions. Hence, it is essential to check the sensitivity of the value conclusion to changes in critical assumptions and value drivers. Starting from an analysis of the impact of single-value drivers, sensitivity analyses can also be performed for alternative scenarios comprising simultaneous modifications of a set of both qualitative and quantitative key variables. The precise degree to which value drivers are likely to vary can be analyzed using simulation techniques such as the Monte Carlo method (Hertz, 1964, 95ff; Kautt and Hopewell, 2000, 91ff.; Nawrocki, 2001, 93ff.; Gruber and Venter, 2006).

1.2 Functions of valuation

As with a company valuation, any patent valuation must reflect the specific purpose and guiding paradigm of the valuation project (Bausch, 2000, 488ff.). At least four different paradigms are possible: First, valuation projects facilitate and support the making of decisions (advisory function). Second, a precise idea about the (private) value of a patent portfolio to a company and to an unrelated third party significantly increases the efficiency of and the bargaining power during a negotiation process (function of reasoning). Third, valuation projects can also attempt to find an appropriate solution that meets the expectations of both parties involved (intermediary function). Finally, due to the transparency created by any thorough analysis prior to and during a valuation, these projects increase communication and understanding of complex interactions of business, technological, and legal issues (communication function).

2 Reasons for valuation

Patent-valuation projects are motivated by a variety of different reasons. For the following analysis, I differentiate between reasons driven by management needs and value reporting for accounting purposes. In the former case, the need for valuation projects results from specific business circumstances (see section 2.1). In the latter case, the accounting framework and accounting rules define methods and value of patents (see section 2.2.). Their primary aim is to disclose information to shareholders. This book perspective, however, may be of little value for specific business situations and management purposes.

2.1 Valuation for management purposes

2.1.1 Sale, purchase, or licensing of patents

Like any other resource, patents and knowledge assets can be subject to sales transactions. Particularly in the context of cross-border transfers to affiliated companies, tax authorities demand detailed and transparent descriptions of the underlying valuation rationale and the resulting transfer prices. Property rights to patents can also be temporarily transferred through licensing agreements (see chapter 1 in Part IV). In both cases, any serious decision requires an assessment of the underlying monetary value (Contractor, 2001, 114).

2.1.2 Cooperation between companies

Alternative methods for a definite transfer of patents include various forms of cooperation between companies, ranging from joint ventures and alliances to acquisitions and mergers. Patents, like any other tangible and intangible resource, are part of a due-diligence process prior to signing and closing the agreement. Patents can play a major role in this process since they can be used to assess the technological strength of candidates (Breitzmann et al., 2002). They comprise and express explicit knowledge in a standardized way which facilitates evaluation and valuation processes. However, for merger and acquisitions, valuation processes do not only take place prior to agreeing on the purchase price. Often, they are conducted after the transaction has taken place in order to split up the acquired goodwill (purchase-price allocation).

2.1.3 Spin-off activities

One way to commercialize the value of knowledge assets, especially of patents, is to hive off a patented technology field in cooperation with a venture capitalist. Here, patents play various roles: In the pre-investment phase they serve as a signal to underline the competitive advantage of the new company. Furthermore, they might also be seen as a liquidation benefit for the venture capitalist, given that the most important patents can be sold or redistributed in case of a bankruptcy. Over the course of the holding period, patents are used in a number of ways. They serve as means for blocking competitors, as a strategic device to protect competitive advantages, and as a source of income through licensing agreements, as well as a bargaining chip in negotiations and the establishment of strategic partnerships. In the exit phase, venture capitalists can use them to convince the capital market and/or future shareholders of the quality and economic potential of the company (Rivette and Kline, 2000, 60–61; OECD, 2005, 12–13).

2.1.4 Patent securization

In recent years, patent and intellectual property (IP) securization has developed out of the increased awareness of knowledge and intellectual property as major drivers of a firm's success. The basic idea is that a royalty stream generated from a patent is transferred to a special-purpose vehicle (SPV). An SPV is a legal entity created for a particular purpose and acts as a depository for a specific group of assets in a securitization. It issues securities to capital market investors. Proceeds from these securities are passed back to the patent holder. The royalty stream is used to pay investors back over a fixed period with an interest rate (Wagner, 1999).

For investors, one main advantage of this deal structure is that patents are no longer available to creditors of the original patent holder and are solely used to pay investors in securities. In addition, securities issued by SPVs are usually backed by numerous assets, thus facilitating a risk diversification on investor's side. For patent holders, major advantages of IP and patent securization include lower financing cost (compared to loans), immediate availability of capital (compared to annual royalty income over several years), and the possibility of a higher credit rating on the securization than the originator's rating. Especially for non-profit institutions such as universities with applied research programs or smaller companies with insufficient access to capital, patent securization can be an important liquidity tool (Borod, 2006).

2.1.5 Compensation of employee-inventors

In large organizations, most inventions result from the research efforts of employee-inventors. In the case of an invention made by an employee, questions about the rights and duties of both the employee and the employer arise. In addition, employee-inventors expect to receive a reasonable share of the value of their invention as compensation. There are only a few countries in the world in which compensation schemes are governed by a specific legal institution. In Germany, these questions are defined in the German Employee's Invention Act (Gesetz über Arbeitnehmererfindungen; ArbnErfG). Comparable legal regulations can be found in Denmark, Finland, Norway, and Sweden. In other countries, regulations dealing with employee-inventions are part of the respective national patent laws (United Kingdom, France, Italy, Austria, Netherlands, and Japan). In the Unites States and Canada, issues concerning compensation of employee-inventors are regulated by individual contractual agreements between employer and employee and guided by a set of prior court decisions (Cherensky, 1993; Harhoff and Hoisl, 2007, 1145–1146).

2.1.6 Patent portfolio management

Value-based management theory is grounded on the premise that each investment must yield future returns exceeding capital cost. It requires that investment opportunities and all other strategic and operating decisions are analyzed with regard to this paradigm (Copeland et al., 1995, 93–94; Hahn and Hungenberg, 2001, 191ff.).

In line with this value-based management approach, the overall aim of patent portfolio management is to maximize the contribution of the patent portfolio to firm success (Moser and Goddar, 2007, 598). It is of major importance to create a proprietary and defensible competitive advantage by establishing and maintaining a monopolistic market position (Rivette and Kline, 2000, 56).

The main tasks of patent portfolio management comprise: (1) the creation and (2) maintenance of a comprehensive patent portfolio, protecting technological fields that are of importance for the company (Davis and Weitz, 1998, 69). This also includes the institution of legal proceedings in case of patent-infringing activities by third parties (see section 1.6 of Part II). Furthermore, patent portfolio management should (3) provide useful and reliable information for decision-making at the corporate and business-unit level and (4) facilitate planning and exploiting the economic potential of the given patent portfolio (Ernst, 1998, 281ff.; Wurzer and Reinhardt, 2006, 32ff.).

Patent strategy serves these aims by defining the ways and deploying the resources necessary to achieve these preselected goals. Given the predominance of an economic perspective, the consequences of decisions relating to the patent portfolio of a company have to be analyzed with regard to their economic impact. This comprises not only decisions relating to the exploitation of a given portfolio. Additionally, the creation and structure of the patent portfolio – decisions, for example, about patent applications and renewals, as well as patent scope and procedure choice – should reflect the basic economic rationale of profit maximization. Managers need detailed information on the content and structure of a company's patent portfolio, not only for assessing the cost and benefits connected to legal options given by the patent law in the case of an infringement of the company's patent portfolio by a third party but also to estimate risks associated with the breach or circumvention of patents of competitors.

Patent-related decisions usually involve a high degree of risk since the future in general and R&D investments in particular are uncertain (Tritle et al., 2000, 47). Comparisons to other existing patents are only possible to a limited extent due to the heterogeneous nature of patents and innovations. Therefore, patent managers are more likely to create patent portfolios that do not follow the economic principle of maximizing value but rather aim at reducing risk. In other words: "*When in doubt, file an application*" (Grubb, 1982, 47). Hence, patent strategy and patent-related decisions tend to be dominated by a discussion of risk and not by an analysis of economic benefits or utility (Wurzer and Reinhardt, 2006, 34–35).

The impact of this behavior on patent values is straightforward. In combination with poorly drafted patent claims and weak patent regimes, uncertainty can lead to numerous patents of low legal quality (Anton et al., 2006). However, as already outlined above, patent values are driven by both legal quality and economic profitability. Even in the case of high profitability, low legal quality must result in low patent values. This fact underlines the importance of a sound and comprehensive evaluation of the legal quality during a valuation project.

2.2 Disclosing information to shareholders

The primary task of financial statements is to provide useful and reliable information to shareholders. The criticism that the usefulness of accounting information is declining with the increasing relevance of intangible assets for corporate performance and value (Egginton, 1990, 193; Napier and Power, 1992, 85; Lev, 2003) has motivated the introduction of new accounting rules. They focus on measuring the value of intangible assets in general and patents in particular.

2.2.1 German HGB and DRS 12: Recognition criteria

According to § 246 Abs. 1 HGB, the annual report of an enterprise must contain an overview of all assets as long as there are no options or interdictions for disclosure defined elsewhere (Förschle and Kroner, 2003, 81). IPRs must be shown under the item "intangible assets" (§ 266 HGB). Besides HGB, further disclosure requirements for group accounting can be found in the Deutscher Rechnungslegungsstandard 12 (DRS 12). This standard defines an intangible asset as being an identifiable, non-monetary asset without physical substance that is controlled by an enterprise and that is required to produce goods and services or creates utility by either transferring it to a third party or through use by the owner (DRS 12.7).

2.2.2 German HGB and DRS 12: Disclosure and measurement

Under German HGB and DRS 12, the origin of the intangible asset determines its disclosing value. If a patent has been acquired, value equals the sum of the acquisition cost. These costs comprise not only the purchase price of the respective patent but also all costs needed to enable its full utilization (Richter, 1990, 91; Schmidbauer, 2003, 2041). In the case of a barter trade, the value of the patent obtained equals the book value of the asset given away less possible income taxes. Alternatively, a prudent estimation of the value at the transaction date can be conducted (Kußmaul, 2000, 51).

In the past, inventors were not allowed to book a self-created patent as an asset (§ 248 Abs. 2 HGB and DRS 12.13). This general principle is revised by the draft of the Bilanzmodernisierungsgesetz (BilMoG), published in November 2007 and scheduled to be effective in 2009. According § 255 HGB n. F. the process of developing an intangible asset (patent) includes a research stage and a development stage. Thus, all cost for self-creation is divided in research cost and development cost. Development cost (for an invention) must be capitalized if an intangible asset (patent) can be identified. Research cost must not be shown on the balance sheet. Needless to say, the focal point of such a split is on determining the end date of the research stage and the starting date of the development stage (Mindermann, 2008, 276ff.).

After the initial recognition, patents are to be depreciated over their expected useful life – which can differ from the maximum duration of a patent. In fact, according to

DRS 12.14, a variety of factors, such as product life cycles and technological progress, have to be taken into account when determining the useful life of a patent. In the past, German jurisprudence defined the useful life to be, on average, eight years (see BFH III 58/62, III R 75/66). However, several authors support the idea of a shorter period, between three to five years, due to increasing technological progress (Glade, 1986, 111; Richter, 1990, 119).

In addition, DRS 12.22 and DRS 12.23 define an exceptional depreciation to be conducted should the fair value of a patent fall below its book value. If the reasons for the exceptional depreciation no longer apply, an appreciation to amortized cost is required. Finally, the income statement must show benefits and costs connected to patents (Richter, 1990, 120), and accruals must be set up in case of patent litigation (Berger and Ring, 2003, 100).

2.2.3 International Financial Reporting Standards: Recognition criteria

Patents match the definition of an intangible asset as defined by IAS 38.8, since a patent is an identifiable, non-monetary asset without physical substance. In order to meet the criterion of identifiability, an intangible asset must be distinguishable from goodwill (IAS 38.11). A sufficient condition for identifiability is given if an intangible asset is separable or if it arises from contractual or other legal rights (IAS 38.12). Finally, patents meet the criterion of having no physical substance. Although the patent specification is of a physical nature, the most important part of a patent is the protected and incorporeal invention (Epstein and Mirza, 2003, 310).

An asset is a resource that is controlled by the enterprise as a result of past events (for example, purchase or self-creation) and from which future economic benefits (inflows of cash or other assets) are expected. In sum, the three critical attributes of an intangible asset as described by IAS 38.8 are: (1) identifiability, (2) control (power to obtain benefits from the asset), and (3) future economic benefits (such as revenues or reduced future cost).

Whether a patent has been purchased or self created, IAS 38.21 requires an enterprise to recognize it if (1) the enterprise expects to obtain future economic benefits that are attributable to this patent and (2) if the cost of the patent can be measured reliably. As for the first, the probability of future economic benefits must be based on assumptions, both reasonable and supportable, about the circumstances and situations the patent will face over its lifetime. IAS 38.33 states that this probability criterion is always satisfied if the patent is acquired separately or in a business combination.

In the case of self-created intangible assets, the enterprise has to distinguish between two stages in the process of creating intangible assets – a research and a development stage (see also the discussion of the BilMoG in subsection 2.2.2 of this Part). If the respective intangible asset has to be allotted to the research stage, all costs are to be charged as resource costs affecting the income of this period (IAS 38.43). However, costs connected to the intangible asset can be capitalized if an intangible asset has already entered the development stage. In order to distinguish between the research and development stages, IAS 38.57 defines six criteria regarding technical and commercial feasibility that have to be met cumulatively. If this is not the case, the enterprise must treat all expenditures as if they were incurred during the research stage only.

As for patents, this distinction between research and development stage is of minor importance since they must always – be they acquired or self-created – be recognized and shown in the balance sheet (Alexander and Archer, 2003, 20.06; Epstein and Mirza, 2003, 312).

2.2.4 International Financial Reporting Standards: Disclosure and measurement

Initially, intangible assets are measured at cost (IAS 38.24). The measurement of cost depends on the way by which the enterprise obtains control over the resource. If the patent is acquired separately, acquisition cost is the price after deduction of allowances. In addition, all direct costs incurred to make the patent ready for its expected use must be assessed (IAS 38.27). If the patent is obtained in exchange for another resource or a similar patent, then cost equals the fair value of the resource or combination of resources given away (IAS 38.45). In the case of an acquisition of a company, the fair value of a patent has to be determined (IAS 38.35). IAS 38.39 generally considers the price on an active market to be the most reliable estimate for a fair value. However, due to their heterogeneity and uniqueness, an active market does not exist for patents (IAS 38.78). Therefore, the fair value must reflect the value that would have been obtained if the patent had been transferred between willing, competent, and independent parties (IAS 38.40). If an enterprise is involved in transferring intangible assets on a regular base then other methods for estimating the fair value may also be used. IAS 38.41 specifies multiple approaches, for example, relief from royalty or a discounted net cash-flow method, as appropriate techniques.

A self-created patent must be measured at production cost; this also includes patent registration fees (IAS 38.66). Subsequent to the initial recognition, intangible assets can either be carried at cost less any amortization and impairment losses (cost model, IAS 38.74) or at a revalued amount (revaluation model, IAS 38.75). As for the latter, revaluation amount is based on the fair value of the intangible asset at the date of revaluation less any subsequent amortization and any subsequent impairment losses. However, the revaluation model requires the existence of an active market for the intangible asset, which is not given in the case of patents (IAS 37.78). Thus, patents have to be carried using the cost model. As a patent has a finite life defined by patent law (20 years), it must be depreciated over its useful life. According to IAS 38.94, the useful life can not exceed the maximum patent lifetime of 20 years, but may be shorter, depending on the expected period over which the patent will be used. The depreciation method should reflect the pattern of benefits. If this pattern cannot be determined reliably, the straight-line method must be used (IAS 38.97). In addition, a residual value shall only be assumed to be not equal to zero if either a commitment to buy the asset at the end of its useful lifetime by a third party exists or if the asset is traded on an active market. The amortization charge is recognized in the profit or loss statement if not IAS 38 or any other standard permits or requires it to be included in the cost of another asset. In accordance with IAS 38.104, the amortization period should be reviewed at least annually. Furthermore, an impairment test must be conducted in accordance with IAS 36 (IAS 38.111).

2.2.5 United States Generally Accepted Accounting Principles: Recognition criteria

SFAC 6.25 defines an asset referring to probable future benefits that can be controlled or obtained by the asset owner due to a past transaction or event. Probable future benefits contain benefits the asset owner enjoys by selling, exchanging, or using the respective asset either alone or in combination with other assets. Furthermore, the acceptance of an asset in a settlement of a liability by creditors also fulfills the criterion of future economic benefits (SFAC 6.173). These assets must be recognized if they can be measured reliably and if information connected to them is relevant. Relevance means that the information has an impact on decisions of information users. Reliability requires the information to be faithful, verifiable, and neutral (SFAC 5.63). In addition, classifying an asset as being intangible necessitates that the asset is not classified as a financial asset and lacks physical substance (SFAS 142). If an intangible asset has been acquired in a business combination, it must be recognized as an asset apart from goodwill if it either arises from legal or contractual rights or if it is separable (SFAS

141.39). In general, patents meet all the criteria of an asset as defined in SFAC 5 and SFAC 6. Furthermore, SFAS 141.A14 e identifies patents as one example of intangible assets that meet the criteria for recognition apart from goodwill.

Acquired intangible assets must be shown in the balance sheet. The cost of developing, maintaining, or restoring a self-created intangible asset must be recognized as an expense if the asset is either not identifiable, has an infinite life span, or belongs to an entity as a whole (SFAS 142.10).

2.2.6 United States Generally Accepted Accounting Principles: Disclosure and measurement

According to SFAS 142.9, an intangible asset must be carried at its fair value. In case of an acquisition, fair value equals acquisition cost. This consists of the price after all allowances have been taken into account plus all other costs incurred to make the item ready for use (SFAS 141.5). If a combination of assets is subject to the transaction then the purchase price must be allotted according to the relative fair values of the different assets. If these allotted costs per asset exceed its fair value this can indicate that not only a group of assets but also a whole business operation has been acquired, which in turn requires the application of SFAS 141 (Dawo, 2003, 137–138). If an intangible asset is obtained through a barter trade, then measurement depends on the fair value of the given or acquired asset, depending on which of them can be assessed more reliably (SFAS 141.6).

Prices on active markets are considered to be the best evidence for fair values (SFAS 142.23). However, if an active market does not exist, a fair value must be calculated using present value techniques as described in SFAC 7. This standard defines two calculation techniques – the traditional approach and the expected-cash-flow approach (SFAC 7.40). Following SFAC 7.23, calculating present values requires an examination of the following five steps: (1) Analyzing the stream of future cash-flows, (2) creating expectations about possible variations regarding amount and timing of the underlying cash-flows, (3) determining a risk-free interest rate for assessing the time value of money, (4) defining a risk premium to reflect uncertainty, and (5) reviewing other factors such as illiquidity or market imperfections that can have an impact on fair values.

The traditional approach and the expected-cash-flow approach differ regarding the way they account for risk and uncertainty (see also the discussion on income-based valuation in sub-subsection 3.1.3.1 in Part III). Under the traditional approach, fair value is determined by discounting the most probable pattern of future cash-flows at a single discount rate reflecting steps 2 to 5 and summarizing all risky aspects in the discount rate (SFAC 7.42–44). However, a risk premium is to be included for risks that are identifiable, measurable, and significant. If this is not the case, then SFAC 7.62 expects the risk-free interest rate to be the best available estimate to calculate a fair value. According to SFAC 7.69ff., various models can be used for determining risk premiums (Hitz and Kuhner, 2000, 895; Starbatty, 2001, 548).

In contrast, the expected-cash-flow technique does not concentrate on the most likely stream of cash-flows; rather, all expectations about possible future patterns of cash-flows and their probabilities are to be taken into account. The cash-flows used to calculate a fair value equal the sum of all expected streams of cash-flows weighted with the probability that they may occur in the future. These probabilities contain all risk factors besides the time value of money. Therefore, the discount rate applied for calculating fair values equals the risk-free interest rate (SFAC 7.45-46). The fair value depends on production cost if the patent is self-created. Patent registration fees as well as court and lawyer fees in case of a successful litigation can also be capitalized (Kieso et al., 2001, 603; Siegel et al., 2004, 3.78).

After the initial recognition, a patent value is to be depreciated over its useful life (SFAS 142.11). The amortization method should reflect the pattern of consumption of the economic benefits associated with the respective patent. If this pattern cannot be determined reliably, straight-line amortization should be used (SFAS 142.12). The maximum duration for the useful life of a patent is 20 years. According to SFAS 142.B 46, assessing the useful life of a patent depends on the period over which a patent contributes to the creation of cash-flows. In each reporting period, the remaining useful life of a patent must be reviewed. The overall amortization volume equals the amount initially assigned to the patent less any residual value. In general, the residual value is assumed zero to be (SFAS 142.13). An exception to this general rule is given, in the case that a third party commits to acquiring the patent before it expires (SFAS 142 Appendix A, Example 2). Additionally, an impairment test must be conducted according to SFAS 144 (SFAS 142.15), substituting the regulations of SFAS 121.

3 Patent valuation – A review of existing approaches to value

The discussion in the previous chapters already indicates that the task of valuing patents is a challenging one since it takes place in the presence of a high degree of uncertainty. However, the importance of patents in general for securing a leading competitive edge as well as the increasing willingness to exploit the economic potential of these rights through market transactions (see Part IV) have supported the emergence and application of several valuation methods.

For the following analysis, I distinguish between two different groups of valuation techniques. The first group, which I refer to as direct valuation techniques, comprises models that allow a direct calculation of financial values (section 3.1). These approaches rest on the basic assumption that patents fully or partly protect technology embedded in sophisticated and marketable products or services. They can be clustered into three main groups according to their underlying approach to value, which can be either cost, market, or income (Reilly and Schweihs, 1998).

Indirect patent valuation measures form the second group of valuation techniques (section 3.2). They take advantage of the fact that patent documents are fully available to the public and contain a considerable amount of standardized information. These bibliographic patent value indicators are considered to be fundamental drivers of patent values. They are used to approximate the intrinsic patent values with sufficient reliability.

Of course, the various approaches to value each have their own strengths and weaknesses. Based on these existing approaches and the analysis of their adequacy (section 3.3), as well as the findings of the previous Parts, I conclude this Part with a detailed description of a comprehensive approach to value (section 4).

3.1 Direct patent valuation: Three approaches to value

A variety of methods and processes can be used for the appraisal of patents, and they all strive for the same goal: arriving at a reasonable indication of a value for a specific patent or patent portfolio. For further analysis and discussion, however, it is advisable to group these methods according to their underlying economic principles of substitution, equilibrium, and anticipation.

3.1.1 The principle of substitution: Cost approach

3.1.1.1 General introduction

The basic idea of all cost approaches is that an unrelated third party or a prudent investor would not pay more for a patented technology than the cost to obtain this technology elsewhere or to develop a substitute for it. Hence, the cost approach defines an upper value limit. Although a valuation based on expected economic benefits might exceed this value, a rational-acting economic agent would not pay more for a patented technology than the cost to obtain a suitable substitute (Moser and Goddar, 2007, 596).

Hence, the value of a patented technology depends on (1) the number and (2) the availability of substitute technologies. To understand this principle of substitution it is important to recall that from an economic point of view, all technologies qualify as substitutes as long as they offer a comparable utility to the customer. This does not necessarily imply that they also exhibit the same technological functionality. Functionality refers to the way in which a utility is created. Thus, several technologies can result in the same utility. This is one basic prerequisite for circumventing activities by competitors. For further discussion, a suitable classification of cost-based approaches to value is offered by the following three dimensions: (1) components of cost, (2) type of cost, and (3) temporal dimension of cost.

3.1.1.2 Components of cost

Cost accrues during the production process. For patents this process comprises not only development cost for the invention but also all costs incurred for gaining and maintaining patent protection. Consequently, for patents, the main components to be considered are: (1) R&D expenditures if the substitute is assumed to be developed by a member of the organization or acquisition cost if it can be bought in a market transaction and (2) legal expenditures such as patent application fees, renewal fees, and court costs in case of legal disputes. In addition, one might add cost for prototypes and specific tools as a third cost component, given that their impact on the utility of the patented technology can be determined reliably. Some authors further argue that a comparable utility on the patentee's side requires additional, supportive marketing expenditures (Rings, 2000, 842–843). Needless to say, a reliable cost based valuation calls for a careful assessment of the cost components to be included. An additional main challenge lies in estimating an adequate formula for allocating cost if several patents and related know how are expected to result from one R&D project.

3.1.1.3 Type of cost

Cost-based valuation theory distinguishes between two different types of cost: reproduction and replacement (Smith and Parr, 2000, 202–203; Park and Park, 2004, 388). Reproduction cost is the estimated cost to produce an exact replica of the patent to be valued; replacement cost equals the estimated cost to develop a patented invention with equivalent utility.

In both cases, cost should be measured at current prices as of the valuation date. If information on historical cost for the valuation object is available, one approach for estimating current cost is to trend these historical cost (arrow 1 in Figure 16). This can be achieved by using an inflation index such as a consumer or producer price index (Reilly and Schweihs, 1998; Smith and Parr, 2000, 204).

For an aged patented invention, (current) cost must be depreciated to account for obsolescence. This is due to the fact that the (aged) valuation object is theoretically inferior to the brand-new asset that is the basis of this cost estimate (Mard, 2000, 27). Four forms of obsolescence can be considered: (1) physical deterioration, (2) functional, (2) technological and (3) external (economic) obsolescence.[8] This classification of different types of obsolescence is conceptually derived from the valuation of real estate property. If the item to be valued is a building site or a building, external obsolescence comprises two subcategories – locational and economic obsolescence. Clearly, locational obsolescence is of little importance for patent valuation; thus, economic obsolescence becomes a synonym for external obsolescence.

Deductions for functional obsolescence reflect the fact that the patent endows the patentee with a lower degree of exclusivity than anticipated by the patent holder at the point in time at which the patent was granted. This can be due to numerous reasons, including poorly written patent claims, overly optimistic market expectations, and limited geographical coverage (given for patent families). Technological obsolescence can arise due to improvements in technology. Clearly, new technological discoveries may offer substitutes for the patented invention, thus reducing its value generation potential. Finally, external obsolescence must be taken into account if patent protection is reduced, either as a consequence of legal proceedings or because of successful inventing-around activities initiated by competing companies. In order to classify a reason

[8] I do not discuss physical deterioration here since a reduction of value due to wear and tear is not applicable in the case of patents (Reilly and Schweihs, 1998, 127) .

for obsolescence as external, the reduction of value must result from effects, events, or conditions that are external to – thus not controlled by – the patentee.

In contrast to this, patentees might be able to cure functional and/or technological obsolescence. Hence, for these two forms of obsolescence a further distinction can be made with regard to the degree to which they can be cured. In general, any deficiency of an asset is considered to be curable if the benefits of modifying this asset exceed its modification cost. Clearly, whether or not any of these reasons for obsolescence can be cured depends on the specific situation. In case of a granted patent, a change of claims to cure functional obsolescence after the granting date is not possible. In contrast to this, changes in the claims are possible during the patent application process, but they are also limited since any modification may not exceed the scope of what was initially covered by the application. If the patentee wishes to extend the geographical coverage, then additional national applications must be filed within one year after the priority date (see also chapter 1 in Part II). This, however, does not constitute a shortcoming on the part of one single national patent. Nevertheless, it is of importance if the valuation object is an entire patent family.

The distinction between curable and incurable obsolescence is important for understanding the relationship between reproduction and replacement cost. The replacement cost approach assumes equivalent utility. This implies using modern materials and production techniques allowing the production of a well-defined utility at lower cost. All curable (and costly) inadequacies and obsolescence are excluded. In contrast to this, the replication cost approach focuses on an exact replica and presumes the use of the same material and production techniques and devoting the same quantity and quality of human resources. Thus, the replica includes also the same inadequacies and obsolescence as the subject patent. If a considerable amount of time and human resources must be devoted to the interactive process between patent applicant and patent authority, then this cost should also be considered in a reproduction cost approach (Wurzer and Reinhardt, 2006, 221).

Hence, reproduction and replacement cost differ with respect to curable obsolescence (arrow 2 in Figure 16). Adjusting (current) reproduction cost by curable obsolescence leads to (current) replacement cost. For an aged patent, this cost may further be depreciated due to account for incurable obsolescence (arrow 3 in Figure 16) in order to come to an indication of its current value (Reilly and Schweihs, 1998, 128).

The specific amount for depreciation depends on the age of the patent on the valuation date (arrow 7 in Figure 16), the remaining useful life (arrow 6 in Figure 16), and the amortization method. Using the concept of depreciation, valuation theory focuses on quantifying changes – or more precisely, decreases in value (due to physical, functional, or economic causes) – rather than on systematically allocating cost from an accounting or tax perspective (Smith and Parr, 2000, 563–564).

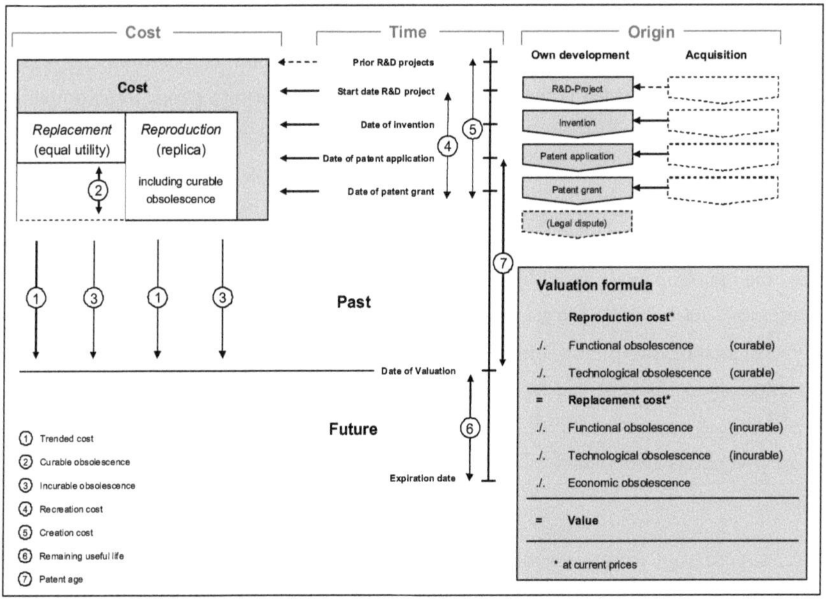

Figure 16: Cost Approach

3.1.1.4 Temporal dimension of cost

Given path-dependent research and development projects (see section 4 in Part I), the question arises how far back in the process of developing a patented invention costs should be measured. For cumulative inventions, in particular, a match between one invention and one single R&D project is difficult to achieve. In contrast to tangible goods it may therefore be not easy to separate the amount of knowledge required for the creation of a specific patent.

Two different classifications for cost deal with this question. They distinguish themselves by the number of periods over which cost is measured. An analysis of creation cost assumes that all the intellectual content of an invention was to be created only for the patent to be valued (arrow 5 in Figure 16). In contrast, the application of a recreation-cost perspective (arrow 4 in Figure 16) rests on the assumption that the invention was developed based on already existing knowledge (Reilly and Schweihs, 1998, 123–124).

3.1.2 The principles of equilibrium and competition: Market approach

3.1.2.1 General introduction

The market approach is based on the principles of equilibrium, competition, and substitution. The general idea is that equilibrium prices of substitute goods in a competitive market provide an indication for the value of the valuation object (Reilly and Schweihs, 1998, 101). It is noteworthy, though, that these prices heavily depend on market conditions and on non-market specific influences affecting the transaction at the time the asset or patent was transferred. In particular, (historical) market prices reflect the participants' specific negotiation strategies and bargaining positions (Contractor, 2001, 12ff.). Furthermore, a market approach implicitly assumes a certain degree of homogeneity between the subject of the valuation project and an adequate reference object. Despite the fact that patent application and patent granting follow a consistent and transparent procedure (see chapter 1 in Part II) the diversity of the protected inventions and related claims might impede any comparative valuation technique.

Any market-based valuation project comprises two main steps. The first step consists of identifying historical transactions which involved patent rights. After collecting and checking a sufficient amount of background information the analyst can derive a value indication for the valuation object (second step). It should be noted that in the first step, not only the selling or buying of single patents and patent families are relevant. Although an observation of single occasions involving a transfer of patent rights is possible, in many cases and for reasons of confidentiality, we can neither clearly identify the circumstances under which a transaction took place nor retrieve the necessary information about the economic conditions of the transfer from public sources only. Therefore additional sources for deriving value indications should be used like e.g. damage awards resulting from patent infringement trials (Reitzig et al., 2007, 137–138). A major advantage of these indemnities is that related background information can be obtained from public sources. This supports the calculation of a fair value (see also section 1.2, in Part I). Furthermore, in recent years we can observe an increase in the number of patent auctions. In 2006 and 2007 important auctions took place in San

Francisco, New York, and Munich. On average, one fourth of all the patents offered were sold at prices between 8,000 and 10,000 USD; very few patents were traded at higher values. From a seller's perspective, auctions have the advantage that they support the finding of potential buyers for patents and can speed up the transaction process. In addition, a seller can obtain a strong bargaining position in case of many interested buyers. However, if an auction fails because the bids do not meet the minimum reserve set by the seller, due to the public nature of these auctions, the seller's position in future negotiations may be weakened (Razgatis, 1999, 189ff.). Finally, at auction, of course, a seller cannot control who the final owner of the patent will be.

The careful use of information from single deals, litigation trials and patent auctions is of particular importance since, at the time of writing, the existence of an efficient and active market in which patents are frequently exchanged between unrelated parties cannot be confirmed. Hence, for the following discussion about the application of market-based valuation techniques, I assume that a minimum of information is available for performing a financial valuation. This includes a sufficient degree of comparability between valuation object and reference object, such that the value of the reference object (*reference value*) can be used to derive an estimate for the value of the valuation object (*target value*). The different market valuation techniques that can be used to derive target values like (1) multiples and analogies, (2) the market replacement cost method and (3) the residual value will be described and discussed in the following sections.

3.1.2.2 Multiple and analogy

Multiples are widely used for company valuation in merger and acquisition projects (Bausch, 2000). In a patent valuation, we can define a multiple as a measure for estimating the value of a target patent. It is computed by dividing the reference value by some relevant variable describing either legal, technical, or economic features of both reference object and valuation target. Besides traditional economic variables likes sales (Moser and Goddar, 2007, 596), income or cash-flows (Reilly and Schweihs, 1998, 150) also bibliographic value drivers can be used for deriving multiples (see section 3.2 of this Part). In contrast to this, an analogy-based valuation implies a holistic comparison of two patents (sales transaction method).

The observation of a transaction between unrelated parties is a necessary condition for applying one of these techniques (see Figure 17). If this criterion is not met, then questions about the objectivity of the reference value arise.[9] By definition, reference transactions occur prior to the valuation date. However, the application of market-based valuation assumes identical or at least comparable market situations. Hence, it is necessary to analyze not only the market conditions of the reference transaction but also the current market conditions in order to control for changes which might result in biased value estimates.

Of course, these two conditions consider neither the features of the subject of transfer nor any kind of compensatory agreement. Therefore, after controlling for relatedness and market conditions, specific transfer characteristics must be evaluated. For patents, it is advisable to analyze not only breadth and scope, and thus the legal quality of the patent right, but also to investigate whether the intended economic use or function of the patent to be valued differs from the past use of the reference patent (see also discussion on patent functions in subsection 2.2.2 of Part II and of value definitions in section 1.2 of Part I).

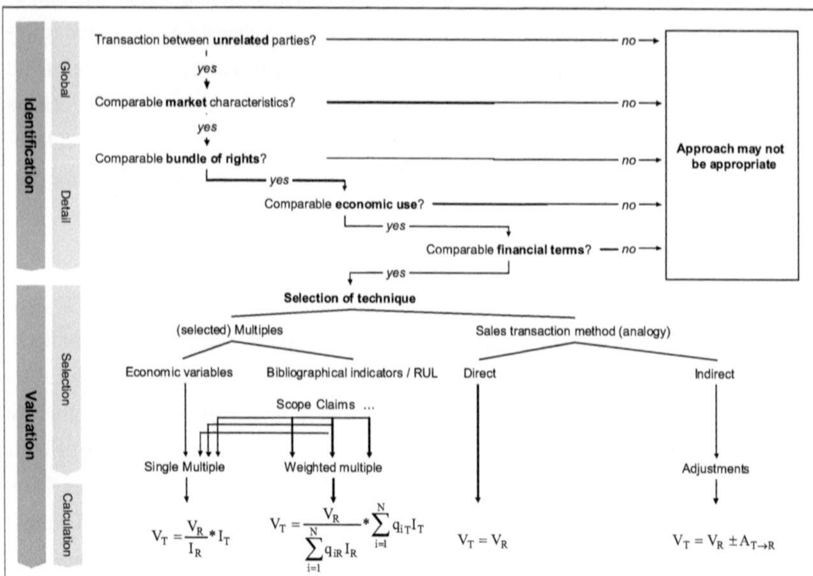

Figure 17: Market approach

[9] If buyer and seller are located in different countries and are legally independent but belong to the same economic unit then any transfer of assets – or more precisely, patents – might also aim at reducing overall tax payments.

A multiple can either consist of one indicator only (single multiple) or can be computed as the weighted sum of N multiples (with q_{iR} as weight for indicator i of the reference patent and $\sum_{i=1}^{N} q_{iR} = 1$). To calculate the value of the target (V_T), we divide the reference value (V_R) by the value of the reference indicator (I_R) or the weighted sum of the values of several reference indicators $\left(\sum_{i=1}^{N} q_{iR} I_R\right)$ and multiply the result by the corresponding value (or the weighted sum of values) of the target patent $\left(I_T; \sum_{i=1}^{N} q_{iT} I_T\right)$.

A second option for valuing patents includes the use of analogies. Analogies might be particularly useful in cases where the patent to be valued has already been transferred between unrelated parties in the past. The simplest approach would be to assume that the reference situation and the target transaction are two of the same kind, thus that V_T equals V_R. However, this might be the exception rather than the rule. Hence, adjustments must be made in order to adapt the target situation to the reference situation ($\pm A_{T \rightarrow R}$). Divergent economic or legal conditions as well as compensation mechanisms of both situations can be reasons for such adjustments (Reilly and Schweihs, 1998, 152). If the compensation model of, e.g., the reference situation, includes nonfinancial positions, a cash-equivalency analysis should be conducted to assess the monetary value of these positions. An additional requirement for modifications can result from the fact that the reference transaction includes additional transaction objects that are irrelevant for the current valuation project. Clearly, these adjustments can also be applied for a single multiple-valuation technique or a weighted-multiple valuation. For the weighted multiple, a second option for reflecting these differences consists of using differing weighting factors (e.g. $q_{IT} \neq q_{IR}$).

3.1.2.3 Market replacement cost method

Replacement cost can be measured (see subsection 3.1.1. of this Part) using the internal records of the patentee. In contrast to this, a market replacement cost approach is based on the estimated cost a knowledgeable, unrelated third party would charge for replacing the utility of the patent and the underlying invention. Of course, the adequacy of a market replacement cost approach depends heavily on availability and reliability of objective arm's-length estimates.

3.1.2.4 Residual value method

The residual value method represents another market valuation technique. In its simplest form, this approach calculates the value of a patent or portfolio of patents (V_{Pat}) by subtracting the value of all tangible (V_{Tan}) and other intangible assets (V_{Int}) except patents from the market value of a company (V_{Mar}), assuming that $V_{Mar} = V_{Tan} + V_{Int} + V_{Pat}$.

The simplicity of such an approach, however, requires simultaneous fulfillment of several rigorous conditions: First, if other intangible assets such as brands or services exist that are not shown in the balance sheet, then any reported goodwill must be split up and an appropriate portion of each group of these nonreported intangible assets must be reliably estimated. Second, if more than one patent or patent family exist then again a consistent and reliable approach must be found to allocate the overall value attributable to patents to the specific valuation object. Finally, the capital market must recognize the impact of selected patents on the patentee's business success. Only if all three of these conditions are cumulatively met, may we consider the application of a residual value method. As for the third condition, several historical examples (Smith and Parr, 2000, 177) and limited empirical evidence (Connolly and Hirschey, 1988; Austin, 1993) show how patent grants and the decision to maintain patent protection affect market values of individual firms. Please note, however, that this method can also lead to values for patents below zero (e.g., in case of $V_{Mar} < V_{Tan}$).

3.1.3 The principle of expectation: Income approach

3.1.3.1 General introduction

The basic idea of all valuation approaches estimating patent values using economic income is that the stream of expected future cash-flows resulting from the existence or use of a patent is uncertain (Damodaran, 2002, 112ff.). Thus, these approaches are based upon the principle of anticipation or expectation (Reilly and Schweihs, 1998, 113). Any valuation perspective that explicitly models an uncertain future must account for the (risk-free) time value of money and the riskiness of the forecasted cash-flows (CF_t) at time t. The way in which these two aspects are conceptually implemented allows for a distinction between two groups of models. The first group discounts expected economic income with an appropriate risk factor (k) to calculate the net present value of an asset or patent (risk-adjusted discount rate method). Thus, the discount factor comprises both aspects – time value (i) and risk (r). An alternative approach (the certainty-equivalent method) to model both factors is to transform the risky stream of income into certainty equivalents (*CE*) and to divide these equivalents by a discount rate that reflects the time value of money only. A certainty equivalent can either be obtained by a direct subjective assessment of an economic agent or via the capital market model and equals the smallest certain amount of money an investor would demand in exchange for this risky cash-flow (Robicheck and Myers, 1966, 728–729).

3.1.3.2 The differences between patent valuation and company valuation

At a first glance, patent valuation using a discounted-cash-flow approach (DCF) is similar to company valuation. In both cases, values are determined by either discounting uncertain cash-flows at an appropriate discount rate or by dividing certainty equivalents of cash-flows by a risk-free interest rate. However, a closer look reveals four principal differences.

First, patents have a limited maximum life of twenty years,[10] whereas business valuation is based on the principle of going concern. A common approach to estimate this infinite remaining life of a business is to split up the valuation period into three different subperiods with decreasing projection accuracy. A detailed analysis of discrete cash-flow projections (subperiod 1) is followed by several periods for which a stable growth rate of cash-flows is assumed (subperiod 2). The third component of a company's value consists of a terminal value. Usually, this value is either calculated as exit value or as perpetuity value and reflects the underlying assumption of infinite existence of the firm (Bausch and Pape, 2005, 477ff.). Patent-valuation techniques using expected economic income do not require a comparable calculation of terminal values due to the legally defined maximum lifespan of twenty years starting with application or priority date (see chapter 1 in Part II). Thus, in contrast to company values, patent values do not face the problem (and criticism) of depending to a large extent on terminal values and the way these values are derived (Damodaran, 2002, 319–320; Henselmann and Weiler, 2007, 354).

[10] In Europe and the United States, an extension of patent protection by a maximum of five years for pharmaceuticals and plant protection products is possible to account for regulatory delays (EEC 1768; EC 1016). Patent applicants may not sell products using the patented invention prior to an official authorization by regulatory authorities (see subsection 1.2.2 in Part II). For pharmaceuticals, the time spent on animal testing and on analyses of safety and efficiency in small and large samples of patients after filing a patent application takes on average 6.5 years (Girotra Karan et al., 2007, 1453). Without an appropriate extension of the patent term this process would reduce the time span of effective patent protection.

The definition of cash-flows to be discounted constitutes a second source of difference. Company-valuation technique uses free-cash-flows to entity or equity, which are either derived on the basis of future income statements or calculated by a detailed analysis of future cash in- and outflows (Hahn and Hungenberg, 2001, 176ff.; Damodaran, 2002, 382ff.). In the case of patent valuation, multiple measures of economic income can be appropriate. In addition to free-cash-flows, saved license fees or other cost savings may also mirror the value of a patent (see sub-subsection 3.1.3.3 in this Part). Adjustments must also be made for the fact that patents represent only one type of a firm's resources. Not all income is relevant for valuation – only that portion of income that is attributable to the patent or patent portfolio (Moser and Goddar, 2007, 598).

Accounting for risk draws a third distinction. A company's risk is usually measured by the weighted average cost of capital. This compound risk rate reflects both equity and debt perspective and assumes for the former that any unsystematic – thus firm-specific – risk is not relevant to the shareholder. In contrast, a patent's risk is driven by specific technological, legal, and economic aspects, and a total diversification of these interdependent types of risks may not be possible (see sub-subsection 3.1.3.5 of this Part).

Finally, patents are national rights. If the patentee is operating in more than one country – for example, (n) countries – but enjoys patent protection in only $(n-m;\, with\ m<n)$ countries, then any income-based measurement of patents must reflect this difference in the geographical range of patent protection and business operations. In this case, not all income realized worldwide by a commercial exploitation of the patented invention is an appropriate measure for estimating patent values. In fact, only an attributable share of these sales or earnings resulting from activities in countries in which a valid patent is in force (see also subsection 4.3 of this Part) should be considered for valuation.

Besides these general methodological differences between company and patent valuation, two specific valuation issues should further be considered. First, if it is a portfolio of patents that is to be valued, the valuation models should reflect any differences in ages and expected lifetime of the members of this portfolio. Assuming that expiring patents are not replaced by new rights during the valuation period, and therefore, that content, breadth, and consequently quality of patent protection change over time requires adequate adjustments of the underlying economic variables in latter periods (see subsection 4.3 in this Part). Second, tax amortization benefits can be an additional source of value. The underlying idea is that a potential acquirer would enjoy benefits due to a reduction of future tax payments resulting from depreciating the acquisition object under a specific accounting regime (Kasperzak and Nestler, 2007, 477). Based on this assumption, the value of a patent is not only driven by an economic exploitation of the underlying invention but also by the present value of the tax savings. Since the patent valuation attempts to calculate reasonable values resulting from this economic exploitation of the protected invention and given that depreciating these values in turn drives any related tax amortization benefits, problems of interdependence clearly arise. These problems can either be solved by iterative calculation methods or by applying a step-up factor.

The derivation of this step-up factor is based on the sum of future tax savings resulting from the amortization of the patent value. Let V denote the patent value, $\frac{V}{n}$ the annual, linear depreciation, T the time constant tax rate, k the capitalization rate, and n the maximum number of valuation periods. The present value of tax amortization benefits (TAB) and the related step-up factor can be described as follows (Herzig, 2004; Beyer, 2005, 152–153; Leibfried and Fassnacht, 2007, 54):

$$\text{Patent value} = \text{Net present value of income stream} + \text{TAB}$$

$$\text{V} = \text{NPV}_{\text{Income}} + TAB$$

$$\text{TAB} = \sum_{t=1}^{n} \frac{V}{n} * \text{T} * \text{k}^{-\text{t}}$$

$$V = \text{NPV}_{\text{Income}} + \sum_{t=1}^{n} \frac{V}{n} * \text{T} * \text{k}^{-\text{t}}$$

$$V - \frac{V * T}{n} * \sum_{t=1}^{n} \text{k}^{-\text{t}} = \text{NPV}_{\text{Income}}$$

$$V = \frac{\text{NPV}_{\text{Income}}}{1 - \frac{T}{n} * \sum_{t=1}^{n} \text{k}^{-\text{t}}}$$

$$\text{Step - up Factor} = \frac{1}{1 - \frac{T}{n} * \frac{k^n - 1}{k^n (k-1)}}$$

$$with \quad \sum_{\text{t}=1}^{\text{n}} \text{k}^{-\text{t}} = \frac{k^n - 1}{k^n (k-1)}$$

Patent values can increase by 20% to 30% on average if a TAB is applied. However, a naïve use of the TAB for any valuation method must be seriously questioned. Market approach and cost approach rest on the assumption that any tax advantage is already fully reflected in the input variables. Hence, a TAB is usually not applied for these valuation methods (Beyer and Mackenstedt, 2008, 347). Furthermore, the application of the TAB implicitly assumes a sustainable economic development. Needless to say, if no or only little profits will be realized in the future, there will also be no substantial relief from tax payments resulting from depreciating patent values (Kasperzak and Nestler, 2007, 477).

In the following chapters I will discuss these specifics of patent valuation in more detail by analyzing each value driver separately and answering the following research questions: (1) Which measures of economic income are appropriate and how can one isolate patent-relevant cash-flows? (2) How can one estimate the valuation period based on remaining useful life analysis? (3) What are sources of risk?

3.1.3.3 Measuring economic income

The decision about the measure for economic income directly affects patent values. Several variables might specify the utility of a patent. Which variable fits best for one specific valuation project depends on the purpose of the valuation and on the underlying valuation model.

In general, patentees can realize economic income either by using the patented technology for producing goods and offering services (exclusive exploitation) or by opting for a collaborative exploitation strategy (cooperative exploitation). In the first case and given a strong patent regime, a patentee can appropriate all income but also faces all potential risk factors. In the latter case, risks as well as income are shared by a patentee and an external partner.

Exclusive exploitation

With respect to innovation, a distinction is commonly made between product and process innovations (see also chapter 2 in Part II). A process innovation leads to a more efficient production process, resulting in lower production cost and, *ceteris paribus,* in higher profits. Thus, patent values are estimated by discounting the stream of future cost savings at an appropriate discount rate. In contrast to this, a product innovation allows the patentee either to meet a by-then unsatisfied demand for which no competitive products exist or to create a higher utility on the customer's side than any existing competitive product (Smith and Parr, 2000, 215ff.). In both cases, sales volume and/or the number of units sold raise. Given a constant profit margin, this increases a company's gross profit.

In the most basic case, an increase in annual sales results from the introduction of a new product which is protected by one single patent (see also discussion on patent value constructs in subsection 2.3 of Part II). This patent's value can be calculated in analogy to the process of company valuation. Given identical geographical scope of patent protection and business operations, the major difference between company and patent valuation results from the fact that a company represents a bundle of resources of which only one resource, the patented invention, is to be valued (see Figure 18).

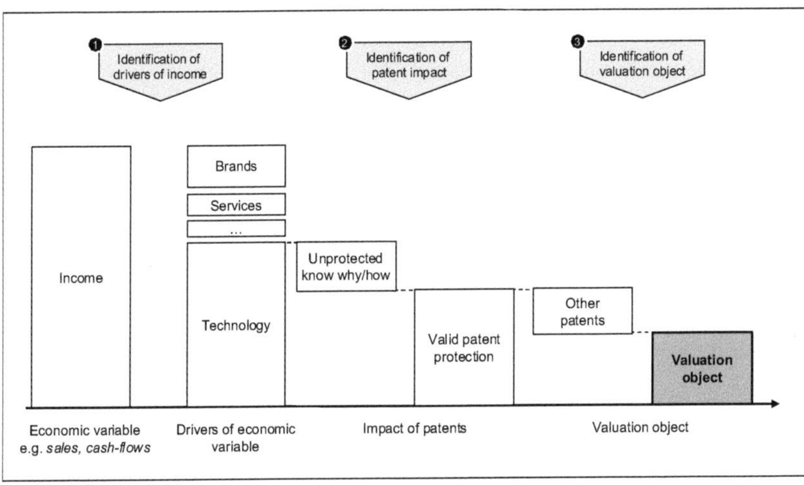

Figure 18: Income approach (exclusive exploitation)

Extracting patent-related cash-flows can be achieved by using two alternative valuation methods, the incremental cash-flow method and the multi-period excess earnings method.

The incremental cash-flow method or comparative income differential method (Reilly and Schweihs, 1998, 153) assumes that a patent-generated income stream can be separated unambiguously (this is also one of the basic assumptions of the theoretical analysis of value constructs in section 2.3 of part II). The net present value of this income stream after taxes equals the patent's value. Examples for this direct assessment of cash-flows include licensing agreements with predefined recurring amount payments over a given period (see sub-subsection 1.3.2.1 in Part IV) or patented inventions that lead to cost-savings in the production process. However, isolating cash-flows is in many cases difficult to achieve. Determining the incremental income of a patent portfolio in fact requires a comparison of all future cash-flows to a company owing a patent with all future cash-flows of a comparable (hypothetical) company or business unit that either does not have this patented invention available or refuses to use it. Needless to say, the absence of any comparable company or business unit in many cases limits the use of this approach.

The multi-period excess earnings method takes into account the common observation that cash-flows result from a joint use of multiple resources and assumes that patents play a major role in generating these cash-flows. In fact, this method requires that the valuation object (e.g. patents) represents the most important resource of the company. If several intangible resources are of equal importance for a firm's success, this method should not be applied. The central idea of the multi-period excess earnings method is to identify the contribution of each asset or resource to the overall income- or cash-flow stream of a company or business unit and to charge an appropriate economic rent for this contribution. The resulting contributory asset charges are a means of allocating cash-flows in a way that an adequate rate of return is provided for the supporting asset. Excess earnings are those that remain after consideration of all contributory assets.

Consequently, this approach, in a first step, requires the identification of all assets that drive cash-flows. The second step focuses on estimating values for all assets. Market values for each asset are most preferable. However, if these are not available, book values may be used as well. The third step includes estimating a fair rate of return on each asset. Theses asset specific rate of returns are than multiplied by the assets' market or book values to come to asset specific capital charges. The sum of these asset-specific capital charges is subtracted from the economic income at the company or business unit level to come to the (net) cash-flow attributable to patents (Reilly and Schweihs, 1998; Moser and Goddar, 2007, 604). Alternatively, one could also assume that all assets expect the valuation object are leased from third parties.

From a theoretical point of view, this approach is similar to the residual value method. In sub-section 3.1.2.4 of this Part, the residual value method is described based on market values. However, the entity value of a company or business unit can also be measured based on discounted future cash-flows. In this case, the value for a specific patent portfolio equals the difference between the sum of the discounted future cash-flows of a company (company's entity value) and the sum of the values of all other resources. In contrast to this, under the excess-earnings approach, the overall cash-flow is first adjusted for contributory asset charges and the resulting excess earnings are then discounted to come to a value indication for a patent portfolio (Moser and Goddar, 2007, 604).

	INCREMENTAL CASH-FLOW METHOD		**MULTI-PERIOD EXCESS EARNINGS METHIOD**
	Δ Sales$_t$		Sales$_t$
-	Δ Cost of goods sold (COGS)$_t$	-	COGS$_t$
=	**Δ Gross profit$_t$**	=	**Gross profit$_t$**
-	Δ Selling, general and administrative expenses (SGA)$_t$	-	Selling, general and administrative expenses (SGA)$_t$
±	Δ Other income/expense$_t$	±	Other income/expense$_t$
=	**Δ Earnings before interest and taxes (EBIT)$_t$**	=	**EBIT$_t$**
-	Δ Taxes on EBIT$_t$	-	Taxes on EBIT$_t$
=	**Δ Earnings before interest after taxes (EBIAT)$_t$**	=	**EBIAT$_t$**
±	Δ Depreciation$_t$/Appreciation$_t$	±	Depreciation$_t$/Appreciation$_t$
±	Δ Change in accruals$_t$	±	Change in accruals$_t$
±	Δ Investments$_t$/Disinvestments$_t$	±	Investments$_t$/Disinvestments$_t$
±	Δ Change in working capital$_t$	±	Change in working capital$_t$
=	**Δ Free-cash-flow (FCF)$_t$**	=	**Free-cash-flow (FCF)$_t$**
		-	Capital charge for other intangible assets
		-	Capital charge for fixed assets
		-	Capital charge for working capital
		=	**FCF$_t$ after contributory asset charges**

Figure 19: Derivation of free-cash-flows using accounting data

After selecting one of these general approaches to estimate an appropriate share of cash-flows, the question of the best measure for these cash-flows arises. Discounted cash-flow analysis for company valuation is usually based on free-cash-flows. As a commonly accepted method, the derivation of these free-cash-flows can either be based on current and future income statements of a company (see Figure 19) or calculated by directly estimating cash in- and outflows. Within the framework of the resource-based view, a future-orientated valuation of a single resource should therefore use a comparable measurement concept.

Cooperative exploitation

If the patentee decides to share both risk and value potential of a technology or a portfolio of patents then entering licensing agreements might be a viable strategy. For any valuation this implies using a different valuation model since economic income is now measured in royalty payments. With a licensing agreement, both parties of the contract agree upon their specific rights and duties in order to transfer property rights with respect to a predefined kind of knowledge from the knowledge owner (licensor) to the recipient of the knowledge (licensee) for a specific period of time in exchange for some form of compensation (Sullivan, 1996; Manfroy, 2002).

Two alternative valuation models can be applied here. First, if the patentee decides to license out a patent portfolio then the value of this portfolio equals the net present value of future licensee fees after taxes that the patentee expects to obtain based on this contract. In contrast to the royalty-income approach, the relief-from-royalty method calculates the value of a patent based on royalty savings. Central to this idea is that patentees would have to pay license fees to a third party if they were not owners of the patent portfolios. Thus, patentees are relieved from paying licensing fees and the sum of these royalty savings equals the sum they would be willing to pay to an unrelated third party.

Both methods assume a running royalty rate and calculate royalty income and savings based on projected sales. However, they differ with regard to the projected sales volume. A royalty-income approach focuses on sales volumes of current or potential licensees. For a relief-from-royalty approach, only the projected sales of the patentee are relevant. Of course, these two perspectives can contain differing sources of risk. Under the royalty-income approach, risk considerations should reflect e.g. the probability that licensees are unwilling or unable to pay the contractually agreed royalty payments. Most important, in both cases, however, is the selection of an appropriate royalty rate. Three alternative ways to arrive at an arm's-length royalty rate can be used. First, royalty rates can be collected from existing licensing agreements used to transfer comparable rights and patents. Of course, this requires an in-depth analysis of licensing contracts (for a detailed discussion see chapter 1 in Part IV). Second, an extensive body of literature with comprehensive lists of industry-wide standard royalty rates can be researched (Smith and Parr, 1998; Groß and Rohrer, 2003; Battersby and Grimes, 2006). Finally, a reasonable royalty rate can be calculated based on heuristic rules (Razgatis, 1999, 102ff). Two widespread heuristic rules are: (1) the 25-percent rule and (2) the

33⅓-percent rule. Both share the idea that the total value in each period resulting from a cooperative exploitation strategy and measured as profit before taxes should be equitably divided between licensor and licensee (profit split analysis). The existing body of literature claims that 25 to 33⅓ percent of the licensee's pre-tax profit margin lead to reasonable royalty rates (Knoppe, 1972, 102; Reilly and Schweihs, 1998; Moser and Goddar, 2007). Please note that in industries with cumulative technologies, a symmetric apportionment (50:50) is more the exception than the rule. A split of 25 to 33⅓ percent is used to reflect higher risks and possible required investments in complementary assets on the licensee's side. A careful assessment is, of course, required to avoid any double counting of risks when selecting royalty rates and discount rates.

These heuristic rules provide a useful way to check the adequacy of existing industry standards, but needless to say, this analytical derivation of royalty rates requires a positive profit margin. For a specific patent or patent portfolio, the decision about the precise value to be used for splitting profits requires a thorough analysis of (1) the functional relationship of how the patent is used and (2) an assessment of its contributory importance to income generation in comparison to all other resources (Reilly and Schweihs, 1998, 193–194). Clearly, limited geographical or technological coverage of the respective patents can motivate adjustments of a selected royalty rate. In the end, the patent value equals the sum of discounted royalty payments (measured as expected royalty income or as hypothetical saved royalty payments) after taxes.

3.1.3.4 Determining the remaining useful life

As already mentioned, the maximum duration of patent protection is limited to a period of twenty years (see subsection 1.1.1, Part II). However, this does not necessarily imply that all patents will be kept in force for this period. Thus, one key issue for income-based valuation is to forecast the time span over which the patentee expects to generate economic income from exclusive or cooperative use of a patent or a portfolio of patents. Of course, remaining-useful-life (RUL) calculations should also be conducted during the application of other valuation approaches. In the case of a cost-based valuation (see subsection 3.1.1 of this Part), RUL analysis is required to estimate obsolescence. When a market approach is used (see subsection 3.1.2 of this Part), an RUL calculation serves as a factor to determine the degree of comparability between transaction objects and to estimate any resulting and required adjustments needed for increasing this comparability.

The service life of an expired patent describes the period in the past extending from the application or priority date to the date on which patent protection ceased due to legal reasons or managerial decisions. The estimate for the service life of a patent or a patent application still in force on the valuation date is called *probable life*. The age of a patent equals the time elapsed between its application date and the valuation date. The RUL of a patent is the time from the valuation date to the future date on which patent protection ends. Consequently, the probable life of a valid patent or patent application equals the sum of its age and its expected RUL. In addition, the average probable (service) life equals the estimated (historical) average life of a brand-new patent application, whereas the average RUL corresponds to the expected, average life of a seasoned patent.

Either qualitative or quantitative analyses can support the decision about an appropriate estimate for this remaining useful life. Qualitative measures mostly focus on an analysis of life cycles. Originating from the biological sciences, life-cycle techniques have widely been applied to various units of analysis such as products and technologies (Rink and Swan, 1979, 220ff.; Basberg, 1987; Silverberg et al., 1988, 1036ff.; Achilladelis, 1993, 295ff.; Achilladelis et al., 1999, 16ff.; Andersen, 1999; Haupt et al., 2007, 388).

A life-cycle analysis attempts to document the income pattern of the respective unit of analysis over its life. In many cases, life-cycle analysis is depicted by a bell shaped revenue line across the following five stages: introduction, growth, maturity, decline, and demise. Given the consecutive nature of these stages, a life-cycle model provides a functional relationship between the utility of an asset and the time over which this asset can be exploited. Of course, time is not the only variable affecting a life cycle's contour and the lengths of its stages (Rink and Swan, 1979, 220ff.). For patents, other factors, such as technological change, market acceptance of patented inventions, and nullity proceedings by competitors, play an important role and can lead to a revenue line with a shape different from the commonly displayed bell curve.

The application of life-cycle analysis to forecasting the RUL of a patent requires one to first determine the stage at which the patented technology belongs on the valuation date. Based on an analysis of historical patterns, interviews with experts (Martino, 1980), and the use of technology substitution models (Meade and Islam, 1998) such as the Fisher-Pry (Fisher and Pry, 1971, 76ff.) or Gompertz models (Chow, 1967) estimates for growth rates and the time spans for the subsequent periods can then be derived.

Quantitative models take advantage of the extensive, publicly available data on historical patent terms. Since patent law requires periodical payments to maintain a patent in force (see subsection 1.1.1 of Part II), historical data on renewal decisions and related patent expirations is used for determining the RUL. The experience band equals the number of periods prior to the valuation date from which historical information is collected to perform a quantitative RUL analysis. It is advisable to select an experience band that comprises patents for which applications were filed twenty years prior to the valuation date. This ensures that, on the valuation date, all patents of the experience band have expired thus avoiding stub survivor curves (Reilly and Schweihs, 1998, 222). Depending on content and reliability of the available data, different methods for estimating the RUL can be taken into account.

The turnover method (Smith and Parr, 2000, 291) and the retirement ratio (Reilly and Schweihs, 1998, 233ff.) both use information on the number of patents at the beginning of each year of the experience band $\left(P_t^b\right)$ and the number of patents that expired $\left(P_t^e\right)$ during this year. For a given experience band of n years, the retirement rate (RR) is calculated as:

$$RR = \sum_{t=1}^{n} \varpi_t \frac{P_t^e}{P_t^b}$$

with ϖ_i as weighting factor for each year and $\sum_{t=1}^{n} \varpi_t = 1$, thus allowing a reduction of the impact of single years in the experience band that are interpreted as outliers. Assuming a constant retirement rate, the remaining useful life is defined as the reciprocal of RR:

$$RUL = \frac{1}{RR} = \frac{1}{\sum_{t=1}^{n} \varpi_t \frac{P_t^e}{P_t^b}}$$

The availability of additional data, such as patent application dates and patent ages, allows one to perform a more comprehensive analysis by constructing reverse S-shaped survivor curves (Smith and Parr, 2000, 289–290). In analogy to population statistics and related actuarial mathematics, these survivor curves graphically describe duration and life expectancy of a (seasoned) patent. Table 10 summarizes key features of existing methods for calculating survivor curves:

Method	Individual unit method	Group method			Annual rate method
		Original group method	Composite original group method	Multiple original group method	
Key features	▪ Number of expired patents in each year ▪ Age of each expired patent	▪ Number of patents applied for in one year (one vintage) ▪ Analysis of the life of each member of the vintage group	▪ Number of patents applied for in several years ▪ Analysis of the life for each member of the vintage groups	▪ Number of patents of multiple vintages ▪ Number of patents surviving one subsequent point	▪ Number of expired patents in each year of the experience band ▪ Age of each expired patent ▪ Number of patents still valid in each year of the experience band ▪ Age of each valid patent

Table 10: Methods for deriving survivor curves

Figure 20 shows a typical S-shaped survivor curve and derived curves such as frequency and probable life curve. The former expresses the relationship between age and percent surviving for a population of patents. Let *m* denote the maximum patent term and *t* serve as time index. If all patents from the experience band have expired on the valuation date, the average life (AL) (arrow 1) is calculated as:

$$AL = \frac{\sum_{t=1}^{m} t * P_t^e}{\sum_{t=1}^{m} P_t^e}$$

The average life corresponds to the area under the survivor curve divided by the percent surviving at age zero (100%). Hence, this average life conclusion of an RUL analysis represents the expected average life for a new unit or patent. The probable life of a patent at age zero equals its average life. In the case of a seasoned patent, the probable life (arrow 2) equals the sum of age (arrow 3) and RUL (arrow 4). RUL is obtained by dividing the crosshatched area (from age 10 to the maximum age 20) under the survivor curve in Figure 20 by the percent surviving at age 10 (26%).

The percentage surviving at age *j* (Ps_j) is given by:

$$Ps_j = \left(1 - \frac{\sum_{t=1}^{j} P_t^e}{\sum_{t=1}^{m} P_t^e} \right) * 100$$

The probable life curve can be calculated for any age x. The horizontal difference between probable life curve and survivor curve corresponds to the average RUL of a seasoned patent.

Period	Age interval	Number of patents at the beginning of this period	Number of patents expired during this period	Survivor ratio (%)	Survivor curve (%)
0		$p_0=p_1$	0	100	100
1	[0-1]	p_1	e_1	$1-e_1/p_1$	$1-e_1/p_1$
2	[1-2]	p_2	e_2	$1-e_2/p_2$	$1-e_1/p_1*1-e_2/p_2$
...	...		...		
20	[19-20]	p_{20}	e_{20}	$1-e_{20}/p_{20}$	$\prod(1-e_i/p_i)$

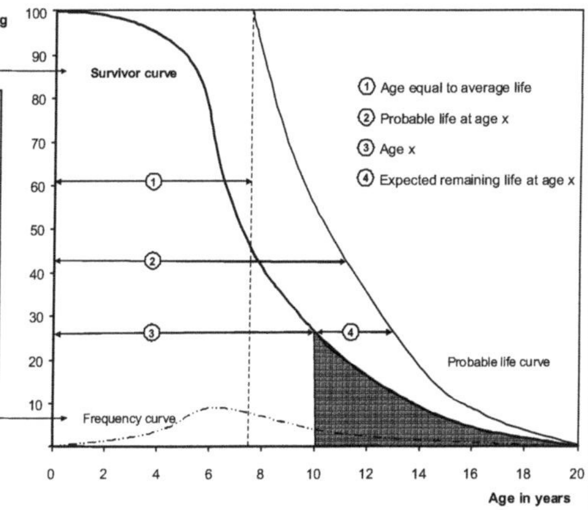

Figure 20: Survivor curve

An alternative way to estimate the RUL is to compare the shape of the survivor curve with the structure of a Weibull function (Weibull, 1951) or one of the 22 "Iowa-type curves". These curves were developed at the engineering institute at Iowa State University (Winfrey, 1953). Originally derived from a comprehensive analysis of various tangible property assets exposed to a variety of different reasons for retirement, these curves have been transformed to allow an application for technology-related intangible assets (Reilly and Schweihs, 1998, 228–229). They comprise seven symmetrical (S0–S6), five right-modal (R1–R5), six left-modal (L0–L5) and four origin-modal (O1–O4) curves. By modification of the underlying parameters of each of the 22 curves, a family of various Iowa curves can be derived. The primary task of this process is to find an Iowa curve that fits best to the survivor curve resulting from an analysis of historical patent applications and patent expiry data. Least-square-fitting analysis and visual inspection represent two common approaches for selecting the best-fitting Iowa curve. After selecting one Iowa curve, RUL and related information can be taken from published probable life tables. Needless to say, this process includes a high degree of subjective judgment and can lead to biased results if the underlying assumptions of the valuation model and the selected Iowa curve differ (Deming and Singpurwalla, 1989).

3.1.3.5 Accounting for time and risk

In a world of non-deterministic outcomes, any future-based valuation method must deal with the uncertainty of future economic rents. As already described in sub-subsection 3.1.3.1 of this Part, two basic conceptual approaches can be implemented to account for risk and time: certainty equivalents and risk-adjusted rate of return. The former separates risk and time aspects, whereas the latter accounts for both factors at once. Common practice in valuation theory and capital budgeting is to assume that accounting for time can be achieved by applying a risk-free interest rate. Thus, under the certainty-equivalent approach, uncertain future cash-flows are transformed into certainty equivalents and than discounted by the risk-free interest rate. In contrast, the risk-adjusted rate of return approach uses a discount rate as the sum of a risk-free interest and a risk premium. Alternative models, such as the capital-asset pricing model (Sharpe, 1964; Litner, 1965; Fama and French, 1995), the three-factor model (Fama and French, 1993; Fama and French, 1997), and estimates of implied cost of equity (Claus and Thomas, 2001; Gebhardt et al., 2001; Easton et al., 2002) can be used to derive this risk premium.

In a multi-period setting both basic approaches seem to lead to different results. Schwetzler (2000) shows that this phenomenon is rooted in the underlying assumptions about the stochastic process governing the cash-flow distributions. If the expected cash-flows of one period are stochastically independent of the cash-flows of the previous period, any periodic-specific risk in one period, say period t, is only relevant for this period. Hence, a risk-adjusted rate of return must only be applied for discounting the risky cash-flow from period t to $t-1$. The resulting, risk-free value for the cash-flows of period t is then to be discounted to the valuation date by the corresponding risk-free interest rate to account for the time-value of money.

In contrast, if risk-factors of a previous period, say $t-2$, have a lasting effect on multiple periods ($t-1$, t, $t+1$ ...), the cash-flows are stochastically dependent. This in turn requires the application of the period-specific risk of $t-2$ premium in the following periods. The certainty-equivalent approach as described in sub-subsection 3.1.3.5 of this Part assumes stochastically independent cash-flows, the risk-adjusted rate of return is traditionally based on the idea of stochastically dependent cash-flows. In a multi-period setting, these different assumptions lead to different net present values. Schwetzler (2000) introduces a set of modifications of the traditional formulas that lead to identical results (Schwetzler, 2000, 472ff.).

Besides these questions of modeling uncertainty and calculating cost of capital as a function of underlying risk, income-based valuation techniques must consider three peculiarities of patents. First, patent-related economic income does not necessarily face the same sources of risk as a company; if economic income results from a collaborative exploitation of a patented invention, moral hazard problems in combination with incomplete contracts can be important risk drivers (see also chapter 1 in Part IV.).

Second, valuation horizons may differ. It is common practice to assume that the return of a long-term government bond is an appropriate measure for a risk-free interest rate (Richter, 2001, 176; 2005, No. 127). Of course, if the RUL of an asset such as a patent differs from the expected lifetime of a company (which is actually assumed to be infinite given the going-concern principle), the risk-free interest rate used for estimating equity cost of capital should be adjusted to account for these divergent time horizons (Damodaran, 2002, 155). Empirical results show significant differences in the rates of return of long-term and short-term risk-free government bonds (Stehle and Hausladen, 2004, 934).

These two reflections on the differences between a patent's risk and the risk of a company call into question the naïve use of company-wide weighted average cost of capital (wacc) as calculated by the following formula:

$wacc_j = \left[r_f + \beta_j(r_M - r_f)\right]\frac{E_j}{D_j + E_j} + \left[i(1-t)\right]\frac{D_j}{D_j + E_j}$, with r_f as the risk-free interest rate, β_j as the measure of company's j specific risk, r_M as return on the market portfolio, E_j and D_j as current or targeted amount of equity and debt invested in company j, i as interest rate for debt, and t as tax rate.

Clearly, adjustments of a company-wide wacc seem to be one solution to accounting for the different sources of risk. However, besides the question of risk drivers and appropriate measurement, a third peculiarity is rooted in the fact that a patent's risk can change over its lifetime – the likelihood of proceedings for declaration of nullity of a patent decreases with increasing patent age. Furthermore, successfully defending a patent in a patent-litigation trial again reduces its probability of being cancelled in the future. Thus, a patent's legal validity tends to rise with increasing age. However, the use of a single discount rate is not an appropriate measure for this decreasing risk. A constant discount rate would imply that the risk of future cash-flows increases geometrically over the valuation period (Robicheck and Myers, 1966, 728–729, 1968, 479;

Hodder and Riggs, 1982, 131ff.). Dividing the overall valuation period into a sequence of subperiods and applying different discount rates for each of these periods can avoid this problem of a constant discount rate. Of course, number and length of these periods depend on the expected development of the main risk driver identified on the valuation date.

3.1.3.6 Accounting for flexibility and changing risk

Option-valuation techniques and decision-tree analysis represent additional approaches that can be used to model the inherent uncertainty of patent-related future economic rents. A decision tree is a graphical description of a system of alternative decisions at different points in time (Bielza and Shenoy, 1999, 1553). Each decision is represented by a square or decision node, and the way in which these nodes are arranged reflects their chronological order. Uncontrollable probabilistic events are represented by circles or chance nodes. From each decision node, a discrete number of chance nodes can originate for which the related probabilities sum up to one. A decision-tree analysis makes possible the modeling of complex interactions between a limited number of both mutually excluding and sequentially occurring managerial decisions. Each chain of these sequences of decisions and connected uncontrollable events can be graphically described as a branch of the decision tree. Both the number of decisions and the number of uncontrollable events drive the complexity of this analysis.

Starting with the final decisions and going back in time to the valuation date, separate income-based valuations for each course of action (represented by one branch) are to be conducted. For each node separate values can be calculated. For chance nodes, the value is given by the sum of future economic income weighted by the related probabilities attached to all branches emanating from this chance node. If the node represents a decision, values are calculated for each subsequent branch and the highest or lowest value is selected, depending on the overall valuation target (Hespos and Strassmann, 1965, 248–249).

Evaluating alternative decision paths constitutes the core of this analysis and allows an explicit assessment of the underlying flexibility. However, at the same time this also calls into question the appropriateness of using a global discount factor since each decision might differ depending on the type and impact of different risk factors (Loch and Bode-Greuel, 2001, 232ff.; Brandão et al., 2005, 72ff.).

The application of various discount rates reflecting the varying risks created by alternative decisions leads to results consistent with those of option-valuation techniques (Smith and Nau, 1995, 798ff.).

Option-valuation techniques represent a second alternative to account for changing risk and to model flexibility. In general, an option can be defined as a right to purchase (call-option) or sell (put-option) an underlying asset whose price is subject to a form of random variation in the future at a predefined exercise price. American options can be exercised before expiry, European options only at the agreed maturity date (Black and Scholes, 1973, 637). The basic idea of all options is to evaluate managerial flexibility and freedom of action. The value potential of this flexibility results from the irreversibility of many investments in tangible or intangible goods, the high uncertainty in case of multi-period decisions, and the fact that the content and reliability of the underlying set of information on which a decision is based improve over time (Pindyck, 1991, 1116ff.).

Originally developed for valuing financial options (Black and Scholes, 1973; Merton, 1973; Smith, 1976; Cox et al., 1979), the central idea to value flexibility was first applied by Myers (1977) to growth opportunities of a firm he refers to as real options (Myers, 1977, 163ff.). Real options important for patent valuation are presented in Table 11.

Category	**Description**	**Examples in the case of patents**
Option to defer	Decision-maker can wait for a specific period of time to see whether an investment is profitable.	▪ Time between application date and granting date ▪ Priority date claim ▪ PCT application (see subsection 1.4.2 in Part II)
Time to build option	An investment comprises a series of sequential outlays. Each stage may be interpreted as an option on the value of subsequent decisions, thus allowing the valuation as compound option.	▪ Prolongation decisions ▪ Decisions on family size
Option to abandon	Decision-maker can abandon current operations permanently and probably realize the resale value of the underlying assets.	▪ Carve out decision (see subsection 2.1.3 in Part II)
Growth options	An early investment is a prerequisite for a chain of interrelated projects that open up future growth opportunities.	▪ Patent thickets, blocking competitors (see subsection 2.2.2 in Part II)

Table 11: Real options and patent rights

According to Black and Scholes' (1973) well-known formula, the value $w(x,t)$ of a call option at time t is driven by the current share price x, the exercise price c of this call option, the time to expiry (t^*-t), the standard deviation of the underlying asset returns v^2, the risk-free interest rate r, and the distribution function for the asset price N:

$$w(x,t) = xN(d_1) - ce^{r(t-t^*)}N(d_2)$$

with $d_1 = \frac{\ln x/c + \left(r + \frac{1}{2}v^2\right)(t^*-t)}{v\sqrt{t^*-t}}$ and $d_2 = \frac{\ln x/c + \left(r - \frac{1}{2}v^2\right)(t^*-t)}{v\sqrt{t^*-t}}$.

A comparable relationship between these fundamental drivers can be defined in the case of patent valuation as summarized in the following table:

Variable	Financial option	Patent as option
x	Share price	Present value of expected economic income
c	Exercise price	Cost for patent protection
(t^*-t)	Time to expiry	Remaining useful life
v^2	Standard deviation of underlying share returns	Standard deviation of present patent values
r	Risk-free interest rate	Risk-free interest rate

Table 12: Financial options, patent options, and variables

The patent application process as described in Figure 12 on page 67 and Figure 13 on page 71 and its related decisions comprise a series of options. Along with the initial decision to file a patent application, decisions about the request for examination, the geographical range of patent protection, and, of course, the payment of renewal fees represent some of the most important options. Table 13 gives an exemplary overview of selected decisions and options during the patent-application-and-granting process:

Stage of a patent's life	Decision	Cost of decision	Benefits of decision
Filing of a patent	Examination of patentability of an innovation	Cost of legal advice	Call options on application, foreign applications and on continuation
	Filing a patent application	Cost of application	Call options on foreign applications and on continuation
Request for examination	Examination of state of the art	Cost of examination procedure	Call options on foreign applications and on continuation
Patent grant and maintaining patent protection	Payment of annual renewal fees	Cost of maintaining patent protection (renewal fees, defending patents during a trial, etc.)	Call options on foreign applications and on a monopolistic technology position

Table 13: Patents as call options

Despite the intuitive similarity between financial options and real options, three main differences do exist (Trigeorgis, 1998, 128–129). First, financial options are frequently traded in efficient markets whereas real investments are very often not reversible and are not traded in an open market. Second, many real options are shared options, which means that the option holder cannot fully exclude competitors from profiting from this investment. Of course, given an effective patent protection this should be of minor concern. Finally, as already illustrated (Table 13), real options and especially patent-related decisions consist not only of one option but comprise a series of compound options. Given the numerous interdependencies between the members of such a chain of options, single option values are not necessarily additive and require more complex analysis (Trigeorgis, 1993, 7ff.). In addition, the assumption of a constant variance for underlying returns as defined by Black and Scholes (1973, 652) does not hold in case of a chain of options. In particular, the idea of technology cycles and related economic income (see sub-subsection 3.1.3.4) contradicts this assumption of a constant variance of future returns.

3.2 Indirect patent valuation: The analysis of bibliographic value indicators

3.2.1 Valuation approach

The extensive amount of publicly accessible information presented in patent documents has motivated a large body of research (Griliches, 1990). One stream focuses on analyzing the relationship between monetary patent values and bibliographic value indicators (see Figure 21).[11] The basic idea is to develop and test causal models describing how bibliographic information can be used to explain (1) the probability that a patent will be attacked by competitors and (2) the economic value of patents (Pavitt, 1984, 79–80). Since the question of the legal validity of a patent is essential for patent valuation, I also include empirical studies analyzing this topic in the following discussion.

The absence of an open and competitive market from which value indications can be derived requires first the development of a proxy for patent values. Since patent renewal fee schedules are published by patent authorities and renewal decisions can be tracked over time, economic theorists analyze renewal decisions (Pakes et al., 1989). They derive values for patents by applying the basic rationale of option analysis and by assuming deterministically (Pakes and Schankerman, 1984; Schankerman and

[11] In general, bibliographic indicators are parts of text documents that can be coded for statistical analysis. Bibliometrics is the science of studying and measuring texts and information.

Pakes, 1986; Sullivan, 1994; Schankerman, 1998) or stochastically (Pakes, 1986; Lanjouw, 1998) distributed future returns. Alternative approaches for determining patent values include surveys of patent holders (Sanders et al., 1958; Harhoff et al., 1999; Scherer and Harhoff, 2000; Harhoff et al., 2003a; Ceccagnoli et al., 2006; Giuri et al., 2007) and estimates of the impact of a firm's patent stock on its share price and market value (Pakes, 1985; Austin, 1993; Lerner, 1994; Bloom and Van Reenen, 2002; Hall et al., 2005).

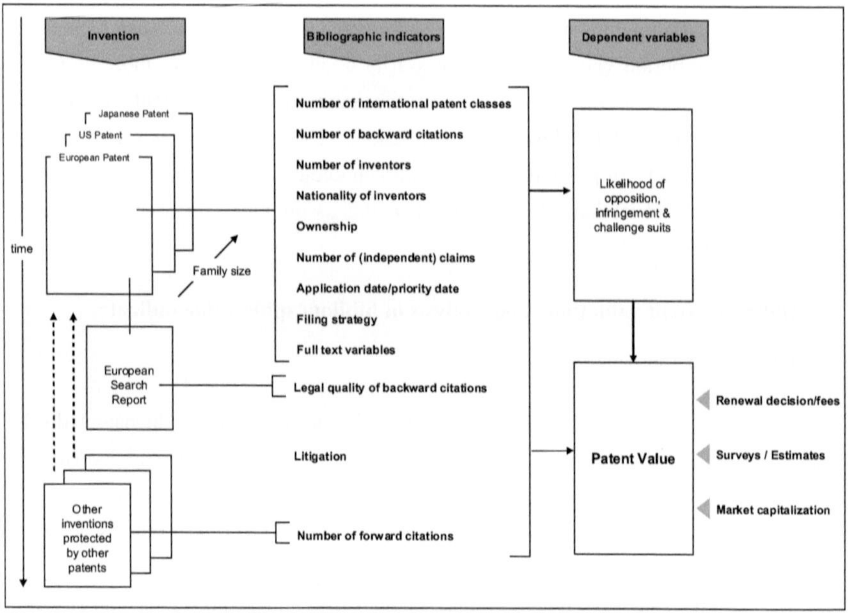

Figure 21: Bibliographic patent data

A review of the existing body of literature shows that several patent value indicators have been identified and tested so far. Table 14 summarizes the definitions, economic rationale, and empirical results for these variables. These bibliographic indicators can be clustered into three main groups (Reitzig, 2004a). First-level indicators focus on general and traditional economic considerations and comprise backward citations (Narin et al., 1987), forward citations (Trajtenberg, 1990), family size (Putnam, 1996), and market value of the corporation (Griliches, 1981; Cockburn and Griliches, 1988; Connolly and Hirschey, 1988; Hall et al., 2005). Second-level indicators consist of information connected to the patent-application-and-granting procedure, such as the number of International Patent Classifications (IPC) classes, the filing strategy, and the legal quality of backward citations (Lerner, 1994; Harhoff et al., 2003a; Harhoff and Reitzig, 2004).

Additionally, some researchers have also used the information presented in the full text of the patent document, such as information on claims (Tong and Frame, 1994; Lanjouw and Schankerman, 2001; Harhoff and Reitzig, 2004; Reitzig, 2004a). Reitzig (2004a) argues that these third-level indicators are attractive, as they are available after the patent has been published and as they are based on a relatively strong theoretical foundation. But at the same time, they are the result of the strategic considerations of the patentee or the respective patent attorney, who might try to optimize the effectiveness of the patent protection by creating strong (broad) patent claims and simultaneously reducing the probability of (1) losing patent protection in a legal argument and (2) disclosing more information than actually required to fulfill the needs of the patent system and the respective patent examiner. Assuming this kind of strategic behavior reduces the objectivity of the information collected from the full text of the patent document.

Indicator	Definition	Economic rationale	Empirical results
Backward citations (to other patents and to scientific literature)	Number of other patent documents or scientific publications that are cited by a patent. The novelty of an invention is tested against these prior publications.	The number of backward citations serves as a proxy for the attractiveness of an invention (Carpenter et al., 1980; Narin et al., 1987). Citations of scientific documents can be interpreted as an indicator for the relatedness of an invention to new scientific knowledge and discoveries. Citations referring to other patents give an indication about the attractiveness of a technological field and the economic potential of the invention.	▪ Negative (but insignificant) effect on the likelihood of infringement and challenge suits (Lanjouw and Schankerman, 2001, 143). ▪ Positive, significant impact on patent values (Ceccagnoli et al., 2006, 44; Harhoff and Hoisl, 2007, 1358). ▪ Positive, significant impact on the likelihood of opposition (only for non U.S. owners) (Harhoff and Reitzig, 2004, 472).
Forward citations	Number of times a patent is cited by subsequent patent documents.	The number of forward citations serves as a proxy for the impact of an invention on a specific technological field (Trajtenberg, 1990; Albert et al., 1991).	▪ Positive, significant effect on the likelihood of infringement and challenge suits (Lanjouw and Schankerman, 2001, 143). ▪ Positive, significant impact on the likelihood of opposition (European patents) (Harhoff and Reitzig, 2004, 472). ▪ Positive, significant impact on patent values (Harhoff et al., 2003a, 1358; Ceccagnoli et al., 2006, 44). ▪ Frequently cited patents are of significantly greater technological importance than patents that are not cited (Albert et al., 1991, 258). ▪ Positive significant correlation between mean forward citations and financial performance (Narin et al., 1987, 151–152). ▪ Positive, significant effect on patent values (Lanjouw and Schankerman, 2001, 143; Harhoff and Hoisl, 2007, 1159). ▪ Broader patents receive more citations. One standard deviation increase in patent scope increases the expected number of citations by 11% (Lerner, 1994, 322). ▪ The inverse relationship seems to hold as well: Patents with higher (subjective) values are more often cited by subsequent patents (Harhoff et al., 1999, 513ff.).
Number of inventors/ international cooperation	The quality of an invention, thus the value of a patent, is driven by number and diversity of inventors.	If highly specialized knowledge workers create an invention through a joint effort, this invention may be of higher quality than an invention made by only one single inventor (see also sub-subsection 2.2.6.1 in Part I).	▪ Significant impact of different nationalities on the likelihood of opposition (Harhoff and Reitzig, 2004, 472). ▪ A significant positive impact on the probability of a patent grant (2000) (2007) and on a patent's value (Harhoff and Hoisl, 2007, 1159) can be shown if the invention was made by more than one inventor.
Key inventors	The quality of an invention, thus the value of a patent, is driven by the skills of the inventor.	The technological competence of a company, thus the ability to create and sustain a leading competitive position, is rooted in the quality of the scientific output and mainly depends on the inventive capabilities of a firm's R&D personnel.	▪ Lotka's law also applies for R&D personnel; thus, only a small fraction of highly skilled inventors is responsible for a large share of inventions and patents (Narin and Breitzmann, 1995; Ernst et al., 2000).

Indicator	Definition	Economic rationale	Empirical results
Age	The age of a patent equals the time lapsed between the current date and the application date.	Cost-benefit analysis. Patent protection is limited to a period of up to twenty years. However, patent applicants must periodically pay (increasing) renewal fees in order to keep their patent in force. From an economic point of view, the patent value must justify this cost (Schankerman and Pakes, 1986).	▪ Positive, significant relationship between patent values and age is confirmed by multiple studies (Pakes, 1986, 767ff.; Schankerman and Pakes, 1986; Lanjouw et al., 1998, 416–417; Reitzig, 2004b, 470–471).
Family size	Number of countries in which the same invention is protected by patent rights.	Cost-benefit analysis. Patent rights are national rights. Increasing the number of countries in which patents protect inventions broadens exclusive exploitation options in different national markets. However, this also increases costs, which a rational acting applicant will only be willing to accept if these costs are outbalanced by expected economic rents (Guellec and van Pottelsberghe de la Potterie, 2000).	▪ Positive, significant impact on patent values (Ceccagnoli et al., 2006, 44; Harhoff and Hoisl, 2007, 1358). ▪ Positive, significant impact on the likelihood of opposition (Harhoff and Reitzig, 2004, 472). ▪ Positive, significant effect on patent values (Lanjouw and Schankerman, 2001, 143; Harhoff and Hoisl, 2007, 1159).
Number of International Patent Classifications (IPC) classes	Number of IPC classes to which an invention is assigned to.	The measure of the scope, thus the breadth of a patent (Lerner, 1994) and the diversity of an invention (Guellec and van Pottelsberghe de la Potterie, 2000).	▪ Negative, significant effect on the likelihood of infringement and challenge suits (Lanjouw and Schankerman, 2001, 143). ▪ No significant impact on patent values (Harhoff et al., 2003a, 1358). ▪ Positive impact on the value of biotech firms (Lerner, 1994, 327).
Filing strategy	Patent protection for a European country can either be obtained by filing a national application, a European application, or using the PCT procedure.	Priority rights endow the patent holder with the right to postpone decisions, which in turn creates a (valuable) option to wait or defer (see sub-subsection 1.4.2.2 in Part II).	▪ The probability of a patent grant is more likely if the application is filed at the EPO through the PCT-Chapter II process, followed by applications first filed with national patent offices. Direct applications to the EPO are less likely to be granted (Guellec and van Pottelsberghe de la Potterie, 2000, 112). ▪ Positive and significant relationship between the filing according to Chapter II PCT and the likelihood of opposition (Reitzig, 2004a, 951).
Ownership	Property rights to a patent may either belong to an individual or a corporate owner.	Corporate owners enjoy economies of scale over the entire patent application process as well as during patent litigation (Harhoff and Reitzig, 2004, 476).	▪ When reputation is relevant, the probability of a patent suit is higher for corporate owners than for individual owners. Foreign corporate owners are less likely to be engaged in an infringement suit than national corporate owners. (Lanjouw and Schankerman, 2001, 145–146). ▪ No significant impact of ownership on the likelihood of opposition (Harhoff and Reitzig, 2004, 472).

Indicator	Definition	Economic rationale	Empirical results
Legal quality of backward citations	In European search reports, each citation is marked with an "*A*," "*Y*," or "*X*" to define the degree to which it is harmful to the novelty of the invention.	The number of backward citations may not only be an indicator of the technical or economic importance of a patent. Some citations may be introduced because they contain a good description of prior art (Schmoch, 1993, 195). Thus a further assessment of the legal quality as presented by *A*-,*Y*-, and *X*-references is useful as, e.g., an *X*-reference indicates that the claimed invention cannot be considered as being new or inventive with respect to this citation (Michel and Bettels, 2001). Such an analysis of the legal quality of patent rights allows one to better judge the risk that a patent will be found invalid during any legal dispute (Harhoff and Reitzig, 2004).	▪ Positive, significant impact on the likelihood of opposition in case of X-and Y-references (Harhoff and Reitzig, 2004, 472). ▪ Positive, though insignificant impact on the likelihood of opposition in case of X-references (Reitzig, 2004a, 951).
Number of (independent) claims	An invention is described by patent claims (Tong and Frame, 1994).	Patent claims may serve as a proxy for a patent's breadth (Lanjouw and Schankerman, 2001). The broader the monopolistic right of a patent, the higher its value will be.	▪ Positive, significant effect on the likelihood of infringement and challenge suits (Lanjouw and Schankerman, 2001, 143). ▪ Positive, significant impact on the likelihood of opposition (Harhoff and Reitzig, 2004, 472). ▪ Positive, significant impact on patent values (Ceccagnoli et al., 2006, 44). ▪ Positive and significant correlation between the number of independent and dependent patent claims (European patents) and the likelihood of opposition (Reitzig, 2004a, 953).
Litigation	Patents are legal documents of which content and validity can be questioned through legal disputes.	The legal quality of a patent increases after it has been successfully defended in a legal dispute (Harhoff et al., 1999).	▪ Positive, significant impact on patent values (Harhoff et al., 2003a, 1358) ▪ Broader patents are more likely to be litigated. One standard deviation in patent scope increases the probability of litigation by 41% from 1.3% to 1.8% (Lerner, 1994, 323). ▪ Patentees have a high probability of winning at trial; however, inter-industry differences exist. Engine patents are found to be more difficult to defend than textile patents and pharmaceutical patents (Lanjouw, 1998, 690–691). ▪ Positive, significant relation between litigation (opposition) and patent values (Lanjouw and Schankerman, 2001, 143; Harhoff and Hoisl, 2007, 1159).

Indicator	Definition	Economic rationale	Empirical results
Full-text variables	Full-text variables comprise data collected not from the front page of the patent but from the text of the patent document.	▪ Number of words describing the state of art reflects the novelty of an invention (Reitzig, 2004a, 948ff.). ▪ Number of words describing the technical problem is a measure for the degree of inventive step (Reitzig, 2004a, 948ff.). ▪ Number of mentioned technical advantages serves as a proxy for expected market demand or the economic potential of an invention (Reitzig, 2004a, 948ff.). ▪ Number of technical preferences of the invention operationalizes the disclosure of the patent. According to Article 83 EPC, opposition may be substantiated by referring to an insufficient degree of disclosure (Reitzig, 2004a, 948ff.). ▪ Number of independent claims describes the degree of inventive step and patent breadth (Reitzig, 2004a, 948ff.). ▪ Number of dependent claims, process claims, and application claims describes the degree of inventive step and patent breadth, and creates fall-back options (Reitzig, 2004a, 948ff.).	▪ Positive and significant correlation between the number of words describing the technical problem (European patents) and the likelihood of opposition (Reitzig, 2004a, 953). ▪ Negative and significant correlation between the number of technical preferences (European patents) and the likelihood of opposition (Reitzig, 2004a, 953).

Table 14: Bibliographic value indicators and empirical results

3.2.2 Empirical results for patent values

Overall, several empirical studies have shown that patent values follow a highly skewed distribution (Pakes, 1986, 777; Schankerman and Pakes, 1986, 1067; Putnam, 1996, 124ff.; Lanjouw, 1998, 694; Scherer and Harhoff, 2000, 560–561; Harhoff et al., 2003b, 287ff.). Thus, a very small fraction of all patents is highly valuable and the majority of patent rights contains little or no economic value. However, as shown by Figure 22, country- and industry-specific differences seem to exist.

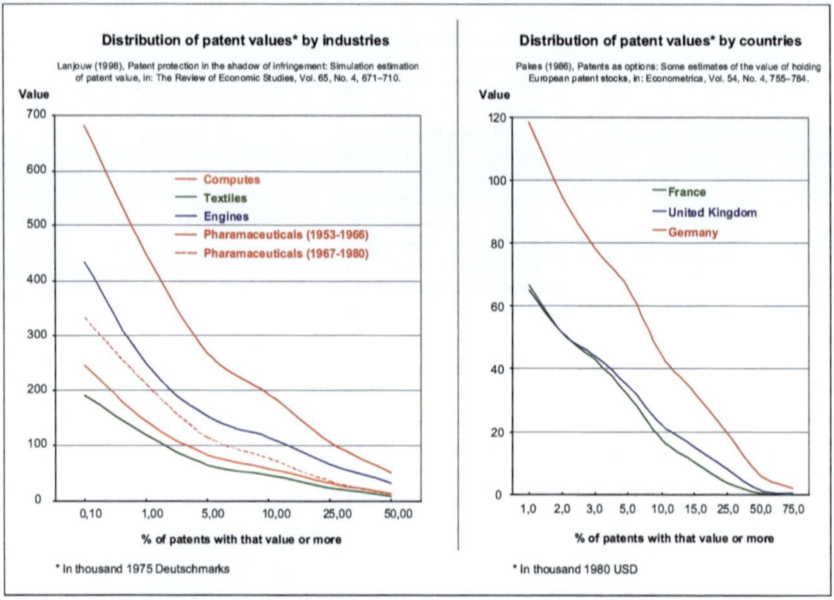

Figure 22: Patent value distributions by industry and country

In addition to this, the geographical breadth of patent protection (family size), the number of times a patent is quoted by subsequent patent rights (forward citations), and the type of owner of the patent (company or single inventor) show strong theoretical and empirical validation. The tables on the following pages summarize existing empirical results grouped according to their underlying value constructs.

RENEWAL VALUE				
Author	**N**	**Industry**	**Time**	**Results**
Barney (2002)	70,860 US patents	▪ All industries	1986	▪ The bottom 10% of patents have an implied value equal to or less than about 430 USD (in 2001 inflation adjusted dollars). ▪ The top 10% of patents have an implied value equal to or greater than about 112,500 USD (in 2001 inflation adjusted dollars). ▪ Aggregate value of all 70,860 patents was 5.2 Billion USD (in 2001 inflation adjusted dollars), 780 patents account for 55% of this amount.
Lanjouw (1998)	20,000 patents (U.S., Japan, Western Europe)	▪ Computers ▪ Textiles ▪ Combustion engines ▪ Pharmaceuticals	1955–1988	▪ Learning about the possibilities of the inventions and about the market is over by age six or seven. ▪ Rapid depreciation. However, interindustry differences do exist ▪ Mean values (in 1975 DM) per industry: Computer (23,495); Textiles (17,486); Engines (49,728); Pharmaceuticals (54,546).
Pakes (1986)	All patent applications in France and the U.K. as well as all patent grants in Germany.	▪ All industries	France: 1951–1979 U.K.: 1955–1978 Germany: 1955–1974	▪ On average, German patents are more valuable than French and English patents. ▪ Learning about the possibilities of the inventions and about the market is over by age five. ▪ Median patent values (in 1980 US Dollars): France 553.96; U.K. 1,516.84; Germany 6,252.93 ▪ Mean patent values (in 1980 US Dollars): France 5,3631; U.K. 7,357; Germany 16,169 ▪ Patent value distribution is extremely skewed.
Sullivan (1994)	All patent applications and grants in Great Britain and Ireland.	▪ All industries	1870–1872; 1970	▪ Mean patent value: 298 GBP (1870/72); 254 GBP (1970) ▪ Median patent value: 74 GBP (1870/72); 68 GBP (1970) ▪ Patent value distribution is extremely skewed.
Schankerman & Pakes (1986)	All patent applications in France and the U.K. as well as all patent grants in Germany.	▪ All industries	France: 1970–1980 U.K.: 1955–1981 Germany: 1955–1981	▪ On average, German patents are more valuable than French and English patents. ▪ Median patent values (in 1980 US Dollars age five): France 847; U.K. 1,861; Germany 5,710 ▪ Mean patent values (in 1980 US Dollars, age five): France 6,656; U.K. 6,963; Germany 19,124. ▪ Patent value distribution is extremely skewed. ▪ Over time the number of patent applications per year and the quality of patents varies: Until the late 1960s the number of patents rose. Than it began to fall whereas the quality of patents increased ▪ On an aggregate, macroeconomic level returns to patents seem to be only a small fraction (on average 5.5%) of the domestic R&D (U.K. 5.7; France 6.8%; Germany 5.6%).
Schankerman (1998)	All patent applications in France.	▪ Pharmaceuticals ▪ Chemicals ▪ Mechanical ▪ Electronics	1959–1982	▪ 50% of the patents lapse before reaching the age of ten. ▪ Renewal rates differ depending on nationality of the patent holder and on the industry, indicating that each country specializes in different technologies. ▪ Median patent values (in 1980 U.S. dollars) for pharmaceuticals: 1,631; chemicals 1,594; mechanical 2,930; electronics 3,159. ▪ Median patent values (in 1980 U.S. dollars) for pharmaceuticals: 4,313; chemicals 4,969; mechanical 15,120; electronics 19,837 ▪ Percentage of the total value of all rights, the top 1% (5%) of patents account for in each industry: pharmaceuticals: 12% (34%), chemicals: 14% (38%); mechanical 21% (50%), electronics 24% (55%).

Table 15: The renewal value construct and empirical results

ASSET VALUE				
Author	**N**	**Industry**	**Time**	**Results**
Lerner (1994)	1,678 patents, 173 firms, 535 financing rounds	▪ Biotechnology	1973–1992	▪ Patent scope has an impact on a firm's valuation (one standard increase in average patent scope leads to a 21% increase in firm's valuation).
Pakes (1985)/ Pakes & Griliches (1984)	120 firms, 968 patents	▪ Drugs and chemicals ▪ Machinery ▪ Office, computing and accounting machinery ▪ Electronic components and communications	1986–1975	▪ Unpredicted changes in a firm's R&D policy lead to a revaluation of the firm. A 1% increase in R&D above the predicted level results in a firm value increase of 0.39%. ▪ Current and past changes in a firm's R&D policy have a significant effect on changes in current patent applications. ▪ On average patents have a significant effect on firm's value: a 1% increase in patents leads to a 1.56 % increase in the market value of the firm. However, patents are a noisy indicator, supporting the idea of an extremely dispersed distribution of patent values.
Conolly & Hirschey (1988)	390 firms	▪ Fortune 500	1977	▪ Robust, large, positive, and significant relationship between the number of unexpected patents and excess value. ▪ One anticipated patent increases the excess value of Fortune 500 firms by 5.33 million USD.
Trajtenberg (1990)	456 U.S. patents	▪ Computer tomography	1971–1986	▪ Weighted patent counts are correlated with the value measures of innovation, simple patent counts are not.
Harhoff, Scherer, Vopel (Harhoff et al.)	752 German patents	▪ Drugs and chemicals ▪ Electronics ▪ Mechanical ▪ Others	1977	▪ 27% of the patents in this sample are valued at an amount less than 100,000 DM. ▪ 26.6% of the patents in this sample are valued at an amount between 100,000 DM and 399,999 DM. ▪ 20.5% of the patents in this sample are valued at an amount between 400,000 DM and 999,999 DM. ▪ 17.2% of the patents in this sample are valued at an amount between 1 million DM and 5 million DM. ▪ 3.7% of the patents in this sample are valued at an amount between 5 million DM and 10 million DM. ▪ 2.1% of the patents in this sample are valued at an amount between 10 million DM and 20 million DM. ▪ 2.0% of the patents in this sample are valued at an amount between 20 million DM and 40 million DM. ▪ 0.7% of the patents in this sample are valued at an amount between 40 million DM and 80 million DM. ▪ 0.3% of the patents in this sample a valued at an amount more than 80 million DM.
Gambardella et al. (2006).	20,236 European patents	See results	1993–1997	Median / Average value (in euros) of patents overall: 305 / 3,024 Median / Average value (in euros) of patents by sector: ▪ Organic fine chemistry: 679 / 6,261 ▪ Pharmaceuticals, cosmetics:605 / 5,260 ▪ Chemical & petrol, basic materials chem.: 580 / 5,298 ▪ Materials, metallurgy: 467; 4,187 ▪ Macromolecular chemistry, polymers: 449 / 3,980 ▪ Space technology weapons: 414 / 3,854 ▪ Agriculture, food, chemistry: 408 / 3,637 ▪ Materials processing, textiles, paper: 367 / 3,325 ▪ Engines, pumps, turbines: 361 / 3,344 ▪ Environmental technology: 354 / 3,250 ▪ Medical technology: 351 / 3,279 ▪ Biotechnology: 336 / 3,134 ▪ Chemical engineering: 335 / 2,992 ▪ Thermal process and apparatus: 327 / 3,012 ▪ Surface technology, coatings: 325 / 2,924 ▪ Optics: 308 / 2,960 ▪ Transport: 298 / 2,782 ▪ Semiconductors: 284 / 2,555 ▪ Machine tools: 276 / 2,568 ▪ Civil engineering, building, mining: 275 / 2,546

ASSET VALUE				
Author	N	Industry	Time	Results
				▪ Nuclear engineering: 274 / 2,421 ▪ Handling, printing: 269 / 2,441 ▪ Analysis, measurement, control technology: 252 / 2,358 ▪ Telecommunications: 247 / 2,331 ▪ Mechanical elements: 243 / 2,208 ▪ Audio-visual technology: 236 / 2,296 ▪ Information technology: 235 / 2,265 ▪ Electrical devices, engineering, energy: 211 / 1,938 ▪ Consumer goods and equipment: 193 / 1,814 ▪ Agricultural & food-proc. machin.-apparatus: 170 / 1,544

Table 16: The asset value construct and empirical results

COMPETITION VALUE				
Author	N	Industry	Time	Results
Austin (1993)	565 U.S. patents	▪ Biotechnology	1991	▪ Patents readily identifiable with end products tend to be more valuable. ▪ Patents announced in press are highly valued. ▪ Patents have an effect on competitors' performance; the impact on rivals' performance is weaker than on the performance of the patent holder.

Table 17: The competition value construct and empirical results

3.3 Evaluation of different approaches to values

3.3.1 Evaluation of direct patent valuation methods

A wide variety of methodological approaches can be identified for patent valuation. This leads to the question of which method is the most appropriate. Of course, assessing the adequacy of one method always depends on the specific valuation model and the underlying economic rationale. However, certain key criteria can be used for evaluating these methodologies.

3.3.1.1 Key criteria for evaluation

Due to the intangible nature of patents, one of the most important evaluation criteria is objectivity. Valuation methods differ with regard to the quantity of information needed for performing patent valuations and involve different degrees of subjective judgments. Hence, each valuation necessitates a trade-off between methodological requirements and an inherent degree of subjectivity. This general criterion further includes the criteria of relevance, reliability, versatility, and credibility.

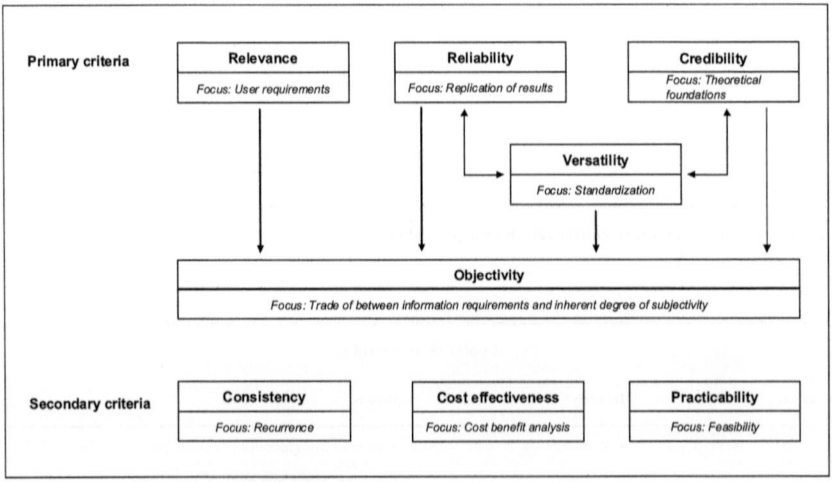

Figure 23: Key evaluation criteria for direct valuation methods

Relevance focuses on a user's requirements. Clearly, any valuation must fully reflect the underlying valuation model and the aim of the valuation project. Thus, a valuation technique should exhibit a certain degree of flexibility, allowing a perfect fit to the respective peculiarities of a valuation project.

Despite this need for flexibility, any valuation should also be verifiable – a knowledgeable third party should be able to replicate the valuation process. The criterion of reliability reflects this fundamental requirement. A valuation method meets the criterion of credibility if it has a strong theoretical foundation and is respected in practice. Versatility links and supports the criteria of reliability and credibility by focusing on the degree of standardization of each method and its degree of applicability across companies, industries, and jurisdictions.

In addition to these primary criteria, consistency, cost effectiveness, and practicability are further relevant. Consistency concentrates on the degree to which a method can be repeated on a temporal basis to assure up-to-date values. The criterion of cost effectiveness assures an adequate degree of economic efficiency of the entire valuation procedure. Finally, practicability refers to the fact that any method should be clearly described and, of course, feasible.

3.3.1.2 General assessment of different direct valuation approaches

Given the complexity and diversity of reasons for patent valuation, the aim of the following comparison of main patent valuation approaches is to provide an overall picture of the general strengths and weaknesses of each valuation method. Clearly, situations may exist in which certain advantages or disadvantages play a major role, which in turn can change the ranking and qualitative assessment of existing valuation techniques.

Figure 24 reports individual strengths and weaknesses for the various approaches to value. The table in the lower part shows the degree to which each of the presented valuation techniques meets the evaluation criteria as defined above. Since patents endow their owner with the right to exclude a third party from exploiting valuable knowledge in the future, a patent valuation method should take future economic rents generated by this patent into account. Hence, income-based valuation techniques represent the most suitable approaches. Their adequacy is further supported by the fact that patent protection is limited to a period of twenty years, thus excluding problems of determining terminal values. Within this family of valuation techniques, royalty-based valuation is very appropriate in case of a collaborative exploitation strategy or given a high degree of licensing activities in an industry.

The quality of a royalty based valuation first of all depends on finding an appropriate and comparable royalty rate. This in turn requires a careful analysis of market based royalty agreements (see also chapter 1 in Part IV). Option valuation is of particular use for young patents or patent applications. However, real option models exhibit a degree of complexity that can make it difficult to understand the underlying economic rationale (Amram, 2005, 80).

In most cases, income-based valuations model specific-use values. A cooperative exploitation strategy, for example, assumes that value is only exploited through the licensing of activities. In contrast to this, decision-tree analyses facilitate joint analyses of different use values and therefore lead to owners' values (see also section 1.2 in Part I). The basic requirement of identifying incremental cash-flows limits the occasions on which an incremental cash-flow approach can be used. Yet, it might be particularly suitable for valuing patented inventions that lead to cost savings. A multi-period excess earnings method takes into account the additional resources that a full exploitation of patents requires. However, this approach tends to overestimate the value of a patent given portfolio effects resulting from the joint use of all resources or in case that not all contributing resources can be identified or valued (Moser and Goddar, 2007, 605).

Approach	Strengths	Weaknesses
Cost	+ Reliable indicator of value in case of a recent acquisition and most applicable when detailed data on this transaction is available + Improved data availability if historical costs are fully and consistently recorded in the books + Easy to calculate and to perform on a periodical basis + Appropriate when the objective of the analysis is to estimate cost	– Focuses on past, not on future benefits – No consideration of risk – No direct correlation between cost, price and value – Subjective nature of replacement cost – Less applicable when the aim of the valuation project is to calculate the a patent's to a third party and not to the current owner – Less applicable for old patents
Market	+ Increased objectivity if comparable transactions or patents can be identified and reliable information on these transactions is available + Easy to calculate (especially in case of the residual value method) + Market replacement cost: Objective nature of cost	– Absence of an open market for patents limits the identification of comparable transactions and thus the applicability of this approach – Requires comparable market conditions and a minimum degree of homogeneity – No direct assessment of future benefits and risk – Difficult to apply if patents are sold in combination with other assets.
Income	+ Focus on future economic benefits (royalty savings, earnings or cash-flows) + Systematic and transparent assessment of (varying) risk + No terminal value problem + Detailed identification of important value driver. Industry specific royalty rates can be collected form public sources (royalty approaches) + Analysis of supporting resource bundle (multi period excess earnings method) + Allows an analysis and comparison of different scenarios and explicitly models future options (option valuation, decision tree analysis) + Adaptable and flexible approach; emulates the actual decision making process + Well known and widely recognized across various valuation and appraisal disciplines + Most rigorous and structured analysis tool. Requires a consideration of all critical economic variables and an explicit description of underlying assumptions.	– Requires a considerable amount of input data – Quality of the result depends on a large extent on the quality of the input data – Subjective assessment of future market conditions and related economic benefits required – Option values decreases with increasing patent age (option approach) – The inherent complexity increases the probability of making honest mistakes and offers the possibility to influence sensitive variables and bias the result – May lead to overestimating patent values

*Evaluation citeria**	*Focus*	*Cost*		*Market*				*Income*				
		Rpl	Rpr	Mul	Ana	MRpl	RV	ICF	MPEE	RfR	RI	OV
Relevance	User requirements	◔	◔	◑	●	◔	◑	◕	◕	◕	◕	●
Reliability	Replication of results	◕	◕	◕	◔	◑	◕	◕	◕	●	◕	◑
Versatility	Standardization	●	●	◑	◑	◑	◑	●	●	●	●	◑
Credibility	Theoretical foundations	◑	◑	◕	◕	◑	◕	●	●	●	●	●
Objectivity	Trade of : Information requirements vs. degree of subjectivity	◑	◑	●	●	●	◑	◕	◕	●	●	◔
Consistency	Recurrence	●	●	◔	◔	◔	◔	◕	◕	◕	◕	◑
Cost effectiveness	Cost benefit analysis	◕	◕	◔	◔	◔	◔	◔	◑	◕	◑	◔
Practicability	Feasibility	◕	◕	◑	◑	◑	◑	◔	◑	●	●	◑

* Harvey balls indicate the degree to which a particular method meets a particular criterion

Rpl: Replacement Cost / Rpr: Reproduction cost / Mul: Multiple / Ana: Analogy / MRpl: Market replacement cost / RV: Residual value (market based) / ICF: Incremental cash flow / MPEE: Multi-period excess earnings / RfR: Relief from Royalty / RI: Royalty Income / OV: Option valuation

Figure 24: Evaluation of patent valuation methods

Furthermore, it should only be applied in case that the valuation object represents the most important intangible resource. Of course, for each future-oriented valuation technique, an analysis of tax amortization benefits can be conducted, making possible a broader perspective on the cost and benefits of a single transaction and its impact on company results. Despite these advantages, the quality of income-based valuation approaches is directly linked to quality of the forecasted economic benefits and a proper analysis of inherent risk factors.

The application of a market approach rests on the assumption that the price of a comparable patent fully reflects future economic value and risks. Needless to say, a thorough analysis for identifying comparable transactions requires a (1) an open market on which patents are frequently traded and (2) a considerable amount of background information – possibly even exceeding the data requirements of income-based approaches. At the time of writing, however, the first condition, in particular, has not yet been met. However, an increasing volume of patent transactions and auctions can be observed, which could lead to the emergence of such a market. This is of particular importance since, if properly performed, market valuation exhibits the lowest degree of subjectivity, which in turn increases the objectivity of the analysis. Cost-based approaches do not account for any kind of future economic rents. They define the maximum amount an investor should pay instead of analyzing the value potential of an invention. A relationship between cost, price, and value exists, but this is not necessarily one of equality. Cost-based valuation may be applicable when the valuation object was transferred in the past. Clearly, the appropriateness of such a valuation then depends on the quality of the historical information.

3.3.2 Evaluation of the indirect valuation approach

Of course, the question remains as to what extent an indirect valuation approach can support the valuation of single patents and patent portfolios. First of all, it is useful to recall that these empirical studies can identify trends on an industry- and country-wide level. Second, the use of sophisticated statistical methods and large sample sizes increases the validity of these findings.

However, the quality of the analysis is driven by the quality with which patent values are measured. An analysis of renewal decisions implicitly assumes rational behavior of patent applicants following the general economic principle of cost-benefit analysis. However, patent-related decisions seem primarily to be driven by a consideration of risk, rather than a proper analysis of cost and benefits (see also the discussion on patent portfolio management in subsection 2.1.6 of this Part). Furthermore, especially in cumulative industries, benefits from holding extensive patent portfolios may also result from improvements in the patentee's bargaining position during (cross-) licensing deals. In this case, the portfolio value exceeds the sum of the values of all portfolio members. Thus, weak patents, too, may be renewed – in spite of their low stand-alone value. This portfolio logic depends mainly on industry- and firm-specific characteristics and is only partly reflected in renewal value analysis (see also the discussion on the renewal-value construct in sub-subsection 2.3.1.5 of Part II).

If patent values are measured by asking inventors or patentees to give an indication of the value of their inventions or patents, results may be biased by overly optimistic expectations and strategic behavior at the respondent's level. One methodological way to reduce this problem is to ask patentees after twenty years what their minimum price would have been on the filing date if they had known the contribution this patented invention would make to business success (Harhoff et al., 2003b, 283). However, this limits the availability of up-to-date information, which is essential for direct patent valuation. In addition, one further methodological issue is worth mentioning. Almost every questionnaire asks patentees to opt for one value interval out of a predefined set of value ranges when estimating the value of their patent rights. Needless to say, the number and breadth of these value intervals directly affect the results.

Market valuation of companies is strongly driven by expectations. Without stressing the point about the degree of rationality and reliability capital markets exhibit in valuing firms, deriving patent values referring to market values of companies is based on two main assumptions: First, that the patent information is somehow so important to shareholders that they consider this information and introduce it in their valuation model; second, that they have a more or less precise idea of the patent portfolio of a company and how this portfolio affects major economic variables such as sales, earnings, and finally dividends. However, since not all patents are shown in a firm's balance sheet (see section 2.2 in this part) shareholders must gather this information from other public sources.

Econometric indicator analysis certainly helps in dealing with entire patent portfolios and can be used to distinguish "more valuable" from "less valuable" patents. However, the quality of these indicators is driven by the quality of the model in general and the measurement of patent values in particular. If a proxy for patent value does not measure the intrinsic patent value with sufficient reliability then the results for these selected indicators may be questionable.

Hence, I conclude that, given the rich information revealed by patent documents, indirect valuation offers a sophisticated approach for statistical patent analysis. However, in order to improve our understanding of patent value indicators and to increase the validity of this valuation approach, these indicators should be tested with real market values. I present the result of such an analysis in chapter 2 of Part IV.

4 The valuation of patents: A comprehensive approach to value

In view of the analysis in the preceding chapters of all parts, I present a comprehensive approach for valuing patents in this section. After a presentation of a suitable way to compile the required database (section 4.1), I discuss the question of selecting an appropriate valuation horizon (section 4.2), review alternative definitions of economic benefits (section 4.3) and value exploitation strategies and patent specific risk drivers (section 4.4).

4.1 Basic rationale and database compilation

The basic rationale in valuing patents is given by the relationship between patented inventions, technological innovations, and the resulting economic consequences (see section 3 in Part II). Hence, a consistent valuation of patents requires linking the legal nature of patents with the economic realm of profit and cost analysis. A valuation approach based on expected economic benefits is most appropriate for patent valuation, given: (1) the fact that patents have a maximum term of twenty years and protect new technological know-why, (2) the basic economic principles of the supreme irrelevance of sunk cost, and (3) the idea that any investor focuses on a future, but uncertain, stream of profits.

Patents protect inventions. In cumulative industries more than one invention prepares the ground for a new technological field. Multiple inventions from different technological fields are implemented in complex products and system solutions. Thus, any valuation project should first start with matching the sample of patents subject to this specific valuation (valuation sample) with technologies and these technologies with products. This can be achieved by using two matrices. The first matrix, which I refer to as the Patent-Technology-Product Matrix (PTPM), matches all patented inventions or patent families with technological product features. The overall aim of this matrix is to connect all patented technologies of the valuation sample with the members of all product families that result from applying these technologies. This process comprises two steps. First, all products must be matched with the technologies used during their creation. Second, after listing all these technologies, all patents of the valuation sample must be grouped according to the extent to which these patents protect each of the identified technologies. Depending on the degree of complexity and maturity, one technology might be implemented in a variety of different products. If an invention can be applied in more than one technological field, this might be a first indication of a valuable patent. In the end, the PTPM depicts technology and products in rows and patents in columns.

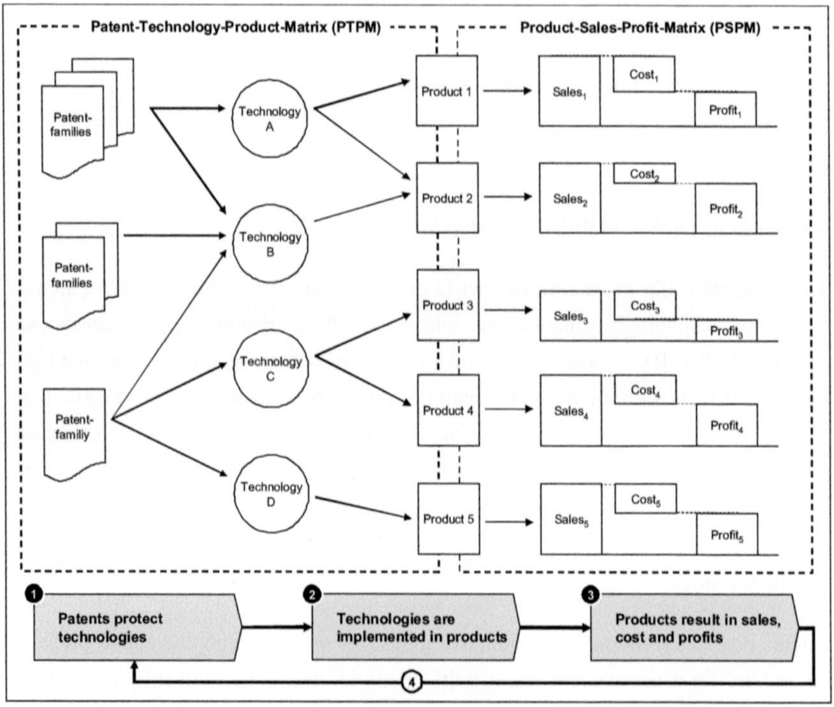

Figure 25: Patent-Technology-Product Matrix (PTPM) and Product-Sales-Profit Matrix (PSPM)

For each product, key economic variables such as sales, cost, and profit margin are to be collected and structured in a Product-Sales-Profit matrix (PSPM), with products in rows and profits and cost in columns. The compilation of these two matrices allows us to establish a transparent link between patented protection and economic variables (see also sub-subsection 3.3.2.3 in Part I). This in turn supports any subsequent thorough analysis and valuation.

4.2 Definition of valuation horizon

A valuation approach based on future income implies adding a time dimension to both the PTPM and the PSPM. The valuation horizon is defined as sum of discrete valuation periods for which data is forecasted. Since only those patents and patent applications can be valued that exist on the date the PTPM is compiled, the maximum number of valuation periods within the valuation horizon can be no more than twenty years from the application date of the youngest patent family within the valuation sample. This time span defines the maximum remaining term of patent protection. However, two important issues must be taken into account: (1) The remaining life of a seasoned patent is not twenty years. In fact, survivor curve analysis often reveals that it is even less than the difference between the maximum life of twenty years and the current age of a patent (see sub-subsection 3.1.3.4 in this Part). (2) A definition of the valuation horizon should not only rely on this expected remaining legal life only since patent management should also follow the basic rationale of cost-benefit analyses (see subsection 2.1.6 in this Part). Thus, we might expect that patent-renewal decisions are also driven by technology cycles and that patents will not be renewed if the protected technology is no longer profitable. With the exception of basic inventions, in fact, only a very few economic reasons might exist that can credibly justify why a patent should be renewed even if the technology no longer constitutes a competitive advantage to the company or other third party. Basic inventions can be very valuable if they represent key technological ideas that are used for multiple product generations and induce a stream of additional and dependent patent rights. Hence, maintaining and defending patent protection over the maximum patent term seems likely in this case.

In the end, the valuation horizon should reflect the remaining useful life as a time span over which benefits can be generated through exploitation of the patented invention. The focus is thus put on the economic dimension, but this in turn is driven by the expected remaining legal lifetime of the valuation sample and the position of the underlying technologies in their life cycles.

4.3 Definition of economic benefits

In most cases, economic benefits are tied to a stream of sales that can be generated through implementation of the patented technology in sophisticated products. Of course, e.g. cost savings, expected royalty income, and any advantages resulting from blocking competitors can also serve as input for defining the expected economic benefits. The discussion in section 2.2 of Part II shows a variety of different patent functions. Needless to say, the heterogeneous nature of these functions leads to diverse benefits that in turn result in different value conclusions.

Sales result from multiplying the number of units sold by the price for each unit in one or more national markets. For valuation purposes, these prices should be defined as prices on a competitive and open market. The fact that patents are first of all national rights calls for a careful analysis and matching of national product markets and geographical scope of patent protection. Competitors can be successfully blocked from using patented technology by obtaining patent protection either in countries where products are produced or in national markets where they are sold to customers. Needless to say, the most comprehensive, but also most expensive, patent protection results from securing all countries in which either of these two criteria applies.

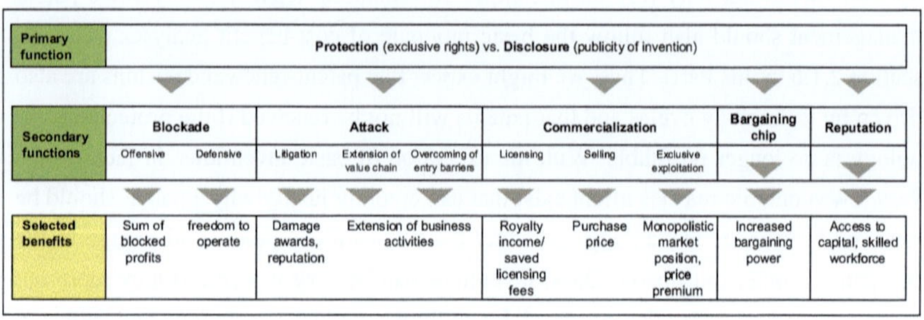

Figure 26: Patent functions and selected benefits of patent protection

In addition, due to the specific characteristics of the relationship between patents, technologies, and products, more than one patent family usually protects sophisticated goods. Due to the underlying path-dependency of research and development processes and resulting patent application decisions, the patent families in the valuation sample differ with regard to their age. The valuation horizon equals the remaining useful life of the youngest patent (family). Hence, the concentration of patent families required for comprehensively defending one product is likely to decrease over time. Theses changes in the concentration over time reduce the degree of effective patent protection in latter periods of the valuation horizon. Therefore, the size of the valuation sample must be forecasted for each valuation period. The analyst should take this reduction of patent protection into account, for example, by introducing a factor to weight future economic benefits according to the number of patent families still in force in each valuation period.

4.4 Valuing cooperative and exclusive exploitation

As already discussed in subsection 3.1.3 of this Part, the value potential of patents can either be exploited exclusively or through cooperation with a third party. Two alternative valuation methods mirror this dualism. A discounted cash-flow approach calculates patent values by assuming an exclusive use by the patent holder, whereas the application of the royalty method implies a (hypothetical) licensing agreement between two unrelated parties.

In both cases, a key issue of any valuation is the analysis of product profit margins. The selection of a reasonable royalty rate should reflect the profitability of a technology. As for the licensee, royalty rates reduce the profit margin, all else being equal. Thus, setting a royalty rate that exceeds the product profit margin constitutes a questionable assumption. For a discounted cash-flow valuation, in contrast, profit margins can be used to derive cash-flows.

However, since sales and consequent cash-flows not only stem from exploiting patented technology but are also motivated by other tangible and intangible assets of a company, only a reasonable share of these sales volumes and cash-flows can be used for calculating patent values. Three considerations must be taken into account here. First, the analyst must estimate or derive the impact of technological product features on product sales. Clearly, since patents protect technological innovations, only that part of sales that can be traced back to the underlying product technology can provide a basis for further valuation. It is plausible to assume that the share of sales that can be traced back to technological features is higher (1) in case of high-tech products than it would be for products with a strong brand that do not rely on technological aspects or (2) in the presence of a high impact of service efforts on sales (see also subsection 3.3.2 in part I).

I define this degree of technological dependence as technology share (*Tech-share*). *Tech-share* can take values between one and zero; due to its impact on patent value, a careful determination of its exact value is obligatory. Delphi-analysis, customer interviews, and a thorough analysis of competitors' products and reputations are three alternative and mutually supporting techniques to derive a reasonable value for the *Tech-share*.

Second, after weighting sales and cash-flows by *Tech-share*, an additional question may arise regarding the degree to which the underlying product technology is protected and revealed by explicit descriptions in patent documents. Given the case that successful economic exploitation of a technology requires the simultaneous ownership of patents and access to unprotected know-why and know-how and assuming that the valuation focuses on estimating the stand-alone value of patents, the portion of sales induced by technological product features must further be adjusted. Unprotected know-why (e.g., manuals, blueprints) and tacit knowledge (know-how) can both be sources of technological competitive advantages (see section 2.2 in Part I). However, if a patent portfolio is valued on a stand-alone basis, only the exclusive right is subject to valuation and any other technological asset that drives the commercial success is not included. Therefore, an additional deduction for this know-how and unprotected know-why contributions might be applicable.

Finally, any valuation must reflect the legal quality of the patent protection. Two issues are worth mentioning here. First, the valuation model must differentiate between patent applications and patent grants. The patent application endows the applicant with only limited, preliminary legal options against infringing parties. Second, if the patentee decides to exclusively exploit a patented invention (e.g. by offering patented products and related services) the strength of the patent regime directly affects the underlying risk of not being able to enforce the exclusive right of a patent. This general uncertainty depends on (1) the attractiveness of the patented technology from a competitor's perspective, (2) the expected difficulty a competitor might face in inventing around a specific patent, and (3) the ability of patentees to detect and successfully enforce their rights under a specific patent regime (see Figure 27). The first driver of risk, attractiveness from a competitor's perspective, again depends on the technological features of the invention, the resulting competitive advantage, and the anticipated remaining time-to-market for this invention. The difficulty of inventing around an existing patent is driven by the scope of the patent and the availability of substitute technologies, whereas the probability of successfully enforcing an infringed patent depends on the monitoring of competitors' activities, the resources devoted to related legal means, and the patentee's reputation – which might also have an impact on the attractiveness of a technology (see also the discussion on cost and benefits of litigation in section 1.6, of Part II).

All these reflections can be described by qualitative statements and either (1) be summarized in a patent protection factor (*PPF* with $0 \leq PPF \leq 1$) to weigh the nominator in a standard discounted cash-flow model or (2) be accounted for in determining an appropriate discount rate. The advantage of the *PPF* is that it easily allows the mirroring of varying degrees in the strength of patent protection in different valuation periods and consequently increases transparency. The cost of such an approach results from splitting risk considerations. This in turn requires a careful sensitivity analysis in order to avoid any double counting of the same risk in nominator and denominator.

The inclusion of patent risks in the discount rate raises the question about determining an appropriate risk premium for patents. Of course, management estimates and the qualitative assessment of the legal strength of a patent can be sources for defining risk premia. However, measuring the precise amount of a risk premia for specific assets should be linked to the overall company risk. The risk of a resource reflects the volatility of cash-flows a resource generates. For companies or business units, value-based management defines specific hurdle rates by calculating weighted average cost of capital (wacc). All (marketable) resources of a company together therefore must yield a return that equals (or exceeds) the wacc.

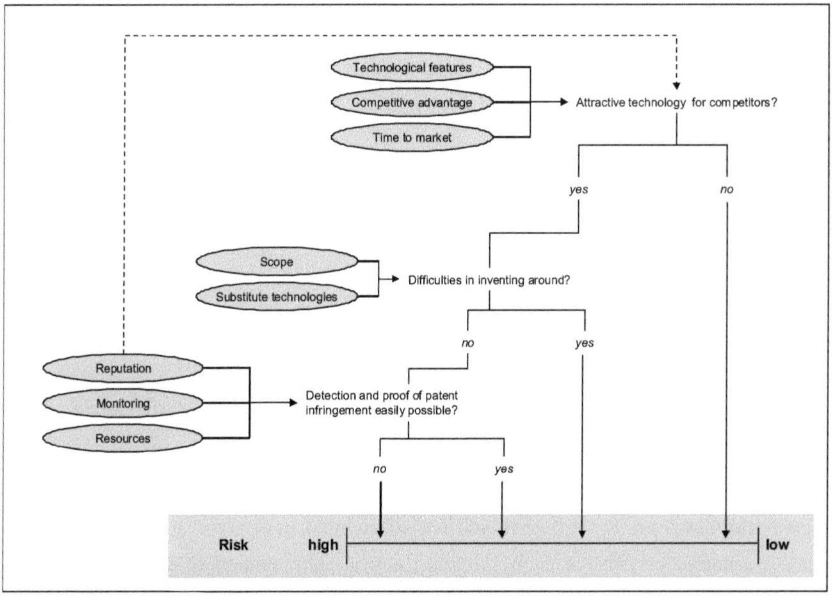

Figure 27: Patent risks (exclusive use)

Of course, not all resources exhibit the same risk profile. In contrast to tangible resources like property, plant and equipment or the net working capital, cash-flows to intangible assets are highly volatile due to e.g. the intangible nature of these assets, their underlying specificity and irreversibility.

Within the group of intangible assets, the risk of a patented technology might be lower than the risk associated with a company's goodwill. Hence, all resources (R_i) of a company can be arranged according to their resource specific risk(ρ_i) (Moser and Goddar, 2007; Beyer and Mackenstedt, 2008). It is plausible to assume that the risk of tangible (intangible) resources is on average lower (higher) than the wacc. Based on the idea that the weighted sum of these resource-specific risks should be equal the wacc and assuming comparable RUL for all resources, risk premia can be derived. Resource specific weights (ω_i) can be calculated based on present book values (ω_i^p) or expected future (book) values (ω_i^f).

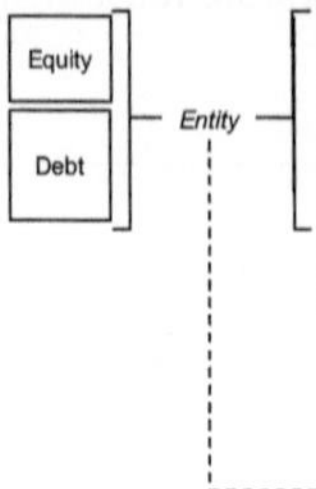

Resources	Risk	(Book)Value	Weight	Risk premium	Resource specific risk	Weighted risk
Goodwill	high	10	0,0625	5,10%	15,10%	0,94%
Patents	↕	30	0,1875	4,20%	14,20%	2,66%
Property, Plant, Equipment		45	0,2813	-0,90%	9,10%	2,56%
Working Capital	low	75	0,4688	-1,83%	8,17%	3,83%
		160	1,0000			10,00%

Assumptions

1. $\rho_1(R_1) > \rho_2(R_2) > \ldots > \rho_n(R_n)$
2. $\sum_{i=1}^{n} \omega_i^p \rho_i(R_i) = wacc \qquad \sum_{i=1}^{n} \omega_i^p = 1; \omega_j^p = \frac{Bookvalue_j}{\sum_{i=1}^{n} Bookvalue_i}$
3. $wacc = 10\%$
4. *Equal remaining life for all resources*

Figure 28: Resource-specific risk premia

These peculiarities of a DCF approach can be cumulatively reflected in a royalty-based valuation by choosing a reasonable royalty rate. The advantage of such an implicit and cumulative approach is given in view of time and cost constraints. However, a detailed analysis of the driver in a DCF approach significantly increases both transparency and credibility of the valuation project. For both approaches, royalty payments or cash-flows after taxes are to be determined and discounted to arrive at a present value of these economic benefits in each valuation period. The sum of these present values equals the financial value of the valuation sample.

In a final step, tax shields from depreciating this value can further be considered by applying a step-up factor (see also detailed description of the TAB in sub-subsection 3.1.3.2 of this Part).

4.5 Getting robust results

The quality of the results and the process of patent valuation as described in the preceding chapters rest on three pillars: a comprehensive and well-structured database, a set of reasonable and explicitly defined assumptions, and a correct and precise calculation. Of course, due to the inherent uncertainty of future events, values depend on making the right assumptions. In order to substantiate the final results extensive sensitivity and scenario analyses are useful (see also subsection 1.1.4). Furthermore, the discussion of strengths and weaknesses of existing valuation approaches further supports the application of more than only one approach to value (see section 3.3 of this Part). In fact, using multiple valuation techniques for estimating patent values increases transparency and, again, the reliability of each value conclusion.

In light of this, initial empirical evidence on the impact of selected bibliographic indicators on patent value can be helpful (see section 3.2 of this Part). In combination with the rare occasions on which real-market transactions can be observed, we can derive comparables based on family sizes or forward citations (see chapter 2 of Part IV). These results should be interpreted with caution, but can of course support the results obtained through a direct valuation approach. In addition, valuation based on historical cost in combination with expected or projected return on investment rates can be additional criteria against which the resulting value is benchmarked.

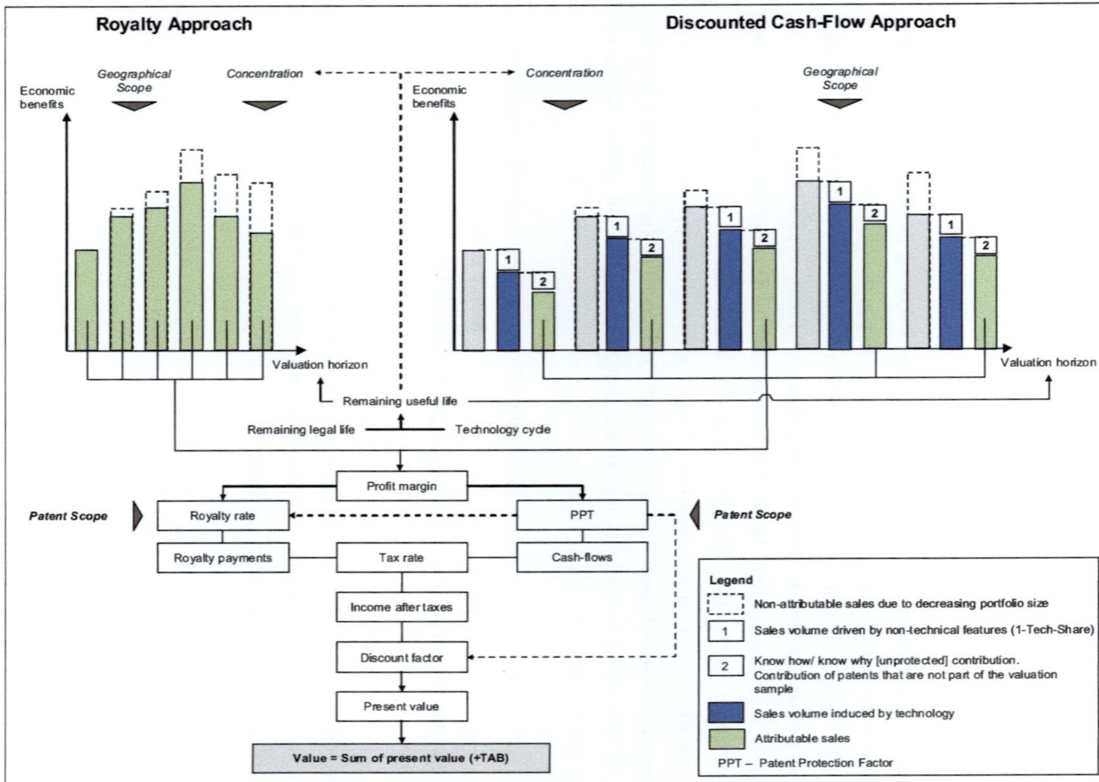

Figure 29: Patent valuation – A comprehensive approach

Part IV: Exploiting patent protection of knowledge-based competitive advantages through market transactions

1 Transferring the economic potential of knowledge and patents through licensing: Which contractual features affect the value of knowledge?

1.1 Introduction

The discussion in Part III shows that cooperative exploitation represents one strategic option for solving Arrow's (1962; 1971) information paradox and consequently allows the effective appropriation of value from knowledge assets in general and patents in particular. In the case of innovations, licensing agreements are one type of performance-oriented contracts used to exploit the value embedded in technical knowledge (Teece, 1986). Licensing activities have motivated a large body of literature, covering topics such as reasons for (Mottner and Johnson, 2000; Saracho, 2002; Arora and Fosfuri, 2003; Lichtenthaler, 2007) and results of (Arrow, 1962; Rockett, 1990) granting licenses, profit-maximizing licensing strategies (Katz and Shapiro, 1986; Kamien and Tauman, 2002; Poddar and Sinha, 2004; Fosfuri, 2006), ways to distribute the value created between licensor and licensee (Kamien and Tauman, 1986), timing of licensing (before or after developing a technology) (Gallini, 1984; Gallini and Winter, 1985; Shapiro, 1985), and the types of innovations that are transferred (Katz and Shapiro, 1985; Arora, 1995).

One stream of research analyzes in detail the information given by licensing agreements. Major contributions have been made by Taylor et al. (1973), Caves et al. (1983), Rostoker (1983), Contractor (1981; 1985) Macho-Stadler et al. (1996), Aulakh et al. (1998), Bessy et al. (1998), Anand et al. (2000), and Nagaoka et al. (2006). Most of the research carried out in this field, so far, has focused on describing the different features of licensing agreements. The following analyses go on to make a particular contribution to research by investigating the relationship between the financial value of a licensing agreement and its content, thereby answering the following research questions:

(1) Does an effective market mechanism for technical knowledge exist?

(2) Which contractual terms drive the value of a licensing agreement?

An earlier version of the model and the empirical results shown in the next sections were presented at the 66th Annual Meeting of the Academy of Management 2006 in Atlanta. I thank two anonymous reviewers for their valuable feedback.

1.2 Drivers, purpose, and objectives of licensing contracts

Lichtenthaler (2007) identifies monetary and strategic drivers that motivate and influence licensing decisions. Monetary reasons comprise voluntary as well as compulsory licensing. Strategic drivers consist of (1) product-oriented (entry into foreign markets, selling products and services in combination with licenses, setting industry standards), (2) technology-oriented (guaranteeing freedom to operate, gaining access to the licensor's technology portfolio, establishing and maintaining a leading technological position), and (3) mixed-strategic (enabling learning effects, enhancing reputation, and strengthening interorganizational networks) drivers (Lichtenthaler, 2007, 69ff.).

This wide variety of drivers for licensing decisions is due to the flexibility of licensing contracts. In fact, the main advantage of licensing agreements is that they can deal with any type of knowledge (see also Part I). They can be used to transfer not only explicit knowledge in the form of intellectual property rights (IPRs) or documents such as manuals, blueprints, and technical handbooks, but also tacit components through offering technical assistance and educational services (Arora, 1995; Anand and Khanna, 2000). By granting licenses for explicit knowledge, licensors can overcome appropriability problems, since a licensing contract reduces the public nature of explicit knowledge. Furthermore, if licensors do not grant an exclusive license, they can take advantage of the feature of nonrivalry in consumption. This allows multiple transactions of the same knowledge content with different licensees. In the case of tacit knowledge, licensing agreements are one way to control knowledge flows between licensor and licensee. One major advantage of the flexible nature of licensing contracts for licensees is that they can avoid the risk of being sued for infringing property rights related to explicit knowledge and – with the same contract – can profit from implicit or tacit components of knowledge.

The primary objective of a licensing agreement is to define the specific rights and duties of both contracting parties. Based on this agreement, the licensor transfers property rights to the subject of the contract to the licensee for a specific period of time. In exchange, the licensor receives financial and non-financial compensation (Sullivan, 1996; Manfroy, 2002). In contrast to a contract of sale, the licensor or knowledge owner retains title to the property and only temporarily allows the licensee to exercise a well-defined bundle of owner-specific rights (Contractor, 1985).

According to Teece (1986) and his influential work on profiting from innovations, licensing agreements are particular advantageous under a strong appropriability regime and in the presence of complementary assets. However, if the subject of the contract is an unprotected innovation or other technical knowledge then such contract can hold a danger of opportunistic behavior on both sides. Bessy and Brousseau (1998) further emphasize that any knowledge transfer can induce the creation of new knowledge that in turn can substitute or devalue the knowledge originally transferred. Due to these limitations, complex contractual agreements are needed in order to exploit the economic potential of knowledge in the marketplace.

Although neither content nor structure of licensing agreements are legally defined, several recurring features can be found in each contract (Contractor, 1985; Merwin and Warner, 1996; Bryer, 1999). They allow comparative and statistical analyses of content and features of these agreements. In fact, all licensing agreements contain information about the identities of licensor and licensee, subject of the contract, purpose of the contract, number and characteristics of rights granted, compensation provisions, and expected lifetime.

1.3 The life cycle of a licensing contract: A two-stage model

The lifetime of an agreement is made up of two consecutive stages. During the first stage, the negotiation period, licensor and licensee discuss and bargain on the specific features of the licensing agreement. Like any other market transaction, this period is characterized by a series of negotiations and compromises. If both parties eventually agree, they will draft a licensing agreement to come into force on the effective date (end of stage one, start date for stage two).

During the second stage (contract period), the licensee may use the subject of contract as defined in the agreement. In a world with deterministic outcomes, licensor and licensee *ex ante* know the future costs and benefits associated with this agreement. However, in reality, both contracting parties face a high degree of uncertainty regarding the economic and legal consequences of their decisions. Particularly in an economic surrounding such as the electronics industry, where we observe rapid technology development of cumulative technologies protected by extensive, overlapping patent portfolios (Grindley and Teece, 1997; Reitzig, 2004b) and scarcely predictable customer behavior, drafting and entering appropriate licensing agreements is a key factor for sustainable economic success.

Therefore, I assume that both parties try to reduce this multifaceted uncertainty by choosing appropriate contractual terms. During the negotiation period it is most important for them (1) to achieve a common understanding about the subject of contract, (2) to clearly define which rights are transferred, and (3) to agree on the features of these rights. With regard to the unknown future, the parties must implement contractual clauses that define not only (1) the duration and (2) termination of the contract, but also (3) how the licensee shall compensate the licensor for the transfer of rights.

1.3.1 Stage one: Negotiation period

Before and during the negotiation period, both parties form expectations about the strategic and economic value that will result from a possible licensing contract. A successful outcome of any negotiation requires that their expectations coincide, at least partially (see also section 1.3 in Part I). Since each party also takes into consideration the value expectations of the other party and since all expectations are based on a set of assumptions, licensee and licensor will estimate not only single values but entire value ranges for the respective technology. Following the model of Contractor (1985), the borders of each value range can be identified based on expected costs and benefits.

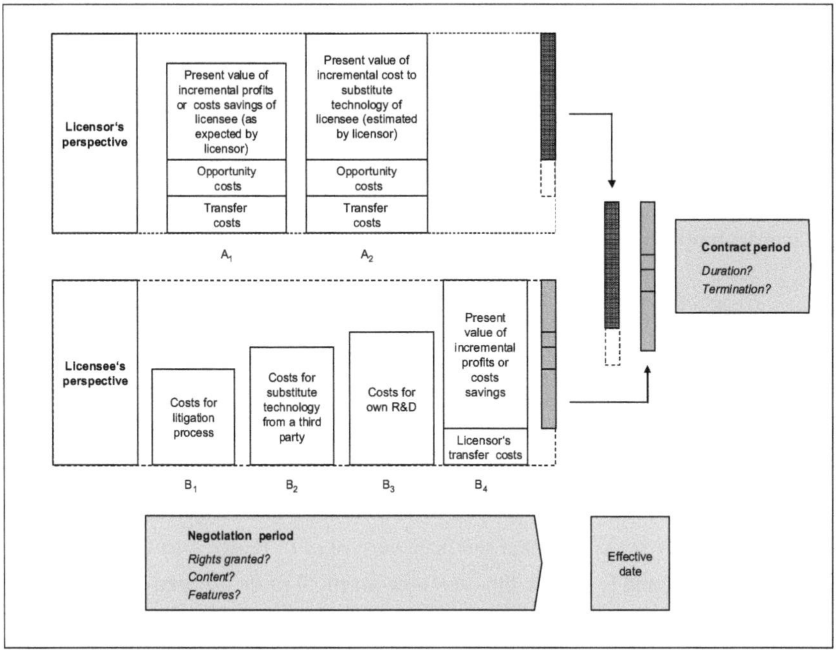

Figure 30: Value ranges and the life cycle of a licensing agreement

1.3.1.1 Negotiation period: Licensor's perspective

The transfer of technological knowledge is costly (Teece, 1977; Gambardella et al., 2007, 1174ff.). These transfer costs define the minimum acceptable value from the licensor's perspective. They comprise, for example, costs for delivering explicit knowledge such as documents, manuals, and patents and costs for transferring implicit knowledge induced by e.g., teaching licensee's engineers and offering support and ongoing assistance over the entire duration of the agreement. If the purpose of the contract is to penetrate a foreign market or if an exclusive license is granted, then opportunity costs have to be added. They increase the threshold value since the choice of licensing as form of market entry theoretically rules out the possibilities for export or foreign direct investment (Contractor, 1981). In case of granting an exclusive license, opportunity costs arise since the licensor is bound by the contract not to grant this specific license to other potential licensees.

The maximum value from the licensor's perspective equals either the sum of transfer costs, opportunity costs, and the present value of all cash-flows the licensor expects the licensee to obtain over the lifespan of the agreement (A1) or the sum of transfer costs, opportunity costs, and the present value of all costs, the licensor expects the licensee to incur in order to obtain the respective technology elsewhere (A2). As for the latter, I accept Farok Contractor's argumentation, but with respect to the former I would suggest that for both licensee and licensor, not only the present value of future cash-flows is of importance but also the degree to which both licensor and licensee expect an appropriation of these cash-flows.

1.3.1.2 Negotiation period: Licensee's perspective

From a licensee's perspective, the most favorable contract would grant a license free of charge. However, since both parties have entered a negotiation process, the licensee will form expectations about the licensor's transfer costs and take these into consideration in assessing a minimum value for the respective technology. The maximum cost the licensee will be willing to accept depends on the options available to gain access to the technology. If we assume that the licensee wishes to bridge a technological gap through licensing and to exploit the economic potential of the respective technology, the maximum value equals the sum of the discounted incremental profits or cost savings that can be yielded by using this technology (B4). This has been the predominant motivation for the sample of licensing contracts analyzed here. However, value expectations can be driven by other factors as well. Instead of asking for a license, licensees could also set up their own R&D project to either develop a similar technology or to invent around (B3) the licensor's patents (see sub-subsection 3.3.2.1 in Part I). Alternatively, the licensee could try to find a similar technology offered by a different licensor in order to substitute the negotiated technology (B2). If the licensee requires permission to use a specific technology to avoid an infringement process, a fourth option includes calculating a net present value of the costs for such a litigation process (B1). These costs include more than the expenses for legal advice and legal proceedings. Since the patent owner can obtain a preliminary injunction (see also section 1.6 in Part III) against any further value exploitation activities conducted by the infringing party, costs of lost sales and earnings must also be taken into account (Grudziecki and Michel, 2002).

If the expected value ranges of licensor and licensee overlap, a successful signing of the contract will appear likely (see also section 1.3 in Part I). The contractual features mirror the expectations of both licensor and licensee, as well as their individual bargaining powers. I recognize that the latter can hardly be measured reliably. But since these agreements are negotiated by experts led more by clear interests and less by emotions, I make the assumption that the contracts I am investigating are "wise agreements" (Fisher and Ury, 1982) that meet the interests of both parties, allow for a fair solution of conflicting interests, and are durable.

1.3.2 Stage two: Contract period

1.3.2.1 Contract period: Compensation provisions

Empirical results show a considerable variety of compensation provisions (Merwin and Warner, 1996; Aulakh et al., 1998; Bessy and Brousseau, 1998). Apart from lump sum payments, the most common means to determine license fees are recurring-amount payments and royalty rates. Royalty rates can either be defined as an absolute amount to be paid on a per unit basis or as a percentage of sales volume – or more precisely, as a percentage of the net selling price. This price is usually calculated as the price of contract products charged to customers after allowing deductions for value-added tax, costs for packing, transport and insurance, applicable import-export and excise duties, returns, and trade discounts. In addition to these two bases, royalty rates might also be defined as percentage of the gross margin or the profit before or after taxes (Perlitz, 1980).

A royalty rate furthermore either remains stable (flat royalty) or changes with regard to the development of the royalty basis. In the latter case, licensor and licensee agree upon a schedule defining the adjustments of the royalty rate to be made if the basis, e.g., the sales volume or the number of units sold, exceeds predefined thresholds. Finally, recurring amount payments are either due after the completion of various steps in an overall process (e.g., product development) or at predefined future dates. The contracts belonging to the sample analyzed here show three main compensation mechanisms: (1) a fixed component, comprising lump sum and (2) recurring amount payments; and (3) a variable component, consisting of a schedule of declining royalty rates.

If both parties agree upon a running royalty rate, then the licensor's revenue (royalty income) is directly linked to the exploitation of the respective technology by the licensee (Cho, 1988). From the perspective of the licensors, the financial value of a license therefore depends not only on the economic potential – or more precisely on the stream of profits the licensees generates by exploiting these rights – but also on the degree to which licensors can appropriate a satisfactory part of this stream via the compensation formula. Therefore, the transaction value of a license agreement $V(L_0)$ from a licensor's perspective at time $t = 0$ is given by:

$$V(L_0) = \left[\sum_{t=1}^{T} \frac{V(r_b)_t * rr_t}{(1+c)^t} + \sum_{t=1}^{T} \frac{RA_t}{(1+c)^t} + LS_0 \right] * \varphi_0$$

with $V(r_b)_t$ as the value of the royalty base in t, rr_t as royalty rate in t, RA_t as recurring amount payments in t, LS_0 as lump sum payment in period 0, c as cost of capital and T as the duration of the agreement. The variable φ_0 $(0 \leq \varphi \leq 1)$denotes an appropriability factor which determines the extent to which the licensor can appropriate the value calculated by the compensation formula.

In addition to this financial value, both parties might agree upon a reciprocal exchange of knowledge or patents. From the perspective of the parties, such a cross-license (Taylor and Silberston, 1973, 116) creates the advantage of avoiding development costs for a complementary technology and allows an earlier introduction of a product based on each partner's technology. But at the same time this also provokes the creation of substitutes for the products of each partner (Fershtman and Kamien, 1992). Moreover, cross-licensing might foster collusive behavior of both parties since it increases (in the case of imperfect substitutes) the probability of a market entry (Eswaran, 1993) and/or enables each party to directly influence the pricing or distribution strategy of the respective partner (Shapiro, 1985).

1.3.2.2 Contract period: Duration and termination

The compensation provisions answer the question of how the licensee shall compensate the licensor during the contract period. However, before the parties can decide on this specific feature, they must first agree upon a clear definition of the lifetime of the agreement. If the contract deals with patents, it usually terminates on the expiry date of the last patent. For the electronics industry, Taylor and Silberston (1973) report that inasmuch as the subject of contract in most cases also comprises unprotected know-why and know-how (see section 2.3 in Part I), licensor and licensee define a shorter period and implement prolongation clauses. If both contracting parties fail to give notice by a certain predefined date that they do not wish to extend the duration of the term then these clauses automatically extend the validity of the agreement. In contrast to this prolongation, both parties can also define situations in which one party can void the contract. These termination rules are important should a party infringe a substantial condition of the agreement.

1.4 Development of hypotheses

1.4.1 Hypotheses: Negotiation period

The overall aim of a licensing agreement is to determine the rights and duties of both parties. In general, we can identify four classes of property rights (Coase, 1960; Demsetz, 1967; Alchian and Demsetz, 1973) that can be licensed. A licensee can obtain the right (1) to use, (2) consume and (3) obtain income from, and (4) to alienate attributes of the subject of contract. Attributes comprise all operation modes and application areas of this resource (Foss and Foss, 2005).

Since a contract is one of the primary sources of information in case of any legal proceedings and provides the basis for a successful business relationship, it must not only cover all important aspects of subsequent transactions but also be written in a clear and precise style (Ramsay, 2002). Of course, multiple formulations can be used to express the rights granted. The right to use is reflected in a licensing agreement by giving the permission to utilize the subject of contract as defined in the agreement. In contrast to this, granting rights to produce or manufacture specific goods based on the traded technology corresponds to the right of the licensee to exploit this technology within the production process in every way that might seem suitable. Hence, the licensee obtains the right to consume this technology in order to produce a specific output. The granting of rights to market or to sell products and services enables the licensee to obtain income from the attributes of this technology. The right to sublicense qualifies the licensee to generate profits from selling thus, alienating the respective technology.

The impact of these different classes of rights derives from the fact that they not only determine the size of the market in which the licensees can operate but also the means by which they can penetrate this market. Furthermore, by a precise and extensive specification of the license, licensee and licensor can reduce uncertainty regarding the rights granted. Based on these considerations, I hypothesize:

Hypothesis 1: The more rights that are granted, the higher the transaction value.

A clear and precise formulation of the rights granted first requires a common understanding of the concepts that describe specific rights and duties. Therefore, every contract contains one section in which definitions of key contractual terms, such as "contracting products" and "transferred rights" are given.

The introduction of definitions for key contractual terms allows a clearly arranged description of the license. Additionally, an extensive definition of these terms again reduces uncertainty during the negotiation period and facilitates an efficient problem-solving process in case of any future problems between the contracting parties. Thus, I assume:

Hypothesis 2: The more accurately that contractual terms are defined, the greater the transaction value.

Having exclusive access to important resources is vital for achieving and securing competitive advantages (Barney, 1991). The highest offer a licensor can make is the grant of an exclusive license to a third party. This decision narrows the window of opportunity for the licensor; in fact, it rules out the possibility of profiting from the feature of nonrivalry in consumption. These limitations drive opportunity-costs considerations. In the presence of an efficient market mechanism, these additional costs should increase the licensor's threshold (Merwin and Warner, 1996). Therefore I hypothesize:

Hypothesis 3: The decision to grant an exclusive license (in contrast to a non-exclusive license) increases the transaction value.

1.4.2 Hypotheses: Contract period

Based on an analysis of 46 contracts, Bessy and Brousseau (1998) identify five different classes of licensing agreements. One feature that distinguishes between these five classes is the existence of contractual terms referring to cross-licenses. In one class, which Bessy and Brousseau (1998) refer to as "development technology licenses," no compensation mechanisms are implemented other than a pure cross-license. In the case of cross-licensing agreements, licensor and licensee may not only consider technology primarily as a source of future revenue but also as a currency or a bargaining chip to be used during the negotiation process in order to achieve their individual objectives (Nickerson, 1996; McEvily et al., 2004). In view of these considerations, I interpret the existence of contractual terms referring to cross-licenses as an equal means to compensate the licensor and, therefore, assume:

Hypothesis 4: Cross-licensing clauses reduce transaction value.

Based on their analysis of the semiconductor and electronics industry, Grindley and Teece (1997) distinguish two types of (cross-) licensing contract: (1) a capture model that entitles the licensee to use all the patents within a technology field, not only during the license period but until they expire, and (2) a fixed-period licensing model, in which the contract is only valid for a predefined life span. In order to prolong this kind of agreement the parties must renegotiate. Grindely and Teece (1997) state that the fixed-period model facilitates greater flexibility since licensor and licensee can periodically adjust the agreement to reflect environmental and technological changes. If both parties agree on a renewal clause, then the existing contract will be automatically renewed after a specific time span. Changes of contractual features will require a renegotiation of the entire contract. Thus, I argue that renewal clauses reduce flexibility and hypothesize:

Hypothesis 5: Renewal clauses reduce transaction value.

Another source of uncertainty is the probability that the existing contract is incomplete. It might be possible that neither party will take all possible future circumstances into account, or that it is too costly to design a contract that reflects all relevant scenarios in sufficient detail (Brynjolfsson, 1994). If contracts are of an incomplete nature, problems may arise such as the unwillingness to fulfill specific contractual duties (Rabin, 1993). In the absence of precise stipulations, these problems can only be solved by costly trials. Therefore, both parties agree upon termination clauses that allow them to react by canceling the respective contract if the environment or their individual situation changes in an unforeseen way. Therefore, I assume:

Hypothesis 6: A high degree of accuracy applied to the definition of termination rules increases transaction value.

1.5 Empirical results

1.5.1 Data collection and transformation

In order to test these hypotheses, I collected 191 single licensing agreements which I obtained by personal contact from various companies active in the electronics industry. I defined five selection criteria to be met by each contract to ensure a high degree of comparability within the sample. First, the contract must have been negotiated by a member of a company-wide licensing department. The existence of a licensing department, either independent or part of a company-wide legal department, is required in order to assure that value exploitation via licensing-out activities is intended to happen on a regular basis. Second, both parties to the contract must have been legally unrelated on the signing date. This criterion is essential for analyzing market transactions at arm's length only and to avoid including intra-firm licensing agreements that define internal transfer prices and may aim at reducing tax payments on a company level (Kopits, 1976). Third, the subject of the contract must either be technological knowledge in explicit form (e.g., a single patent or patent portfolio) or in implicit, thus tacit, form (e.g., training or services). Fourth, I only included contracts that were used to transfer technological knowledge in exchange for (financial) payments in combination with the granting of cross-licenses or financial payments only. I excluded every single purely cross-licensing agreement. Fifth, the licensor's predominant aim must be the commercialization of the value potential embedded in the respective technology. I did not include cases in which licensing agreements served other purposes, e.g., supporting an internationalization strategy.

I carefully went through all contracts and coded them following the model of Srnka and Koeszegi (2007) for transforming qualitative information into quantitative data. This model consists of five separate stages. The first two stages comprise collection and transcription of qualitative data. If the data are already available in written form (as is the case for licensing agreements) these two stages can be omitted. However, most important in these initial stages of the transformation process is creating and ensuring a sufficient degree of comparability within the sample. One major concern here is dealing with language differences. Due to semantic differences and cultural phenomena, comparing documents written in different languages may lead to misinterpretations, which in turn prevent the construction of a comparable dataset. In view of this and since the majority of contracts were drawn up in English, I excluded any licensing agreement written in another language. This reexamination process led to a sample size of 142 contracts.

Stages three (unitization) and four (categorization) focus on defining appropriate units of analysis and on structuring and condensing data. For my sample, I took advantage of the fact that several recurring features and comparable structures can be found in each contract (e.g., the identities of the participating firms, subject of the contract, purpose of the contract, number and characteristics of rights granted, compensation provisions, and time frame). Since I had access to the full text version of the documents, I decided in stage five (coding) to code any common aspect of the contracts. Of course, this implied devoting a considerable amount of time to coding and consistency checks. Such a comprehensive approach allows an in-depth analysis of contractual features, but, given a predefined time span for data collection, it also limits the number of contracts that can be processed.

1.5.2 Definition of variables

1.5.2.1 Dependent variable

In order to calculate the dependent variable "transaction value," I first compute the value of the fixed component by summing up the amount for lump sum payments and the net present value of recurring payments. I then add the net present value of the variable payments based on the royalty schedule defined in the contract and the expected relevant sales volume on the signing date. Finally, I calculate the total value of the licensing agreement as the sum of both the fixed and variable components. Since compensation formulas are defined in two currencies (euro and U.S. dollar), I convert the total euro values into a corresponding U.S.-dollar amount by multiplying the calculated transaction value by the interbank exchange rate effective on the signing date. I assume that both contractual parties either build future expectations about exchange risk on a naïve no-change forecast or apply hedging strategies to avoid currency risks.

As discussed above, compensation formulas comprise four main elements: (1) lump sum payments, (2) recurring amount payments, (3) royalty rate payments, and (4) cross-licenses. All of these elements and combinations of them are found in this sample. The great majority of cases (84.5%) use lump sum payments either as sole compensation mechanism (31.0%) or in combination with royalty rates (26.1%), recurring amount payments (4.2%), or cross-licensing agreements (23.2%).

In the remaining contracts (15.5%), licensee and licensor agree upon more than two compensation mechanisms, such as lump sum, recurring amount, and royalty rate (1.4%); lump sum, royalty rate, and cross-license (10.6%); lump sum, recurring amount, and cross-license (2.8%); and a combination of all four payment schemes (0.7%).

1.5.2.2 Independent variables

From the collection of licensing agreements, I generated six variables which are used for the following empirical analyses. The definition of the license is defined as the number of words used for the description of the license. I assume a positive relationship between the number of words used to describe the license and the rights actually transferred. Of course, this implies that the number of words is not increased by negative formulations such as geographic (or technological) restrictions. Such restrictive clauses are found in a quarter of the contracts (25.4%). In order to create a comparable sample, I carefully read through all contracts and created a net position for this variable by subtracting the number of words used to express restrictions from the total number of words used to describe the license.

I apply the same method of counting and do similar calculations for two other variables. The degree of accuracy in defining key contractual terms equals the number of words used for describing definitions of key contractual terms. I arrive at the degree of accuracy for the definition of termination rules by adding up the number of words used for defining situations in which one party can void the agreement. Contractual terms referring to cross-licenses, renewal options, and exclusive rights enter as dummy variables.

1.5.3 Sample description

Table 18 summarizes the main sample characteristics. The contracts are used to transfer IPRs (patent applications, single patents, patent portfolios, and copyrights) and property rights for inventions, software, software documentation, know-why/how, and hardware.

If the subject of the contract comprises more than just one item (e.g., patent portfolio and know-why/how) I count the number of entries for each variable separately. As can be seen, IPRs play an important role (84.2% of all entries are related to at least one IPR category). In fact, more than half of the entries (52.0%) are connected to a transfer of a portfolio of patents. Furthermore, an analysis of the type of rights granted reveals that in the majority of cases licensors refuse to grant the right to sublicense the subject of contract. I find contractual clauses for exclusive rights in nearly one quarter of all contracts (22.5%).

The earliest date on which licensor and licensee acceded to a licensing agreement was in 1970. However, the majority of contracts were signed either between 1991 and 2000 (47.2%) or 2001 and 2005 (45.8%). This reflects the increasing willingness of companies to extract value from their intellectual assets that we have observed since the late 1980s (Manfroy, 2002).

A final look at geographical restrictions reveals that approximately three-fourths (74.6%) of all contracts contain no explicit geographic restriction and that the rights are granted worldwide. Caves et al. (1983) find geographic restrictions in about one third (34%) of the contracts they investigate and Taylor and Silberston (1973) report that of 29 companies that replied to their question about restrictive provisions, 25 state that they explicitly or implicitly limit the markets in which a product can be sold.

Descriptives		**Number of words**	**Mean**	**Std. Dev.**
Subject of the contract*		Full text	2,666	1,913
Intellectual property rights	84.2%	Preamble	299	364
Patent	15.2%	Definitions	387	491
Patent portfolio	52.0%	License description	262	340
Patent application	15.8%	Compensation formula	275	281
Copyright	1.2%	Termination rules	176	213
Invention	15.8%			
Know-how/why	3.5%			
Software	10.5%			
Software documentation	1.2%			
Hardware	0.6%			
Rights granted*				
Right to produce	31.9%			
Right to use	28.2%			
Right to trade	31.6%			
Right to sublicense	8.4%			
Exclusivity	22.5%			
Technology flow-back requirement	2.1%			
Year of signing				
1970–1980	0.7%			
1981–1990	6.3%			
1991–2000	47.2%			
2001–2005	45.8%			
Geographical extend				
Worldwide	74.6%			
Non-worldwide	25.4%			

* Number of entries per class divided by the total number of entries in the sample.

Table 18: Transferring the economic potential of knowledge (descriptive statistics)

Interviews with licensing managers responsible for the contracts in my sample revealed the fact that a precise formulation of geographical restrictions is often not required or possibly desired. Patent licenses already define the geographical scope in which the licensee can operate (please recall the predominance of IPRs as subject of contract). At the same time, the absence of an explicit formulation of such restrictions can be motivated by the desire to avoid costly renegotiations that occur when the geographical scope of the patent protection is extended after the signing of the contract (see sub-section 1.4.1. in Part II).

1.5.4 Multivariate analysis

Table 19 shows bivariate correlations for all variables. Table 20 reports the results of ordinary least-square regressions for four models with standardized coefficients (beta) and t-values in parentheses. I use SPSS for testing hypotheses and examined the main underlying assumptions of all the statistical tests of hypotheses but found no major violations. In particular, to check for multicollinearity I compute variance inflation factors (for all variables below 2.7) and condition indices (for all variables below 5.0). I begin with a simple model that tests the impact of the breadth of rights granted, the degree of accuracy applied for defining key contractual terms, and the exclusivity of rights. For each of the following four models I add one additional variable; the final model (IV) comprises all variables.

A first look at the results of the full specified model IV ($R^2_{adj.}$ 0.28, $p < 0.01$) shows strong support for hypothesis 1. The breadth of rights granted has a positive and significant ($\beta = 0.44$; $p < 0.01$) effect on the value of a licensing agreement. We also observe a positive and significant ($\beta = 0.24$; $p < 0.05$) relationship between the degree of accuracy applied in defining key contractual terms and the dependent variable. Furthermore, statistical analyses reveal a negative and significant relationship between the value of a licensing agreement and the degree of accuracy applied for defining termination rules ($\beta = -0.26$; $p < 0.01$) and the existence of prolongation clauses ($\beta = -0.16$; $p < 0.05$).

	Variable	1	2	3	4	5	6	7
1	Value	1						
2	Definition of license	0.489 *	1					
3	Definition of key contractual terms	0.351 *	0.544 *	1				
4	Exclusivity of rights	-0.100	-0.164 *	-0.287 *	1			
5	Cross license	0.329 *	0.461 *	0.626 *	-0.306 *	1		
6	Termination	0.086	0.345 *	0.654 *	-0.342 *	0.419 *	1	
7	Duration	0.036	0.317 *	0.247 *	-0.148	0.250 *	0.153	1

* Correlation is significant at the 0.01 level (two-tailed)

Table 19: Transferring the economic potential of knowledge (correlation matrix)

Variable	Model I	Model II	Model III	Model IV
Constant	0.00 (-1.203)	0.00 (-1.355)	0.00 (-0.365)	0.00 (-0.303)
Definition of license	0.42 *** (4.814)	0.41 *** (4.539)	0.40 *** (4.588)	0.44 *** (4.97)
Definition of key contractual terms	0.12 (1.345)	0.07 (0.689)	0.23 * (1.936)	0.24 ** (2.031)
Exclusivity of rights (0/1)	0.00 (0.05)	-0.02 (-0.23)	-0.03 (-0.32)	-0.04 (-0.474)
Cross license (0/1)		0.10 (1.058)	0.10 (1.031)	0.11 (1.196)
Termination			-0.25 ** (-2.573)	-0.26 *** (-2.653)
Prolongation / renewal option (0/1)				-0.16 ** (-2.061)
Beta values (*t*-values)				
N	142	142	142	142
F-Value	15.29 ***	11.75 ***	11.11 ***	10.19 ***
R^2	0.249	0.256	0.290	0.312
$R^2_{adj.}$	0.233	0.234	0.264	0.281
Delta $R^2_{adj.}$		0.001	0.030	0.017

*** $p < .01$
** $p < .05$
* $p < .10$

Table 20: Transferring the economic potential of knowledge (results from OLS-regression analysis)

1.6 Discussion

The first research question addressed in this paper focuses on the effectiveness of the market mechanism for knowledge. An effective market mechanism in turn requires that the traded goods exhibit a degree of homogeneity sufficient for a deduction of values and prices through comparative analyses. This criterion of homogeneity comprises two important aspects. First, we may expect a positive correlation between the quantity or significance of qualitative features of a good and its price. Second, homogeneity implies that market participants share a common understanding of the good's nature and its features. It is widely recognized that market prices therefore serve as good indicators for the value of goods traded on an open and competitive market. Hayek argues that this basic function of the price system is what initially enables a transaction (Hayek, 1945). Consequently valuation techniques based on market data are claimed to be the most suitable approach for determining the value of assets (see 3.3 in Part III).

The intangible nature of knowledge assets can lead to a high degree of uncertainty about their intrinsic value and severe appropriation problems. Hence, the existence of an effective market mechanism for these assets is often denied. Given the results for the first two hypotheses, I cannot support this view. The positive impact on transaction values, I find for both the breadth of rights granted and the clarification of key contractual terms, indicates that a sufficient degree of homogeneity is achievable. This in turn supports the idea of an effective market mechanism.

Furthermore, we may interpret the results for the second hypothesis also with regard to the overall uncertainty, licensor and licensee face during the negotiation and contract period. A reduction of uncertainty through clarification of key contractual terms seems not only possible but also valuable. In view of this, we may conclude that licensing agreements are a suitable tool to exploit the value of knowledge assets.

For patents this result may be less surprising. The underlying idea of a patent is to disclose information to the public, hence to create a common understanding about the quality of the invention. Each invention must meet several fundamental and procedural requirements defined by national patent laws in order to qualify for patent protection. Together with the strong harmonization of national patent laws during the last decades (Jaffe, 2000) these requirements facilitate a certain degree of comparability of various patent rights and thus ensure a minimum level of homogeneity (see also chapter 1 in

Part II). However, in many cases, patents only cover a fraction of the competitive advantages rooted in technological knowledge. In industries with cumulative technologies, in particular, companies need access to unprotected know why and know how in order to fully exploit the value potential of knowledge assets. Licensing agreements seem to be able to deal with the singularity of all these different knowledge assets and to resolve related appropriation problems. Therefore, these findings can also contribute to the debate about the best ways to protect knowledge (see also section 3.3 in Part I).

Licensing agreements are negotiated by highly skilled knowledge workers (Drucker, 1999, 84) using meta-knowledge[12] to evaluate the subject of contract. They first of all enable and facilitate any transfer between licensee and licensor. In view of my results for the first hypothesis, we may conclude that these experts are able to successfully establish a positive relationship between the breadth of rights the licensor grants and the financial value of a contract during the negotiation period. In addition, their function as intermediaries can lead to another interpretation. Given their extensive knowledge about patent rights and other technological knowledge assets, they can guarantee a considerable level of quality in any technology-valuation process. Thus, in the absence of an open and active market, valuation by experts is an appropriate strategy to assess the value for a knowledge asset and allows effective market-like transactions. For patent valuation this implies that information contained in licensing agreements, in particular on compensation schemes (e.g. royalty rates), is highly useful to come to a reasonable value conclusion.

The results for selected contractual features, such as the exclusivity of rights granted (hypothesis three) and the decision to grant cross-licenses (hypothesis four), reveal a small, negative, although insignificant, relationship with respect to the exclusivity of the rights granted. Thus, based on this sample, I cannot confirm hypothesis three. However, this negative relationship is in line with previous empirical results. Kim and Vorontas (2004) show that the complexity of a given technology negatively affects the tendency to grant exclusive licenses. In industries such as the electronics industry, in which cumulative technologies are used, IPRs are weaker and harder to enforce than in industries with discrete technologies. In fact, patent owners in this industry report a lower reliance on the protection of technology through IPRs (Mansfield, 1986; Cohen et al., 2000). However, if IPRs are weak then offering and granting exclusive rights might be less favorable than in other industries with less complex technologies.

[12] Meta-knowledge can be defined as knowledge used in order to assess value and reliability of knowledge as a resource (Spender, 1996; Kakabadse et al., 2001).

In view of the results for hypothesis four, it seems as if cross-licenses have no significant impact on transaction values. This can be explained by the specific characteristics of the electronic industry. Grindley and Tecce (1997) report that in cumulative industries such as electronics, innovations are strongly interconnected. They further argue that this dependency creates mutually blocking patent portfolios leading to a “Mexican standoff” (Grindley and Teece, 1997, 11). In such a situation one major objective is to obtain freedom to operate in a certain technology field. In a recent study on drivers of technology licensing, Lichtenthaler (2007) finds that ensuring freedom to operate is the most important driver of licensing decisions in the three industries (automotive and machinery, chemicals and pharmaceuticals, electronics and semiconductors) investigated (Lichtenthaler, 2007, 73–74). Grindley and Nickerson (1996) state that cross-licensing terms are used in order to solve this mutual blockade. Therefore, granting cross-licenses can be interpreted as a precondition to be met before entering negotiations rather than as a significant value driver.

Furthermore, Anand and Khanna (2000) argue that due to this weakness of IPRs companies working in this industry exhibit in general a higher tendency to grant cross-licenses. Since weak IPRs induce substantial imitation and inventing-around activities by competitors, cross-licensing agreements might be an efficient contracting mechanism in order to avoid costs for reengineering (Anand and Khanna, 2000) and expensive infringement trials. Although Mansfield, Schwartz & Wagner (1981, 913) and Levin, Klevorick, Nelson & Winter (1987, 811) report that patents generally raise imitation costs by only 7 to 15 percentage points in electronics, the probability of litigation including an unfavorable court decision can motivate cross-licensing (Ordover, 1991).

For the negotiation period, we might summarize that two indicators describing the content and range of the rights transferred have a positive and significant impact on transaction values. Turning to the results for the variables of the contract period, the negative and significant relationship between the existence of prolongation clauses and the value of an agreement seems to support the idea that licensor and licensee wish to maintain a high degree of flexibility. Although situations might be possible in which the one party (e.g., licensor) would profit from an extension of the contract at the expense of the second party, this result implies that both parties create negative expectations regarding the future profitability of their present decisions. Two reasons can explain these pessimistic expectations. First, given the predominance of IPRs as subject of transfer in this sample, one important aspect can be that the quality, thus the value, of a patent is not proven until it has been found valid through an infringement trial (Sherry and Teece, 2004). Second, in a world of rapid technological progress, it is generally difficult to create reliable and consistent expectations about how a present decision affects the economic situation of the contracting party in the future.

The results of the statistical analyses do not confirm hypothesis six. Transaction values, in fact, decrease with an increase in the degree of accuracy for defining termination rules. This implies that both contracting parties cannot fully rule out uncertainties during the contracting period. Additional support for this idea comes from Bessy and Brousseau (1998), who argue that uncertainty is reflected in the application of an average royalty fee level. In order to determine whether the royalty rates in this sample differ from average royalty rates, I compared these with royalty rates published by Taylor and Silberston (1973), Contractor (1981), Parr (1995), and Battersby and Grimes (2006) and found no significant differences. Additionally, each agreement can be – as with any other contract – subject to moral hazard problems. In the case of knowledge transfer, Bessy and Brousseau (1998) argue that it might be nearly impossible to create *ex ante* incentive schemes or to implement supervision mechanisms in order to avoid or resolve hidden action problems. Therefore, it is possible to conclude that due to uncertainty and limited information (Caves et al., 1983) – not only about the technology but also about the behavior of each party and the economic consequences of this behavior – licensor and licensee will create prudent expectations and consequently underestimate the economic potential embedded in the licensed technology during the contract period.

1.7 Conclusion and further research

This in-depth analysis of licensing agreements supports the idea of an effective market mechanism for technology transfer. The prices for property rights to knowledge assets are driven by the breadth of the rights granted. Furthermore, it seems that a reduction of uncertainty through an increase of the degree of accuracy in defining key contractual terms has a positive impact on transaction value. My results in fact indicate that licensor and licensee deal with two different kinds of uncertainty. The first type of uncertainty, which I refer to as uncertainty during the negotiation period, can be reduced by choosing appropriate contractual terms. Dealing with the second type, uncertainty during the contract period, seems to be more challenging.

However, the explorative nature of this research design and the focus on one industry reduce the degree to which these findings can be generalized. Lichtenthaler's study (2007) shows that licensing activities in selected industries are motivated by various factors, but he finds no significant industry differences in the relative importance of most drivers of technology licensing. However, turning to the specific features of licensing contracts, prior studies have already revealed certain cross-industry differences. Since cross-licenses play a major role in the electronics industry, the application of this research design to other industries and the analysis of differences between industries could lead to valuable insights.

2 On the reliability of indirect patent valuation – Testing bibliographic value indicators with patent market values

Section 3.2 of Part III presents a literature review on indirect patent valuation. The main weakness of such an approach is the measurement of patent values, which in turn affects the reliability of existing empirical evidence on patent value drivers. With this analysis, I attempt to overcome these measurement problems using data from a real market transaction to test the impact of known indicators on the market values of patents. I analyze a unique set of fair market values for a portfolio of 201 patent families (1,127 national patent rights) that had been transferred in 2006. An analysis of this market transaction has two main advantages. First, the availability of patent values for each single patent family allows a direct analysis of the relationship between value and patent rights at the level of single inventions. Second, market values represent one of the best estimates for objective patent values (see also sub-subsection 3.3.1.2 in Part III).

The empirical analysis builds on theoretical considerations discussed in Part II and Part III of the thesis. In order to reduce redundancy, I will only briefly describe the theoretical background before presenting and discussing the results.

In Part II, I extend the model of Harhoff et al. (2003a) by introducing the degree of diffusion as a second major value driver for patent rights and by adding a new value construct (competition value; see Part II, subsection 2.3.1). As can be seen from the theoretical model, patent values are first of all driven by the underlying value construct and by the strength of the patent regime and the degree of diffusion. In the following analysis of asset values, I present values for both strength of exclusion and degree of diffusion to support comparison with subsequent studies. Patent values are measured following the asset value construct (see subsection 2.3 in Part II).

An earlier version of this paper was presented in August 2007 at the 67th Annual Meeting of the Academy of Management in Philadelphia. I thank two anonymous reviewers for their helpful comments.

2.1 Sample description

The portfolio protects technology embodied in complex systems for measurement and control. Along with European patents and some national patent rights in single European countries, I also find a small subsample (< 4%) of Japanese and U.S. patents. The necessary bibliographic information used to test my hypotheses was gathered from original patent documents. These documents can be collected from the electronic resources of patent authorities.[13] The majority of patent rights (66.89%) are classified in IPC section G (physics). The remaining rights fall in sections F (mechanical engineering, lighting, heating, weapons, and blasting; 19.51%), H (electricity; 11.42%), C (chemistry, metallurgy; 1.51%), B (performing operations, transporting; 0.94%) and E (fixed constructions; 0.09%). Within section G, I find the following classes: G08 (signaling; 46.62%), G01 (measuring, testing; 27.04%), G05 (controlling, regulating; 23.24), G06 (computing, calculating, and counting; 1.90), G02 (optics; 0.70), and G04 (horology; 0.49).

The independent variables of the following analyses result from the literature review on bibliographic value indicators (see section 3.2 in Part III). The market values of each of the 201 patent families enter as dependent variable. These market values follow from a multi-stage valuation project. First, every single patent family was matched with all products and product families that used – or were produced using – the protected invention. In a second step, controlling experts and senior product managers were asked to determine for each product family its current life cycle position and to forecast the expected economic benefits for the valuation period. Patent-related risk factors could be explicitly modeled by using the results of a standardized questionnaire sent in advance to inventors and patent attorneys responsible for the patent portfolio. This questionnaire contained a series of statements concerning the attractiveness of the patented invention, the likelihood of inventing around activities, and the probability of successful patent litigation activities. Respondents were asked to specify their level of agreement to a statement on a seven-point Likert scale. I use the results of this questionnaire to measure the quality of patent protection (mean value for λ: 0.66). Values for the rate of diffusion (mean value for μ: 0.71) come from a series of interviews with

[13] The main source of patent documents was espacenet, the patent database of the European Patent Office.

product managers and specialists of the patent department, who are responsible for monitoring R&D efforts and patent strategies of major competitors. Given this detailed and systematic valuation approach and since the results were checked and audited by a team of certified public accountants, I assume these values to be fair market values (see section 1.2 in Part I) and reliable estimates for patent values. In order to overcome the criticism raised against the indirect approach (see subsection 3.3.2 in Part II), I use them to review the impact of a set of patent value indicators that have been analyzed in the past.

2.2 Development of hypotheses

During the patent-granting procedure, the responsible patent examiner investigates whether the invention meets the essential requirements of the patent law (see also chapter 1 in Part II). Under European patent law, the two most important thresholds are "novelty" and "inventive step" (the U.S. patent law contains similar criteria like "novelty" and "non-obviousness"). In order to determine whether or not an invention is new and contains an inventive step (or is not obvious) both patent applicant and patent examiner refer to the state of the art (prior art) by citing existing patents and other scientific and technical publications. The core idea of these "backward" citations is to describe the background of the invention and how it differs from already existing public knowledge. Citations to patents and other documents, such as scientific articles, are listed on the first page of the patent document. This allows us to investigate the impact of each citation type separately.

Citations to scientific literature seem to positively correlate with excellence in science and technology (Narin et al., 1987). In addition, other empirical results indicate that they also positively correlate with patent values (Carpenter et al., 1980; Harhoff et al., 1997; Narin et al., 1997). They can be interpreted as an indicator for the relatedness of an invention to new scientific knowledge and discoveries. I therefore expect a positive relationship between the number of scientific citations and patent values:

H_1: Patent values increase with the number of scientific citations.

Citations to other patent documents can be analyzed from two different perspectives. They are first of all used to determine the likelihood of a patent litigation (Lanjouw and Schankerman, 2001; Harhoff and Reitzig, 2004; Reitzig, 2004a). A high probability of patent litigation might, in turn, reduce patent values. At the same time, patent citations can also be viewed as an indicator of the attractiveness of the technological field and the economic potential of an invention. Harhoff et al. (1997) find evidence for a positive relationship between patent values and citations to other patents. I therefore assume that:

H_2: Patent values increase with the number of patent citations.

If an inventor files an application with the European Patent Office, a patent examiner begins a search to define the prior art in order to determine whether or not the invention fulfils the substantial requirements of novelty and inventive step. The results of this examination process are listed in a search report (see also subsection 1.3.2 in Part II). This search report thus contains any documents (patents, scientific articles, etc.) that may question the novelty or inventive step of the patent claims. Furthermore, these documents are marked with an "*A*," "*Y*," or "*X*." *A*-references indicate a state of the art not prejudicial to the novelty or inventive step of the claimed invention. *Y*-references refer to documents that in combination with one or more other documents are harmful to novelty, and *X*-references describe documents that on a stand-alone basis negatively affect novelty or inventive step (Schmoch, 1993; Meyer, 2000; Muir et al., 2002). Since *A*-citations are of an explicative nature (Schmoch, 1993), I do not expect to see a significant impact on patent values. However, for *Y*- and *X*-citations, a negative relationship between these variables and patent values seems plausible, leading to the following set of hypotheses:

H_{3a}: Patent values decrease with the number of Y-references.

H_{3b}: Patent values decrease with the number of X-references.

Inventions are made by inventors. Their intellect, education, and experience drive the quality of the invention. Due to the limited capacity of the human brain and the complexity of new technological solutions, the development of sophisticated goods and services generally involves the cooperation of various specialists (Grant, 1996a) and teams (Weinkauf et al., 2004). Guellec and Pottelsberghe de la Potterie (2000) and Reitzig and Burke (2007) find that the probability of a patent grant is higher if the invention was made by more than one inventor. Since patent examiners closely control that an application meets the essential and formal requirements of the respective patent law, it seems plausible to assume that the quality of an invention is positively correlated with the number of inventors. In a recent study, Harhoff and Hoisl (2007) find that the more inventors there are named on the first page of the patented document, the higher a patent's value seems to be (Harhoff and Hoisl, 2007, 1159). In view of these results, I hypothesize:

H_4: Patent values increase with the number of inventors.

Along with the maximum duration of patent protection, the breadth of a patent defines its monopoly power (Gilbert and Shapiro, 1990). Lerner (1994) uses the number of four-digit IPC classes to measure the scope of patents and finds a significant and positive relationship between scope and firm value. However, a closer look at the structure of the IPC hierarchy (Vijvers, 1990) shows that the number of IPC classes might be more related to the diversity of an invention (Guellec and van Pottelsberghe de la Potterie, 2000). Thus, the number of IPC classes does not measure patent breadth but rather signals that it protects a multi-purpose invention. I use the number of IPC classes to measure this degree of diversity of an invention and assume that:

H_5: The broader "the scope" of a patent the higher its value.

Since the number of patent claims delineates the boundaries of the patent, they seem to be a more precise measure for the breadth of patents (Reitzig, 2004a). Empirical results already indicate a significant relationship between number of claims and various macroeconomic variables (Tong and Frame, 1994) and between number of claims and the likelihood of opposition (Harhoff and Reitzig, 2004) and litigation (Lanjouw, 1998). Thus, I hypothesize:

H_6: Patent values increase with the number of claims.

The maximum period during which a patent can be maintained in force is twenty years if patentees regularly pay the required renewal fees (see subsection 1.1.1 in Part II). For a patent at a given age α, the value relevance of α can be investigated using two distinct approaches. First, we can interpret α as the period during which patentees generated income from the patented invention in the past. In this case and all else being equal, we expect older patents to be more valuable, and thus expect to see a positive relationship between α and patent value. This relationship has been validated by previous research (Pakes, 1986; Schankerman and Pakes, 1986; Reitzig, 2004b). Second, if a patent is sold, not past income but future returns are driving its value. The patent values in my sample reflect the net present value of the future income streams a patent holder can expect from the protected technology. In this case the inverse relationship should thus apply. I measure patent age in months and assume:

H_7: Patent values decrease with patent age.

Patents are national rights. An inventor must file for a patent in each country where patent protection is desired. Multinational treaties such as the Patent Cooperation

Treaty (PCT) and regional patents such as the European Patent support patentees in receiving international protection for their invention (see chapter 1 of Part II). Clearly, patent protection in more than one country extends the monopolistic position of a patent holder.

A patent family comprises all patents and patent applications of a patentee that protect the same invention in multiple countries. Putnam (1996) was the first to analyze this phenomenon of family size and finds a positive relationship between patent values and the number of countries in which patentees apply for patent protection (Putnam, 1996; Lanjouw et al., 1998). Additional validation comes from Harhoff et al. (1999) who also report a positive relationship between the logarithm of family size and patent values. Therefore, I assume that:

H_8: Patent values increase with family size.

2.3 Empirical results

As already mentioned above, patent values follow a skewed distribution (see sub-subsection 3.2.2 in Part III). In view of the model proposed by Schankerman and Pakes (1986, 1061), Hall, Jaffe and Trajtenberg (2005), Barney (2002), Harhoff, Scherer and Vopel (2003b), and Lanjouw and Schankerman (2004), I log-transform all variables.[14] Prior to running ordinary least-squares regressions for testing hypotheses, I examined the main underlying assumptions of all the statistical tests of hypotheses and found no major violations. To check in particular for multicollinearity, I computed variance inflation factors (VIF; for all variables below 1.88). Table 21 shows means, standard deviations, and correlations of all variables in this study. Table 22 summarizes the results of several regression analyses.

I report three different models here. Model one contains data collected from the patent document ($R^2_{adj.}$: .136; p < .01). In model two ($R^2_{adj.}$: .134; $p < .01$), I substitute the number of patent citations and scientific references by the number of *A*-, *Y*-, and *X*-

[14] I did not compute the number of times patents in the patent portfolio are cited by following patents (forward citations). The use of forward citations as a measure for the impact of a single patents on subsequent patent rights facilitates the identification of patents that are of particular relevance for a given technological field (Trajtenberg, 1990; Albert et al., 1991). It is plausible to assume that these patent rights are valuable (see Table 14 on page 153). At the same time, however, all else being equal, older patents are more likely to show higher numbers of forward citations than younger patents. Not only because of their significance for subsequent patents but also simply because of their longer existence. Given that the majority of patents in my sample is comparatively young, not enough data for reliably testing the impact of forward citations was available at the time of writing this paper.

citations from European search reports, since the number of citations to other patents and documents alone does not shed light on the quality of a reference and the degree to which this reference influences the patented invention (Schmoch, 1993, 195). Model three ($R^2_{adj.}$: .169; $p < .01$) combines all variables of model one and model two.

I find significant results for six variables, namely, family size, patent age, number of scientific citations, number of *Y*-references, scope of patents, and number of inventors.

	Variable	Mean	Standard deviation	1	2	3	4	5	6	7	8	9	10	11
1	LOGVALUE	5.847	.816	1										
2	LOGNUMINV	.217	.216	-.183*	1									
3	LOGCLAIMS	.963	.203	.010	.321**	1								
4	LOGSCOPE	.259	.257	.175	.043	-.143	1							
5	LOGAGE	.800	.396	-.238**	.053	-.213*	-.091	1						
6	LOGFAMSIZE	.909	.367	.051	.084	.453**	-.366**	-.040	1					
7	LOGCITSCI	.184	.251	.188*	-.011	-.173	.182*	-.049	-.430**	1				
8	LOGCITPAT	.641	.225	.022	.082	.228*	.065	-.245**	.163	.123	1			
9	LOGCITX	.116	.191	-.090	.088	.206*	.057	-.141	.250**	-.201*	.136	1		
10	LOGCITY	.124	.230	-.206*	.016	.197*	-.184*	-.013	.216*	-.049	.238**	.208*	1	
11	LOGCITA	.405	.326	-.105	.034	.268**	-.104	.180*	.421**	-.199*	.409**	.215*	.203*	1

* Correlation is significant at the 0.05 level (two-tailed).

** Correlation is significant at the 0.01 level (two-tailed).

[1] Log(euro)
[2] Log(number of inventors on patent document)
[3] Log(number of claims)
[4] Log(number of IPC classes)
[5] Log(number of months)
[6] Log(family size)
[7] Log(1+number of references to scientific literature)
[8] Log(1+number of references to other patents)
[9] Log(1+number of *X*-references)
[10] Log(1+number of *Y*-references)
[11] Log(1+number of *A*-references)

Table 21: On the reliability of indirect patent valuation (correlation matrix)

	Model I		Model II		Model III	
Independent Variable[a]	β^b	VIF^c	β^b	VIF^c	β^b	VIF^c
LOGNUMINV	-.196** (-2.188)	1.154	-.200** (-2.219)	1.164	-.207** (-2.335)	1.173
LOGCLAIM	.009 (.092)	1.514	.046 (.443)	1.554	.047 (.459)	1.555
LOGSCOPE	.222** (2.436)	1.194	.219** (2.358)	1.240	.210** (2.291)	1.255
LOGAGE	-.207** (-2.330)	1.136	-.193** (-2.113)	1.191	-.180* (-1.898)	1.347
LOGFAMSIZE	.267** (2.443)	1.715	.224** (2.072)	1.674	.322*** (2.867)	1.881
LOGCITSCI	.265*** (2.792)	1.289			.246*** (2.604)	1.328
LOGCITPAT	-.105 (-1.159)	1.175			-.023 (-.225)	1.535
LOGCITX			-.122 (-1.341)	1.177	-.090 (-1.003)	1.200
LOGCITY			-.180** (-2.031)	1.127	-.194** (-.031)	1.173
LOGCITA			-.084 (-.861)	1.365	-.074 (-.695)	1.699
R^2	.185		.190		.236	
$R^2_{adj.}$	.136		.134		.169	
p	<.01		<.01		<.01	
n	201		201		201	

[a] Dependent variable: LOG(Patent value)
[b] *t*-values in parentheses
[c] Variance Inflation Factor
* $p < .10$
** $p < .05$
*** $p < .01$

Table 22: On the reliability of indirect patent valuation (results from OLS-regression analysis)

2.4 Discussion

The significant result for the relationship between family size and patent values in all three models further validates family size as a driver for patent values (see also sub-subsection 3.2.2 in Part III). Given the theoretical background of this relationship and the existing empirical evidence, this result is not surprising. However, since we use fair market values here, we can furthermore interpret this result to be an indicator for an efficient market mechanism for patents and patent portfolios.

The significant, negative relationship between patent age and value is not in line with the positive relationship shown by existing empirical evidence (Pakes, 1986; Schankerman and Pakes, 1986; Reitzig, 2004b). However, these results do not contradict previous research since I do not measure past income but focus on future returns from patents. Clearly, since patent terms cannot exceed twenty years, patent values based on paid renewal fees or past income increase with age whereas values measured as net present values of future income streams decrease with age. This, however, does not imply that assessing values by analyzing renewal decisions and using appropriate fee schedules is inadequate or will become redundant. Serious patent portfolio management should always follow the basic economic principle of optimizing cost and benefits of patent protection. Thus, the decision about maintaining a patent should reflect a positive tradeoff between cost and expected benefits. Renewal decisions are therefore a valuable source of information when no other information about the patent strategy is at hand.

In models one and three I find a highly significant, positive relationship between the number of scientific citations and patent values as predicted given the results of previous studies. A closer look at the results for the number of patent citations shows a negative impact on patent values within the sample. However, since these results are not significant I cannot reject the idea of patent references as being a good indicator for an attractive and established market for technology.

In addition to this quantitative citation analysis, I test the relationship between patent values and qualitative indicators from European search reports in models two and three. Given the low beta and *t*-values for *A*-references in both models, they do not seem to have any impact on patent values. In two recent studies, Reitzig (2004a) and Harhoff and Reitzig (2004) report similar results for the relationship between this variable and the likelihood of opposition to European patents. As for references marked

"*X*" and "*Y*," I find support for the hypothesis of a negative relationship between *Y*-references and patent values. The beta value for *X*-references is negative as predicted, but insignificant. Harhoff and Reitzig (2004) find a positive, though insignificant, relationship between *X*-type citations and the likelihood of opposition. I also used the share of citations marked with an "*X*" among the total number of citations (Reitzig, 2004a), but neither sign nor level of significance changed. One explanation for this insignificant result for *X*-type citations and the significant finding for *Y*-citations could be the fact that the portfolio covers cumulative technologies. These technologies are characterized by complex interactions, which in turn can lead to mutual dependencies between several patents or scientific documents that are described by *Y*-citations (see also subsection 1.3.2 in Part II). All in all, my results indicate that some qualitative indicators from European search reports might be useful for determining patent values. Clearly, more empirical research is needed to finally decide about the reliability of these indicators.

The "scope" variable shows a positive and significant impact in all three models. However, please recall that I do not measure the breadth of patent rights with this variable, as first proposed by Lerner (1994), but rather the degree of diversity of an invention. The results support the conclusion that inventions that can be used in more than one technological field and for the production of a wider range of products are more highly valued than single-purpose inventions.[15] In order to measure patent breadth, I used the number of claims and find small positive but insignificant beta values in all three models; therefore we cannot make a final decision about the reliability of this indicator.

The number of inventors shown on the first page of a patent document seems to have a significant negative impact on patent values. However, this result should be interpreted with caution. The idea of a positive relationship between the number of inventors and patent values rests on the assumption that R&D engineers with individual skills might effectively work together in a team and together be more productive or creative than they would be if all were working on their own. Using the number of inventors might be an inappropriate measure for this team excellence since it implies that all R&D engineers are equally productive. Empirical results, however, show that individual performance within a team of R&D engineers is not equally distributed and that Lotka's law (Lotka, 1926) also applies for R&D personnel. According to this law, the number

[15] Of course, this line of reasoning implicitly assumes a comparable legal quality of several patents.

of scientists producing n papers is proportional to $1/n^2$. For every 100 authors who publish scientific papers within a given period of time, there are, e.g., 25 researchers producing two papers, 11 who publish three, and four who publish five articles. Several authors have analyzed the relationship between R&D personnel and patents and found that the majority of patented inventions is made by a rather small fraction of R&D engineers (Narin, 1993; Narin and Breitzmann, 1995; Ernst et al., 2000; Mariani and Romanelli, 2007). Thus, only a small number of highly skilled key inventors are responsible for the technological performance and competitiveness of a company. Several models and measures for evaluating the quality of R&D engineers using patent data haven been proposed (Narin and Breitzmann, 1995; Ernst et al., 2000; Moehrle et al., 2005). Based on these models, I computed alternative measures for the quality of inventors, but the result (not reported here) did not change and I still found a negative relationship. Of course, this negative relationship could also be partly due to the fact that patents with more than one inventor may be traded at discount. Although patents do reveal information about inventions, a potential buyer cannot acquire the corresponding tacit knowledge or know-how that is crucial for fully exploiting the protected technology. This tacit knowledge might, in fact, be even more valuable than the patent right, but as we know from previous studies, its transfer between two individuals is costly and uncertain (Kogut and Zander, 1992; Grant, 1996a). As already discussed in subsection 3.2.1 of Part I, the acquisition of valuable tacit knowledge in many cases requires the recruitment of an expert (Almeida and Kogut, 1999; Song et al., 2003). Thus, the more inventors that are involved, the more tacit knowledge might be needed to successfully make use of an invention and the less valuable the patent right on a stand-alone base will be. Finally, theoretical and empirical research on innovation processes show that two different types of individuals support innovations, promoters and champions. Promoters have a deep understanding of a particular technological field and can quickly recognize business opportunities even in mature technologies. Champions, on the contrary, exhibit a high degree of architectural or general knowledge to overcome barriers to innovation. Hence, they are particularly successful in fostering radical innovations (Rost et al., 2007, 345ff.). If these two types of individuals exist among the inventors named on a patent document then inventors are not alike. This in turn contradicts the basic assumption of the fourth hypothesis. Consequently the results for the impact of inventors on patent values may be biased.

2.5 Conclusion and further research

All in all, I find further evidence that information contained in patent documents might be a valuable source for determining the economic value of a patent. The application of bibliographic indicators to real-market values further validates the size of the family, its age, the number of scientific citations, the number of *Y*-references, its degree of diversity ("scope"), and the number of inventors.

Of course, with this sample the focus of analysis is on one patent portfolio of one company. Hence, I cannot control for any company- or industry-specific features. However, the calculation of specific values for the degree of diffusion and the strength of the patent system may be of use for conducting comparative analyses with other studies.

In view of the increasing demand for efficient valuation techniques, my results indicate that the quality and value potential of patents can – at least to some extent – be measured by applying patent value indicator analysis. However, since patent values are not solely driven by the technological features of an invention but also by the economic profitability of a new technology and by the legal strength of the respective patent, comprehensive valuation approaches and further empirical research are needed for increasing our understanding of the monetary value of patents.

Conclusion

New knowledge is the most valuable commodity on earth.
The more truth we have to work with, the richer we become
(Kurt Vonnegut, 1922–2007)

Knowledge is valuable. This finding is far from new. From the early days of the first *homo sapiens* to the century of the digital revolution, knowledge has played a key role in fostering economic and social progress. After the predominance of industrial production capabilities in the last centuries, modern economies are more and more based on knowledge assets. Under the paradigm of the resource-based view of the firm, the value of knowledge mainly derives from its intangible nature. This intangibility allows scalability in use and non-rivalry in consumption. In combination with increasing demand for technologically sophisticated products, knowledge has become a major driver for creating and maintaining competitive advantages and sustainable firm success.

In view of this, it is quite surprising that modern economic theory and epistemology fail to provide us with a clear definition for the concept of knowledge. Needless to say, any valuation of any kind of asset or resource first of all requires a clear and precise description of the valuation object. Thus, for this thesis I reviewed both philosophical and economic approaches to knowledge in an attempt to develop a suitable definition.

My definition of knowledge, *the interpretation of facts by the mind of a human being*, highlights two important aspects. First, knowledge is a composite construct that combines external, objective facts with a subjective attitude towards these facts. Second, facts form part of what economic theory usually refers to as explicit knowledge. In contrast to this, implicit or tacit knowledge is driven by the (interpretative) skills and intellectual capabilities of a knowing individual. Clearly, this interaction between (objective) facts and subjective interpretations calls into question any aspect of objectivity with regard to of knowledge. In fact, this objectivity – or more generally, any kind of truth – depends on the similarity of subjective attitudes towards external facts.

An analysis of the content of facts and the impact of implicit parts of knowledge further leads to a definition of four types or levels of knowledge: *know-what*, *know-why*, *know-how*, and *know-who*. The first level, know-what, comprises facts only. The combination and arrangement of a set of various facts by theory leads to the second level, know-why. The third level, know-how, combines theoretical understanding of the relationships between various facts with the skills of an individual. The last level, know-who, contains facts about the knowledge of other individuals.

The emphasis put on the subjectivity of knowledge is in keeping with the economic understanding of the basic functioning of a market system. Based on the assumption of rationally acting economic agents, transactions in a free-market economy require divergent expectations or interpretations regarding the utility or value of external facts. Any quantitative valuation of a resource therefore lies in the eye of the beholder and depends on subjective opinions and assumptions. Strictly speaking, valuation means to apply very specific knowledge about valuation methods, content, and characteristics of the valuation object. Consequently, a reliable valuation comprises three success factors: (1) A sound qualitative analysis of the valuation object and the surrounding economic situation, (2) a clear and transparent transformation of key qualitative findings into numeric values, and (3) a precise implementation of the underlying valuation model trough an adequate valuation formula.

The application of these generic analyses of knowledge and value to patent rights constitutes the core of this thesis. Patents represent one means to protect knowledge-based competitive advantages within the borders of selected countries for a definite period of time. They constitute one option for overcoming problems of appropriating economic rents from knowledge assets. More precisely, they can be used to protect and appropriate benefits resulting from technological inventions. However, in order to assess – i.e., know – their value, it is vital to understand two aspects. First, in many cases patented inventions are only one part of a business success story. In complex technologies, complementary knowledge assets – unprotected know why, know-how, and know-who – are needed to fully exploit a technologically sophisticated and economically attractive field. Second, patent valuation is primarily based on expectations – or subjective interpretations – of the development and impact of current and future economic variables and facts.

Patents have a long history. The origin of multiple national patent systems can be traced back to the 14th century and the first patent law in Venice. A review of fundamental and procedural requirements of the patent systems in Germany, Europe, and the United States shows that the internationalization of business activities has been accompanied by a strong trend toward harmonization of national patent rights. Today, the core of patent protection consists of a patentee's right to exclude any third party from taking advantage of new technological knowledge or know-why for a definite period of time. From an economic point of view, any patent value depends on two factors: the strength of this exclusive right and the marketability – or more generally speaking – the value potential of the protected invention. Only the combination of a profitable product or process innovation with a strong exclusive right leads to high patent values.

Obtaining patent rights is costly. In exchange for a temporal superior position, patentees must fully disclose their invention to the public. In addition to costs for applying, maintaining, and defending patent rights, this disclosure of private knowledge to competitors and the resulting publicity about research and development efforts represent the costs of a patent system from a patentee's perspective. Any valuation should be based on weighting costs and benefits of patent protection.

Various options for measuring costs and benefits of patent protection have led to the definition of two alternative value constructs. Renewal value and asset value. In this thesis, I extend current research on value constructs by adding a third value construct and by introducing the degree of diffusion of inventions as a main value driver. A value construct first of all describes a valuation perspective by comparing specific sets of related costs and benefits in two alternative, counterfactual situations. The construct of renewal value determines a patent's value by comparing the patentee's benefits given a valid patent with the resulting benefits should this patent lapse into the public domain. The basic idea is that a patentee can generate monopoly profits under patent protection and industry-average profits without patent protection. The second value construct, the asset value, contrasts sales or profits when the patent belongs to the patentee with the situation in which the strongest competitor holds the patent – the advantages of a patentee's monopolistic market position are compared to the disadvantages of suffering from the monopolistic market position of the strongest competitor. Following these lines of reasoning, I define a third value construct, the competition value, as being the result of a comparison of a firm's profits given a strong patent held by a competitor with the situation in which this patent lapses into the public domain. This perspective facilitates an estimate of the amount of resources that should be reasonably devoted to destroying the monopolistic market position of a competitor, either by circumventing the patented invention or by attacking the legal validity of the patent right.

Based on this extended version of the basic model and the reflections on knowledge, several conclusions can be drawn for patent valuation. First, the intangible nature of knowledge, together with its evolutionary, path-dependent development and the stickiness of individual skills, calls for a careful assessment of the value of patent rights. Patents can be a source of value, but they might not be the only – maybe not even the most important – source of value. In industries and technologies in which tacit knowledge plays a key role other complementary resources at the firm or individual level must be identified in order to arrive at a reasonable conclusion of a patent's value.

Second, patents are valuable if they endow their holder with a strong exclusive right over a profitable invention. Under a weak patent regime, patentees cannot enforce their rights yet at the same time they face all the disadvantages arising from the disclosure of information. In this case, the better choice would have been not to seek patent protection at all. Then again, even under the strongest patent regime, a patented invention that does not lead to economic rents for the patent holder is of little value.

Third, in the presence of a low degree of diffusion, patents are not required, since competitive advantages based on knowledge are not eroded by competitors. Hence, a patentee only faces costs but no benefits. Low degrees for diffusion result not only from inattentive behavior of competitors. Given a situation in which alternative technological solutions or inventions exist that lead to a comparable economic utility, the uniqueness of an invention does not necessarily transform into superior economic benefits or advanced market positions.

Fourth, the theoretical analysis of patent portfolio values further shows that overlapping patent protection can exhibit a portfolio effect – the value of the portfolio exceeds the sum of the stand-alone values of single patent rights. The existence and magnitude of this portfolio value is driven not only by the drafting of patent claims but also by the type of underlying technology. In complex technologies, patented inventions build on each other. If ownership of the patent rights for one technology is scattered among multiple patentees then a mutual blockade is a possible outcome. In this case, rationally acting economic agents seek freedom to operate by entering (cross)-licensing agreements. Complex patent portfolios can therefore be very valuable because they serve as a bargaining chip or currency. In addition, my empirical analysis of licensing contracts shows, that compensation schemes in licensing agreements also comprise lump-sum and recurring-amount payments or licensing fees based on running royalties. These various elements of the compensation formula can lead to substantial monetary values for the licensor. But this does not necessarily imply that all members of the portfolio exhibit high stand-alone values. Rather it is the complexity of hundreds of overlapping patent rights and the patentee's private knowledge of various patent qualities that create substantial information asymmetries between licensor and licensee and strengthen the bargaining position of the licensor.

Fifth, patent values are driven by the underlying motivation behind a valuation. Patent valuations serve many purposes – not the only selling and licensing of single patents or entire patent portfolios. Patent valuation is required prior to spin off activities as well as during and after M&A transactions. Patent portfolio management needs estimates for financial patent values when making renewal decisions or assessing the costs and benefits of instituting legal proceedings against patent infringement activities by third parties. Since many, or even most, industrial inventions result from the research efforts of employees, they expect to receive a reasonable share of the value they create for the organization. It also facilitates decision-making and improves the bargaining position during the negotiation process prior to a transaction. A consistent patent valuation increases the transparency of complex business transactions; this in turn supports achieving and communicating a common understanding of the nature and value of patent rights to both internal and external parties.

Given the complex relationships between knowledge, patents, and value, it may not be surprising that many patent-related decisions are dominated by a discussion of risk and uncertainty instead of costs and benefits. This underlying high level of uncertainty is reflected in empirical results by a highly skewed value distribution – only a very small fraction of all patents seems to be extremely valuable. Empirical research on the private value of patent rights has been motivated by the richness and availability of information from patent documents. Bibliographic information on patent scope and breadth, forward and backward citations, family size, and inventor characteristics have been used to measure the likelihood of legal disputes and the value of patent rights. Despite the strong theoretical foundation of various variables, the weak point in each approach is the measurement of patent values.

Due to the absence of market values for patent rights, researchers have defined proxies for patent values. These are derived based on observed renewal decisions, subjective opinions of inventors, and from market values of entire companies. Clearly, the content validity of each proxy directly influences the results of any subsequent analysis. With my empirical analysis of bibliographic value indicators, I seek to close this apparent research gap on the validity of past empirical findings. I use detailed information on a recent market transaction of a patent portfolio comprising 201 patent families and more than 1,100 national patent rights to test three alternative models. My results show strong support for six variables, including the size of a patent family, a patent's age and scope, the number of scientific citations on a patent document, the number of *Y*-references in European search reports, and the number of inventors. These findings support the assumption of a causal relationship between bibliographic patent information and financial value. Bibliographic value indicators should therefore not be neglected during the evaluation stage of a patent.

However, a valuation technique that is only based on bibliographic value indicators and attempts to measure financial values according to the coefficients of a set of variables of a current statistical model neglects important aspects of patent valuations. First, patent rights are industry-, firm-, technology-, time-, and country-specific. The propensity to patent varies among industries and for alternative technologies. An analysis of historical patent terms shows different patenting behavior in single time periods and under alternative patent regimes. However, a naïve use of statistical information for patent valuation implicitly assumes at least a sufficient degree of comparability between technologies, industries, firms, countries, and over time. Second, changes in the model specification can lead to changes in the coefficients. These changes can comprise modifications of the structural relationship between dependent and independent variables, the number of independent variables introduced into the model, and finally the measurement of these variables. Third, in many cases, results are neither controlled for underlying value constructs nor for the degree of diffusion or the legal quality of the patent regime. Finally, despite the transparent patent-application-and-granting procedure, empirical results indicate that the disclosure of information in patent documents – hence the specific values for bibliographic indicators – results from a bargaining process between patent applicant and patent examiner. This in turn challenges the comparability of various patent documents.

In view of these objections, quantitative valuation relying only on the statistical analyses of bibliographic value indicators seems unlikely to be a promising approach. Although an automatic valuation methodology based on this information would certainly reduce time and complexity in patent valuation, it would also lead to biased results. In contrast to this, direct patent valuation allows more flexibility to account for the peculiarities of single valuation projects. Thus I review various direct approaches to value and classify them according to their underlying economic principles.

A valuation based on cost focuses on the economic principle of substitution. Hence, the guiding question is which amount of resources a buyer or investor would be willing to spend in order to create a substitute for an existing patented technology. Within this group of cost-based approaches, further distinctions drawn with regard to the components of cost, type of cost, and the time frame over which cost is analyzed can lead to alternative valuation formulas. One main weakness of cost-based valuation is that a relationship between cost and value is plausible, but it is not necessarily one of equality. Furthermore, cost-based valuation contains no explicit analysis of risk. In many cases, though, costs can be assessed with sufficient reliability and can serve as benchmark in combination with additional valuation methods.

Economic theory usually defines any market-based valuation as the gold standard for appraising the value of a specific asset. Prices on active markets mirror the principles of equilibrium and competition. Market-based valuation can be performed either through the application of multiples or analogies, as well as through an analysis of market-replacement cost and the measurement of residual values. The main advantage of market approaches to value lies in their inherent objectivity. Market prices of homogenous assets traded in open and competitive markets are good indicators for the value of these assets. Unfortunately, markets for patents have not yet been established. Only rare opportunities exist where we can fully observe a market transfer of patent rights. Over the last three to five years, however, both, number and publicity of patent auctions have increased. Although these auctions have not fully met the ambitious goals of their organizers, they represent first attempts for increasing the marketability of patents.

Given the primary, future-oriented function of a patent right to obtain a monopolistic market position, a valuation approach based on expected income is most suitable. In contrast to company valuation, an income-based valuation of patents does not face the critique of depending to a large extent on terminal values. In fact, the limitation of the duration of a patent term to twenty years avoids any problems of measuring terminal values. Since only a few patents in selected technologies are likely to be renewed for this entire time span, the main focus is put on estimating the remaining useful life. This equals the number of periods over which a patentee can generate profits out of a patented invention. Determination of the remaining useful life is either based on life cycle models or survivor-curve analysis. I propose that the valuation horizon, hence the remaining useful life, depends on both the number of periods over which patent protection is possible or expected and the current position of a patented technology in its life cycle.

Income-based approaches offer alternative ways to account for risk. Besides discussing general measurement differences between discount-rate and certainty-equivalent approaches, I present a set of factors that drive a patent's risk. The attractiveness of a patented technology from a competitor's perspective, the difficulty in inventing around the patent, and the probability that patentees do not take notice of or can credibly prove an infringement of their rights, are main sources of patent's risk.

For measuring periodical income streams, two alternative models are suitable. First, patentees can opt for an exclusive use. The main task is then to identify the share of economic rents that can be traced back to the patented invention. I propose a two-step approach here. The first step comprises the definition of main sales drivers and the measurement of their impact on total product sales. Besides brands and additional services, technological features can be important sales drivers. The appropriate share of total sales volumes that is motivated by technological features is the starting point of patent valuation. As the analysis of the different levels of knowledge shows, patents can be used to protect know-why. However, this does not mean that all technological features are protected by patent rights. Further deductions are therefore required if additional but unprotected know-why or know-how is needed for offering specific technological product features. This process finally leads to a sales volume that is motivated by protected technology. Based on a profitability analysis, this stream of sales can be transformed into a stream of cash-flows. In order to account for the underlying patent risk, further deductions in the case of a certainty-equivalent approach or an increase of discount rates might be advisable. The sum of discounted, technology-motivated, and patent-protected cash-flows after taxes then leads to a conclusion of value.

Besides an analysis of cash-flows, a second measure for economic income from a patent portfolio focuses on a cooperative exploitation strategy. This means that patentees decide to license out their patent rights. Economic rents are then either measured in terms of licensing revenues (royalty income) or by saved licensing fees (relief from royalty). Consequently, a patent's value equals the discounted sum of these rents after taxes. One key value driver in this case is the selection of a reasonable royalty rate. Heuristic rules, management estimates, and an analysis of published royalty rates offer alternative ways to find a reasonable royalty rate. The main advantage of the structured analysis of patent value drivers described in this thesis lies not only in an increased transparency of patent values. It also allows the running of sensitivity and scenario analyses to evaluate the robustness of the value conclusion.

Two additional points are worth mentioning. First, the amortization of a patent's value leads to tax savings. Depending on the overall valuation model, an additional valuation of these tax savings might be appropriate. Second, in case of a portfolio valuation, the concentration of patents in each period is to be forecasted based on an analysis of the remaining useful life. If the number of patents in a portfolio decreases over time because single patents expire, breadth of patent protection is reduced. Hence, an additional modification of sales or cash-flows or royalty rates is required to account for this reduction.

The fact that in cumulative industries cooperative exploitation strategies are one major source of income has motivated an additional empirical research project. Given the fact that no open and active market for patent rights has so far been established from which market-based conclusions as to value are possible, the question remains as to whether the use of intermediaries supports both transactions as well as reliable valuation. I use a set of 191 licensing agreements to analyze the bargaining process and monetary value of licensing contracts. To the best of my knowledge, this represents one of the most detailed analyses in this field of research. The main findings can be summarized as follows: The values for property rights to knowledge assets correlate with the breadth of the rights granted. This supports the idea of an effective market mechanism in the case of licensing activities. However, licensing agreements are not only used to exploit the value potential of knowledge. They can also be interpreted as a strategic device for reducing uncertainty. In fact, two kinds of uncertainty exit. The first, uncertainty about present situations and rights and duties of licensor and licensee, can be reduced by selecting appropriate contractual terms. This indicates that an efficient market mechanism for valuing knowledge assets can be implemented if valuation is carefully conducted. However, the intrinsic variability of future events leads to a considerable amount of uncertainty about the future. In this context, inflexibility seems to be traded with a discount.

In the end, my theoretical analyses and empirical results lead to the conclusion that Benjamin Franklin was right about the profitability of investing in knowledge assets. Measuring this profitability in the case of patent rights was the main focus of this thesis. Despite its complexity, patent valuation certainly pays off in a world in which knowledge is so crucial for sustainable economic success.

References

Acedo, F., Barroso, C. and Galan, J. (2006), The resource-based theory: Dissemination and main trends, in: Strategic Management Journal, 27 (7), 621-636.

Achilladelis, B. (1993), The dynamics of technological innovation: The sector of antibacterial medicines, in: Research Policy, 22 (4), 279-308.

Achilladelis, B., Schwarzkopf, A. and Cines, M. (1999), The dynamics of technological innovation: The case of the chemical industry, in: Research Policy, 19 (1), 1-34.

Agrawal, A., K., Cockburn, I., M. and McHale, J. (2003), Gone but not forgotten: Labor flows, knowledge spillovers, and enduring social capital, working paper, National Bureau of Economic Research, 1-37.

Albert, M. B., Avery, D., Narin, F. and McAllister, P. (1991), Direct validation of citation counts as indicators of industrially important patents, in: Research Policy, 20 (3), 251-259.

Alchian, A. A. and Demsetz, H. (1973), The property rights paradigm, in: Journal of Economic History, 33 (1), 16-27.

Alexander, D. and Archer, S. (2003), Miller international accounting standards guide, New York: Aspen Publishers.

Almeida, P. and Kogut, B. (1999), Localization of knowledge and the mobility of engineers in regional networks, in: Management Science, 45 (7), 905-917.

Amram, M. (2005), The challenge of valuing patents and early stage technologies, in: Journal of Applied Corporate Finance, 12 (2), 68-81.

Anand, B. N. and Khanna, T. (2000), The structure of licensing contracts, in: The Journal of Industrial Economics, 48 (1), 103-135.

Andersen, B. (1999), The hunt for S-shaped growth paths in technological innovation: A patent study, in: Journal of Evolutionary Economics, 9 (4), 487-526.

Anton, J. J., Greene, H. and Yao, D. A. (2006), Policy implications of weak patent rights, in: NBER Innovation Policy & the Economy, 6 (1), 1-26.

Aristotle (1928), Analytica posteriora, The works of Aristotle: Translated into English under the editorship of W.D. Ross, M.A. Hon. LL.D. (Edin.), I, Oxford: Clarendon Press.

Aristotle (1998), Metaphysics – Translated with an introduction by Hugh Lawson-Tancred, London, New York: Penguin Books.

Arora, A. (1995), Licensing tacit knowledge: Intellectual property rights and the market for know-how, in: Economics of Innovation and New Technology, 4 (1), 41-59.

Arora, A. and Fosfuri, A. (2003), Licensing the market for technology, in: Journal of Economic Behavior & Organization, 52 (2), 277-296.

Arrow, K. J. (1962), Economic welfare and the allocation of resources for invention, in: (Ed.: R. Nelson) The rate and direction of inventive activity: Economic and social factors, Princeton: Princeton University Press, 609-624.

Arrow, K. J. (1971), Essays in the theory of risk-bearing, Amsterdam: Markham Publishing Company.

Arrow, K. J. (1974), The limits of organization, New York: W. W. Norton & Company.

Arrow, K. J. (1975), Vertical integration and communication, in: The Bell Journal of Economics, 6 (1), 173-183.

Arrow, K. J. and Hahn, F. H. (1971), General competitive analysis, San Francisco: Holden-Day.

Arundel, A. (2001), The relative effectiveness of patents and secrecy for appropriation, in: Research Policy, 30, 611-624.

Aulakh, P. S., Cavusgil, T. S. and Sarkar, M. (1998), Compensation in international licensing agreements, in: Journal of International Business Studies, 29 (2), 409-420.

Austin, D. (1993), An event-study approach to measuring innovative output: The case of biotechnology, in: AEA Papers and Proceedings, 83 (2), 253-258.

Ba, S., Stallert, J. and Whinston, A. B. (2001), Optimal investment in knowledge within a firm using a market mechanism, in: Management Science, 47 (9), 1203-1219.

Barney, J. A. (2002), A study of patent mortality rates: Using statistical survival analysis to rate and value patent assets, in: AIPLA Quarterly Journal, 30 (3), 317-352.

Barney, J. B. (1991), Firm resources and sustained competitive advantage, in: Journal of Management, 17 (1), 99-120.

Barton, J. H. (2003), Non-Obviousness, in: IDEA: The Journal of Law and Technology, 43 (3), 475-508.

Basberg, B. L. (1987), Patents and the measurement of technological change: A survey of the literature, in: Research Policy, 16 (2-4), 131-141.

Battersby, G. J. and Grimes, C. W. (2006), Licensing royalty rates 2006, New York: Aspen Publishers.

Bausch, A. (1996), Planung von integrierten Geschäfts-, Funktions- und Regionalstrategien im Industriekonzern, Institut für Unternehmensplanung, Justus-Liebig-Universität, Ferber'sche Universitäts-Buchhandlung Gießen.

Bausch, A. (2000), Die Multiplikator-Methode: Ein betriebswirtschaftlich sinnvolles Instrument zur Unternehmenswert- und Kaufpreisfindung in Akquisitionsprozessen? in: Finanz Betrieb, 7-8, 448-458.

Bausch, A. and Pape, U. (2005), Ermittlung von Restwerten - Eine vergleichende Gegenüberstellung von Ausstiegs- und Fortführungswerten, in: Finanz Betrieb, 7-8, 474-484.

Beier, F. K. (1978), Wettbewerbsfreiheit und Patentschutz, in: GRUR - Gewerblicher Rechtsschutz und Urheberrecht, 80 (3), 123-200.

Berger, A. and Ring, M. (2003), § 249 HGB: Rückstellungen, in: (Ed.: A. Berger, H. Ellrot and G. F. e. al.) Beck'scher Bilanzkommentar: Der Jahressabschluss nach Handels- und Steuerrecht, §§ 238 bis 339 HGB, München: C. H. Beck'sche Verlagsbuchhandlung, 240-302.

Bessy, C. and Brousseau, E. (1998), Technology licensing contracts, features and diversity, in: International Review of Law and Economics, 18 (4), 451-490.

Beyer, S. (2005), Fair Value-Bewertung von Vermögenswerten und Schulden, in: (Ed.: W. Ballwieser, S. Beyer and H. Zelger) Unternehmenskauf nach IFRS und US-GAAP, Stuttgart: Schäffer-Poeschel, 141-189.

Beyer, S. and Mackenstedt, A. (2008), Grundsätze zur Bewertung immaterieller Vermögenswerte (IDW S 5), in: Die Wirtschaftsprüfung, 61 (8), 388-349.

Bielza, C. and Shenoy, P. P. (1999), A comparison of graphical techniques for asymmetric decision problems, in: Management Science, 45 (11), 1552-1596.

Black, F. and Scholes, M. (1973), The pricing of options and corporate liabilities, in: Journal of Political Economy, 81 (3), 637-654.

Blind, K., Edler, J., Frietsch, R. and Schmoch, U. (2006), Motives to patent: Empirical evidence from Germany, in: Research Policy, 35 (5), 655-672.

Blind, K. and Thumm, N. (2004), Interrelation between patenting and standardisation strategies: Empirical evidence and policy implications, in: Research Policy, 33 (10), 1583-1598.

Bloom, N. and Van Reenen, J. (2002), Patents, real options and firm performance, in: Economic Journal, 112 (478), C97 - C116.

Boisot, M. and Child, J. (1988), The iron law of fiefs: Bureaucratic failure and the problem of governance in the Chinese economic reforms, in: Administrative Science Quarterly, 33, 507-527.

Borod, R. S. (2006), What is the future of intellectual property securization, in: International Finance & Treasury, 32 (8), 3-5.

Bouju, A. (1988), Patent infringement litigation costs: A practical worldwide survey, London: Longman.

Brandão, L. E., Dyer, J. S. and Hahn, W. (2005), Using binomial decision trees to solve real-option valuation problems, in: Decision Analysis, 2 (2), 69-88.

Breitzmann, A., Thomas, P. and Cheney, M. (2002), Technological powerhouse or diluted competence: Techniques for assessing mergers via patent analysis, in: R&D Management, 32 (1), 1-10.

Bryer, L. G. (1999), International and U.S. licensing of intangibles, in: (Ed.: M. Simensky, L. G. Bryer and N. J. Wilkof) Intellectual property in the global marketplace, II: Commercial exploitation and country-by-country profiles, 26.1-26.51.

Brynjolfsson, E. (1994), Information assets, technology, and organization, in: Management Science, 40 (12), 1645-1662.

Burke, P. F. and Reitzig, M. (2007), Measuring patent assessment quality - Analyzing the degree and kind of (in)consistency in patent offices' decision making, in: Research Policy, 36 (9), 1404-1430.

Caldwell, L. K. (1975), Managing the transition to post-modern society, in: Public Administration Review, 35 (6), 567-572.

Carpenter, M., Cooper, M. and Narin, F. (1980), Linkage between basic research literature and patents, in: Research Management, 13 (2), 30-35.

Carr, D. (1981), Knowledge in practice, in: American Philosophical Quarterly, 18 (1), 53-61.

Caves, R. E., Crookell, H. and Killing, P. J. (1983), The imperfect market for technology licenses, in: Oxford bulletin of economics and statistics, 45 (3), 249-267.

Cherensky, S. (1993), A penny for their thoughts: Employee-Inventors, preinvention assignment agreements, property, and personhood, in: California Law Review, 81 (2), 595-669.

Cheung, S. N. S. (1983), The contractual nature of the firm, in: IDEA: The Journal of Law and Economics, 26 (1), 1-22.

Chisum, D., Nard, C., Schwartz, H., Newman, P. and Kieff, F. (2004), Principles of patent law, New York: Thomson West.

Cho, K. R. (1988), Issues of compensation in international technology licensing, in: Management International Review, 28 (2), 70-78.

Choi, C. J. and Lee, S. H. (1997), A knowledge-based view of cooperative interorganizational relationships, in: (Ed.: P. W. Beamish and J. P. Killing) Cooperative strategies, San Francisco: New Lexington Press, 33-58.

Choi, J. P. (1998), Patent litigation as an information-transmission mechanism, in: The American Economic Review, 88 (5), 1249-1263.

Chow, G. C. (1967), Technological change and the demand for computers, in: American Economic Review, 57 (5), 1117-1130.

Claus, J. and Thomas, J. (2001), Equity premia as low as three percent? Evidence from analysts' earnings forecasts for domestic and international stock markets, in: Journal of Finance, 56, 1629-1666.

Coase, R. H. (1937), The nature of the firm, in: Economica, 4, 386-405.

Coase, R. H. (1960), The problem of social cost, in: Journal of Law and Economics, 3 (4), 1-44.

Cockburn, I. M. and Griliches, Z. (1988), Industry effects and appropriability measures in the stock market valuation of R&D and patents, in: The American Economic Review, 78 (2), 419-423.

Cockburn, I. M., Kortum, S. and Stern, S. (2002), Are all patent examiners equal? The impact of examiner characteristics on patent statistics and litigation outcomes, working paper, National Bureau of Economic Research, 1-42.

Cohen, M. R. and Nagel, E. (1936), An introduction to logic and scientific method, London: Routledge & Kegan Paul.

Cohen, W., Gotob, A., Nagatac, A., Nelson, R. R. and Walsh, J. P. (2002), R&D spillovers, patents and the incentives to innovate in Japan and the United States, in: 31 (8-9), 1349-1367.

Cohen, W. M. and Levinthal, D. A. (1990), Absorptive capacity: A new perspective on learning and innovation, in: Administrative Science Quarterly, 35 (1), 128-152.

Cohen, W. M., Nelson, R. R. and Walsh, J. P. (2000), Protecting their intellectual assets: Appropriability conditions and why U.S. manufacturing firms patent (or not), Working paper, National Bureau of Economic Research, 1-50.

Comanor, W. S. and Smiley, R. H. (1975), Monopoly and the distribution of wealth, in: The Quarterly Journal of Economics, 89 (2), 177-194.

Conner, K. R. (1991), A historical comparison of resource-based theory and five schools of thought within industrial organization economics: Do we have a new theory of the firm? in: Journal of Management, 17 (1), 121-154.

Conner, K. R. and Prahalad, C. K. (1996), A resource-based theory of the firm: Knowledge versus opportunism, in: Organization Science, 7 (5), 477-501.

Connolly, R. A. and Hirschey, M. (1988), Market value and patents – A bayesian approach, in: Economic Letters, 27 (1), 83-87.

Contractor, F. J. (1981), International technology licensing – Compensation, costs, and negotiation, Lexington, MA: D.C. Heath and Company.

Contractor, F. J. (1985), Licensing in international strategy, Westport: Greenwood Press.

Contractor, F. J. (2001), Valuation of intangible assets in global operations, Westport: Quorum Books.

Cooter, R., D. and Rubinfeld, D. L. (1989), Economic analysis of legal disputes and their resolution, in: Journal of Economic Literature, 27 (3), 1067-1097.

Copeland, T., Koller, T. and Murrin, J. (1995), Valuation - Measuring and managing the value of companies, New York – Toronto – Singapore: John Wiley & Sons.

Corredoira, R. A. and Rosenkopf, L. (1995), Gaining from your losses: The backward transfer of knowledge through mobility ties, working paper, The Wharton School, 1-36.

Coster, R. (2002), From first-to-invent to first-to-file: The Canadian experience, American Intellectual Property Law Association, New York, 1-14.

Cox, J. C., Ross, S. A. and Rubinstein, M. (1979), Option pricing: A simplified approach, in: Journal of Financial Eocnomics, 7, 229-263.

Crampes, C. and Langinier, C. (2002), Litigation and settlement in patent infringement cases, in: Rand Journal of Economics, 33 (2), 258-274.

Cruz, J. (2003), Epistemology, The Nature Encyclopedia of Cognitive Science, London: Macmillan.

Cunningham, M. A. (1995), Preliminary injunctive relief in patent litigation, in: IDEA - The Journal of Law and Technology, 35 (3), 213-259.

Damanpour, F. (1991), Organizational innovation: A meta-analysis of effects of determinants and moderators, in: The Academy of Management Journal, 34 (3), 555-590.

Damodaran, A. (2002), Investment valuation - Tools and techniques for determining the value of any asset, New York: John Wiley and Sons.

Davis, P. and Weitz, D. J. (1998), Creating and maintaining a business focused patent portfolio, in: (Ed.: Patent Yearbook 1998, London: Euromoney, 67-69.

Dawo, S. (2003), Immaterielle Güter in der Rechungslegung nach HGB, IAS/IFRS und US-GAAP - Aktuelle Rechtslage und neue Wege der Bilanzierung und Berichterstattung, Berlin: Verlag Neue Wirtschafts-Briefe GmbH&Co.

Deming, E. W. and Singpurwalla, N. D. (1989), A bear trap in using the Iowa curve methodology for property retirements and depreciation charges, in: The American Statistician, 43 (1), 12-16.

Demsetz, H. (1967), Toward a theory of property rights, in: American Economic Review, 57 (2), 347-359.

Demsetz, H. (1988), The theory of the firm revisited, in: Journal of Law, Economics and Organization, 4 (1), 141-161.

Descartes, R. (1968), Discourse on method and the meditations, Harmondsworth: Penguin Books.

Dewey, J. (1896), The reflex arc concept in psychology, in: Psychological Review, 3, 357-370.

Dewey, J. (1986), Logic: The theory of inquiry, The later works, 1925-1953, 12: 1938, Carbondale: Southern Illinois University Press.

Dewey, J. (1988), The later works: 1925-1953; edited by Jo Ann, 1, Carbondale: Southern Illinois University Press.

Dewey, J. and Bentely, A. F. (1973), Knowing and the known, in: (Ed.: E. C. H. R. Handy) Useful procedures of inquiry, Great Barrington: Behavioral Research Council, 94-209.

Dickens, D. T. (1994), The ECLA classification system, in: World Patent Information, 16 (1), 28-32.

Dolfsma, W. (2006), IPRs, technological development, and economic development, in: Journal of Economic Issues, 40 (2), 333-342.

Dosi, G. (1988), Sources, procedures, and microeconomic effects of innovation, in: Journal of Economic Literature, 26 (3), 1120-1171.

Dosi, G., Teece, D. J. and Winter, S. G. (1992), Toward a theory of corporate coherence, in: (Ed.: R. G. Giovanni Dosi, Pier Angelo Toninelli) Technology and Enterprise in a Historical Perspective, Oxford: Clarendon, 185-211.

Drucker, P. F. (1988), The coming of the new organization, in: Harvard Business Review, 66 (1), 45-53.

Drucker, P. F. (1991), The new productivity challenge, in: Harvard Business Review, 69 (6), 69-79.

Drucker, P. F. (1999), Knowledge-worker productivity: The biggest challenge, in: California Management Review, 41 (2), 79-94.

Duguet, E. and Kabla, I. (1998), Appropriation strategy and the motivations to use the patent system in France: An econometric analysis at the firm level, in: Annales d'économie et de statistique, 49-50, 290-327.

Dyer, J. H. and Nobeoka, K. (2000), Creating and managing a high-performance knowledge-sharing network: The Toyota case, in: Strategic Management Journal, 21 (3), 345-367.

Easton, P., Taylor, G., Shroff, P. and Sougiannis, T. (2002), Using forecasts of earnings to simultaneously estimate growth and the rate of return on equity investment, in: Journal of Accounting Research, 40 (3), 657-676.

Egginton, D. (1990), Towards some principles for intangible asset accounting, in: Accounting and Business Research, 20 (79), 193-205.

EPO (2000), Annual Report, Munich: European Patent Office.

EPO (2005), Annual Report, Munich: European Patent Office.

EPO (2006a), Stakeholders debate future policy on patents, in: Single Market News, 42, 20-21.

Epstein, B. J. and Mirza, A. A. (2003), IAS 2003: Interpretation and application of International Accounting Standards, New York: John Wiley & Sons Inc.

Ernst, H. (1998), Patent portfolios for strategic R&D planning, in: Journal of Engineering and Technology Management, 15 (4), 279-308.

Ernst, H., Leptien, C. and Vitt, J. (2000), Inventors are not alike: The distribution of patenting output among industrial R&D personnel, in: IEEE Transactions on engineering management, 47 (2), 184-199.

Eswaran, M. (1993), Cross-licensing of competing patents as a facilitating device, in: Canadian Journal of Economics, 27 (3), 659-708.

Fama, E. F. and French, K. R. (1993), Common risk factors in the returns on stocks and bonds, in: Journal of Financial Economics, 33, 3-56.

Fama, E. F. and French, R. K. (1995), Size and book-to-market factors in earnings and returns, in: The Journal of Finance, 50 (1), 131-155.

Fama, E. F. and French, R. K. (1997), Industry costs of equity, in: Journal of Financial Economics, 43, 153-193.

Fershtman, C. and Kamien, M. I. (1992), Cross licensing of complementary technologies, in: International Journal of Industrial Organization, 10 (3), 329-349.

Fisher, J. C. and Pry, R. H. (1971), A simple substitution model of technological change, in: Technological Forecasting and Social Change, 3, 75-88.

Fisher, R. and Ury, W. (1982), Getting to yes, in: Management Review, 71 (2), 16-21.

Förschle, G. and Kroner, M. (2003), § 246 HGB: Vollständigkeit, Verrechnungsverbot, in: (Ed.: A. Berger, H. Ellrot and G. F. e. al.) Beck'scher Bilanzkommentar: der Jahressabschluss nach Handels- und Steuerrecht, §§ 238 bis 339 HGB, 5, München: C. H. Beck'sche Verlagsbuchhandlung, 80-120.

Fosfuri, A. (2006), The licensing dilemma: Understanding the determinants of the rate of technology licensing, in: Strategic Management Journal, 27 (12), 1141-1158.

Foss, K. and Foss, N., J. (2005), Resources and transaction costs: How property rights economics furthers the resource based view, in: Strategic Management Journal, 26 (6), 541-553.

Foss, N., J. (1996a), More critical comments on knowledge-based theories of the firm, in: Organization Science, 7 (5), 519-523.

Foss, N., J. (1996b), Knowledge-based approaches to the theory of the firm: Some critical comments, in: Organization Science, 7 (5), 470-476.

Foss, N., J. (2002), 'Coase vs. Hayek': Economic organization and the knowledge economy, in: International Journal of the Economics of Business, 9 (1), 9-35.

Frost, G. E. (1967), The 1967 Patent law debate: First-to-invent vs. First-to-file, in: Duke Law Journal, 5, 923-942.

Gallini, N. T. (1984), Deterrence by market sharing: A strategic incentive for licensing, in: American Economic Review, 74 (5), 932-941.

Gallini, N. T. (2002), The economic of patents: Lessons from recent U.S. patent reform, in: The Journal of Economic Perspectives, 16 (2), 131-154.

Gallini, N. T. and Winter, R. A. (1985), Licensing in the theory of innovation, in: RAND Journal of Economics, 16 (2), 237-252.

Gambardella, A., Giuri, P. and Luzzi, A. (2007), The market for patents in Europe, in: Research Policy, 38 (8), 1163-1183.

Garvey, W. D. and Griffith, B. C. (1971), Scientific communication: Its role in the conduct of research and creation of knowledge, in: American psychologist: Journal of the American Psychological Association, 26, 349-362.

Gebhardt, W. R., Lee, C. M. C. and Swaminathan, B. (2001), Toward an implied cost of capital, in: Journal of Accounting Research, 39 (1), 135-176.

Gettier, E. L. (1963), Is justified true belief knowledge? in: Analysis, 23, 121-123.

Ghemawat, P. (1986), Sustainable advantage, in: Harvard Business Review, 64 (5), 53-58.

Gilbert, R. and Shapiro, C. (1990), Optimal patent length and breadth, in: Rand Journal of Economics, 21 (1), 106-112.

Gilbert, R. and Shapiro, C. (1997), Antitrust issues in the licensing of intellectual property: The nine no-no's meet the nineties, in: Brookings Papers on Economic Activity. Microeconomics, 1997, 283-349.

Girotra Karan, Terwiesch Christian and T., U. K. (2007), Valuing R&D projects in a portfolio: Evidence from the pharmaceutical industry, in: Management Science, 53 (9), 1452-1466.

Giuri, P., Mariani, M., Brusoni, S., Crespi, G., Francoz, D., Gambardella, A., Garcia-Fontes, W., Geuna, A., Gontales, R., Harris, L. J., Hoisl, K., Le Bas, C., Luzzi, A., Magazzini, L., Nesta, L., Nomaler, Ö., Palomeras, N., Patel, P., Romanelli, M. and Verspagen, b. (2007), Inventors and invention processes in Europe: Results from the PatVal-EU survey, in: Research Policy, 36 (8), 1107-1127.

Glade, A. (1986), Rechungslegung und Prüfung nach dem Bilanzrichtlininen-Gesetz: systematische Darstellung und Kommentar, Berlin: Verlag Neue Wirtschaftsbriefe.

Goldfarb, B. (2008), The effect of government contracting on academic research: Does the source of funding affect scientific output? in: Research Policy, 37 (1), 41-58.

Granstrand, O. (2006), Patents and intellectual property: A general framework, in: (Ed.: J. Cantwell) The Economics of Patents (Vol. 1): The Patent System and the Measurement of Invention, Northampton: Edward Elgar Publishing, 3-60.

Grant, R. M. (1996a), Toward a knowledge-based theory of the firm, in: Strategic Management Journal, 17 (Winter Special Issue), 109-122.

Grant, R. M. (1996b), Prospering in dynamically-competitive environments: Organizational capability as knowledge integration, in: Organization Science, 7 (4), 375-387.

Grant, R. M. (2002a), The knowledge-based view of the firm, in: (Ed.: C. W. Choo and N. Bontis) The strategic management of intellectual capital and organizational knowledge, Oxford: Oxford Universitary Press, 133-148.

Grant, R. M. (2002b), Contemporary strategy analysis, 4, Oxford: Blackwell Publishing.

Griliches, Z. (1981), Market value, R&D and patents, in: Economic Letters, 7 (2), 939-957.

Griliches, Z. (1990), Patent statistics as economic indicators: A survey, in: Journal of Economic Literature, 28 (4), 1661-1707.

Grindley, P. C. and Nickerson, J. A. (1996), Licensing and business strategy in the chemicals industry, in: (Ed.: R. L. Parr and P. H. Sullivan) Technology licensing: Corporate strategies for maximizing value, New York: John Wiles & Sons, 97-120.

Grindley, P. C. and Teece, D. J. (1997), Managing intellectual capital: Licensing and cross-licensing in semiconductors and electronics, in: California Management Review, 39 (2), 8-41.

Grochla, E. (1976), Praxeologische Organisationstheorie durch sachliche und methodische Integration - Eine pragmatische Konzeption, in: Zeitschrift für betriebswirtschaftliche Forschung (zfbf), 28, 617-637.

Groß, M. and Rohrer, O. (2003), Lizenzgebühren, Heidelberg: Verlag Recht und Wirtschaft GmbH.

Grubb, P. W. (1982), Patents for chemists, Oxford: Oxford University Press.

Gruber, M. and Venter, C. (2006), "Die Kunst die Zukunft zu erfinden" – Theoretische Erkenntnisse und empirische Befunde des Corporate Foresight in deutschen Großunternehmen, in: Zeitschrift für betriebswirtschaftliche Forschung (zfbf), 58 (11), 958-984.

Grudziecki, R. L. and Michel, A. (2002), Licensing and litigation, in: (Ed.: G. Robert) Licensing best practices - The LESI guide to strategic issues and contemporary results, New York: John Wiley & Sons, 297-311.

Grupp, H. and Schmoch, U. (1999), Patent statistics in the age of globalisation: New legal procedures, new analytic methods, new economic interpretation, in: Research Policy, 28 (4), 377-396.

Guellec, D. and van Pottelsberghe de la Potterie, B. (2000), Applications, grants and the value of patent, in: Economic Letters, 69 (1), 109-114.

Hahn, D. and Hungenberg, H. (2001), PuK - Wertorientierte Contollingkonzepte, Wiesbaden: Gabler.

Hall, B. H., Jaffe, A. and Trajtenberg, M. (2005), Market value and patent citations., in: Rand Journal of Economics, 36 (1), 16-38.

Hall, B. H. and Ziedonis, R. (2001), The patent paradox revisited: An empirical study of patenting in the U.S. semiconductor industry, 1979 - 1995, in: Rand Journal of Economics, 31 (1), 101-128.

Hall, R. (1991), The contribution of intangible resources to business success, in: Journal of General Management, 16 (4), 41-51.

Hall, R. (1992), The strategic analysis of intangible resources, in: Strategic Management Journal, 13, 135-144.

Hall, R. (1993), A framework linking intangible resources and capabilities to sustainable competitive advantage, in: Strategic Management Journal, 14, 607-618.

Harabi, N. (1995), Appropriability of technical innovations: An empirical analysis, in: Research Policy, 24 (6), 981-992.

Harhoff, D., Engel, C. and Möschel, W. (2007), Patentschutz und Innovation, Gutachten des Wissenschaftlichen Beirats, Bundesministerium für Wissenschaft und Technologie, 1-36.

Harhoff, D. and Hoisl, K. (2007), Institutionalized incentives for ingenuity – Patent value and the German employees' inventions act, in: Research Policy, 36 (8), 1143-1162.

Harhoff, D., Narin, F., Scherer, F. M. and Vopel, K. (1999), Citation frequency and the value of patented inventions, in: The Review of Economics and Statistics, 81 (3), 511-515.

Harhoff, D. and Reitzig, M. (2001), Strategien zur Gewinnmaximierung bei der Anmeldung von Patenten, in: Zeitschrift für Betriebswirtschaft, 71 (5), 509-529.

Harhoff, D. and Reitzig, M. (2004), Determinants of opposition against EPO patent grants – the case of biotechnology and pharmaceuticals, in: International Journal of Industrial Organization, 22 (4), 443-480.

Harhoff, D., Scherer, F. M. and Vopel, K. (1997), Citations, family size, opposition and the value of patent rights, working paper, Ludwig-Maximilians-Universität Munich (LMU), John F. Kennedy School, Harvard University, Zentrum für Europäische Wirtschaftsforschung (ZEW), Mannheim, 1-31.

Harhoff, D., Scherer, F. M. and Vopel, K. (2003a), Citations, family size, opposition and the value of patent rights, in: Research Policy, 32 (8), 1343-1363.

Harhoff, D., Scherer, F. M. and Vopel, K. (2003b), Exploring the tail of patented invention value distributions, in: (Ed.: O. Granstrand) Economics, Law and Intellectual Property – Seeking Strategies for Research and Teaching in a Developing Field, Boston/Dordrecht/London: Kluwer Academic Publisher, 1-34.

Haupt, R., Kloyer, M. and Lange, M. (2007), Patent indicators for the technology life cycle development, in: Research Policy, 36 (3), 387-398.

Hayek, F. A. (1945), The use of knowledge in society, in: American Economic Review, 35 (4), 519-530.

Heiman, B. and Nickerson, J. A. (2002), Towards reconciling transaction cost economics and the knowledge-based view of the firm: The context of interfirm collaborations, in: International Journal of the Economics of Business, 9 (1), 97-116.

Henselmann, K. and Weiler, A. (2007), Empirische Erkenntnisse zu Restwertverläufen in der Unternehmensbewertung, in: Finanzbetrieb, 6, 354-362.

Hertz, D. (1964), Risk analysis in capital investments, in: Harvard Business Review, 42 (1), 95-106.

Herzig, N. (2004), Step up-Modelle im Vergleich, in: (Ed.: H. Schaumburg) Unternehmenskauf im Steuerrecht, 3., überarbeitete und erweiterte Auflage, Stuttgart: Schäffer-Poeschel, 131-149.

Hespos, R. F. and Strassmann, P. A. (1965), Stochastic decision trees for the analysis of investment decisions, in: Management Science, 11 (10), 244-259.

Hicks, D. (1995), Published papers, tacit competencies and corporate management of the public/private character of knowledge, in: Industrial and Corporate Change, 4, 401-424.

Hitz, J.-M. and Kuhner, C. (2000), Erweiterung des U.S.-amerikanischen conceptual framework um Grundsätze Barwertermittlung - Inhalt und Bedeutung des Statement of Financial Accounting Concepts No. 7, in: Die Wirtschaftsprüfung, 53 (18), 889-902.

Hodder, J. E. and Riggs, H. E. (1982), Pitfalls in evaluating risky projects, in: Harvard Business Review, 63 (1), 128-135.

Hoisl, K. (2007), Tracing mobile inventors – The causality between inventor mobility and inventor productivity, in: Research Policy, 36 (5), 619-636.

Holström, B. and Roberts, J. (1998), The boundaries of the firm revisited, in: Journal of Economic Perspectives, 12 (4), 73-94.

Horstman, I., MacDonald, G. M. and Slivinski, A. (1985), Patents as information transfer mechanism: To patent or (maybe) not to patent, in: Journal of Political Economy, 93 (5), 837-858.

Huber, G. P. (1991), Organizational learning: The contributing process and the literatures, in: Organization Science, 2 (1), 88-115.

Itami, H. and Roehl, T. W. (1987), Mobilizing invisible assets, London: Harvard Universitary Press.

Jaffe, A. (2000), The U.S. patent system in transition: Policy innovation and the innovation process, in: Research Policy, 29 (4-5), 531-557.

Kakabadse, N. K., Kouzmin, A. and Kakabadse, A. (2001), From tacit knowledge to knowledge management: Leveraging invisible assets, in: Knowledge and Process Management, 8 (3), 137-154.

Kamien, M. I. and Tauman, Y. (1986), Fee versus royalties and the private value of a patent, in: The Quarterly Journal of Economics, 101 (3), 471-491.

Kamien, M. I. and Tauman, Y. (2002), Patent licensing: The inside story, in: The Manchester School, 70 (1), 7-15.

Kant, I. (1998), Critique of pure reason, Cambridge, New York: Cambridge University Press.

Kasperzak, R. and Nestler, A. (2007), Zur Berücksichtigung des Tax Amortisation Benefit bei der Fair Value-Ermittlung immaterieller Vermögenswerte nach IFRS 3, in: Der Betrieb, 60 (9), 473-478.

Katz, M., L. and Shapiro, C. (1985), On the licensing of innovations, in: RAND Journal of Economics, 16 (4), 504-520.

Katz, M., L. and Shapiro, C. (1986), How to license intangible property, in: The Quarterly Journal of Economics, 101 (3), 567-589.

Katzoff, C. (1984), Knowing How, in: The Southern Journal of Philosophy, 22, 61-69.

Kaufer, E. (1989), The economics of the patent system, Fundamentals of pure and applied economics, 30, London: Harwood Academic Publishers.

Kautt, G. and Hopewell, L. (2000), Modeling the future, in: Journal of Financial Planning, 13 (10), 90-100.

Kessler, D., Meites, T. and Miller, G. (1996), Explaining deviations from the fifty-percent-rule: A multimodal approach to the selection of cases for litigation, in: Journal of Legal Studies, 25 (1), 223-260.

Kieff, S. (2003), The case for registering patents and the law and economics of present patent-obtaining rules, in: Boston College Law Review, 45 (1), 55-124.

Kieso, D. E., Weygandt, J. J. and D., W. T. (2001), Intermediate accounting, New York, Singapore, Toronto: Wiley & Sons.

Kim, Y. J. and Vonortas, N. S. (2004), Determinants of technology licensing, Academy of Management Best Paper Proceedings of the Sixty-Fourth Annual Meeting,

Kingston, W. (1995), Reducing the cost of resolving intellectual property disputes, in: European Journal of Law and Economics, 2 (1), 85-92.

Knoppe, H. (1972), Die Besteuerung der Lizenz- und know-how-Verträge, Köln: Verlag Dr. Otto Schmidt KG.

Kobayashi, B. H. and Parker, J., S. (2000), Civil procedure: General economic analysis, in: (Ed.: B. Bouckaert and G. D. Geest) Encyclopedia of Law and Economics, VII, Northampton: Edward Elgar Publishing Ltd, 1-26.

Kogut, B. and Zander, U. (1992), Knowledge of the firm, combinative capabilities, and the replication of technology, in: Organization Science, 3 (3), 383-397.

Kogut, B. and Zander, U. (1993), Knowledge of the firm and the evolutionary theory of multinational corporation, in: Journal of International Business Studies, 24 (3), 625-645.

Kogut, B. and Zander, U. (1996), What firms do? Coordination, identity, and learning, in: Organization Science, 7 (5), 502-518.

Kopits, G. F. (1976), Intra-firm royalties crossing frontiers and transfer-pricing behaviour, in: The Economic Journal, 86 (December), 791-805.

Kraßer, R. (2004), Patentrecht – Ein Lehr- und Handbuch zum deutschen Patent- und Gebrauchsmusterrecht, Europäischen und Internationalen Patentrecht, München: C.H. Beck.

Kußmaul, H. (2000), Immaterielles Vermögen, in: (Ed.: R. Federmann and A. Gnam) Handbuch der Bilanzierung I-L, 1, Freiburg im Breisgau: Rudolf Haufe Verlag, 1-55.

Langlois, R. N. (1992), Transaction-cost economics in real time, in: Industrial and Corporate Change, 1 (1), 99-127.

Lanjouw, J. O. (1998), Patent Protection in the shadow of infringement: Simulation estimations of patent value, in: The Review of Economic Studies, 65 (4), 671-710.

Lanjouw, J. O. and Lerner, J. (1998), The enforcement of intellectual property rights: A survey of the empirical literature, in: Annales d'économie et de statistique, 49-50, 223-246.

Lanjouw, J. O., Pakes, A. and Putnam, J. D. (1998), How to count patents and value intellectual property: The use of patent renewal and application data, in: The Journal of Industrial Economics, 46 (4), 405-432.

Lanjouw, J. O. and Schankerman, M. (1998), Stylized facts of patent litigation: Value, scope and ownership, working paper, The Toyota Centre - Suntory and Toyota International Centres for Economics and Related Disciplines, London School of Economics and Political Science, 1-39.

Lanjouw, J. O. and Schankerman, M. (2001), Characteristics of patent litigation: A window on competition, in: Rand Journal of Economics, 32 (1), 129-151.

Lanjouw, J. O. and Schankerman, M. (2004), Patent quality and research productivity: Measuring innovation with multiple indicators, in: The Economic Journal, 114 (495), 441-465.

Lazarus, R. S. and McCleary, R. A. (1949), Autonomic discrimination without awareness: An interim report, in: Journal of Personality, 18 (2), 171-181.

Lazarus, R. S. and McCleary, R. A. (1951), Autonomic discrimination without awareness: A study of subception, in: Psychological Review, 58, 113-122.

Leibenstein, H. (1966), Allocative efficiency vs. "X-efficiency", in: The American Economic Review, 56 (3), 392-415.

Leibfried, P. and Fassnacht, A. (2007), Unternehmenserwerb und Kaufpreisallokation, in: Zeitschrift für internationale und kapitalmarktorientierte Rechnungslegung, 1, 48-57.

Lerner, J. (1994), The importance of patent scope: An empirical analysis, in: Rand Journal of Economics, 25 (2), 319-332.

Lev, B. (2003), Remarks in the measurement, valuation, and reporting of intangible assets, in: Economic Policy Review, 9 (3), 17-22.

Levin, R., C., Klevorick, A., K., Nelson, R., R. and Winter, S. G. (1987), Appropriating the returns from industrial research and development, in: Brookings Papers on Economic Activity, 1987 (Special Issue No. 3), 783-831.

Lichtenthaler, U. (2007), The drivers of technology licensing: An industry comparison, in: California Management Review, 49 (4), 67-89.

Liebeskind, J. P. (1996), Knowledge, strategy, and the theory of the firm, in: Strategic Management Journal, 17 (Winter Special Issue), 93-107.

Liebeskind, J. P. (1997), Keeping organizational secrets: Protective institutional mechanisms and their costs, in: Industrial and Corporate Change, 6 (3), 623-663.

Litner, J. (1965), The valuation of risk assets and the selection of risky investments in stock portfolios and capital budgets, in: Review of Economics & Statistics, 47 (1), 13-37.

Loch, C. H. and Bode-Greuel, K. (2001), Evaluating growth options as sources of value for pharmaceutical research projects, in: R&D Management, 31 (2), 231-248.

Locke, J. (1975), An essay concerning human understanding, Oxford: Clarendon Press.

Lotka, A. (1926), The frequency distribution of scientific productivity, in: Journal of the Washington Academy of Sciences, 16, 317-323.

Machlup, F. (1961), Die wirtschaftlichen Grundlagen des Patentrechts, in: Gewerblicher Rechtsschutz und Urheberrecht (GRUR) – Auslands- und internationaler Teil, 8/9, 373-460.

Machlup, F. (1967), Theories of the firm: Marginalist, behavioral, managerial, in: The American Economic Review, 57 (1), 1-33.

Machlup, F. (1980), Knowledge: Its creation, distribution, and economic significance, I: Knowledge and Knowledge Production, Princeton University Press.

Machlup, F. and Penrose, E. (1950), The patent controversy in the nineteenth century, in: The Journal of Economic History, 20 (1), 1-29.

Macho-Stadler, I., Martinez-Giralt, X. and Pérez-Castrillo (1996), The role of information in licensing contract design, in: Research Policy, 25 (1), 43-57.

Madhok, A. (1996), The organization of economic activity: Transaction costs, firm capabilities, and the nature of governance, in: Organization Science, 7 (5), 577-590.

Makarov, M. (2006), The eighth edition of the IPC, in: World Patent Information, 28 (3), 122-126.

Mandich, G. (1948), Venetian patents (1450-1550), in: Journal of the Patent Office Society, (March), 166-224.

Manfroy, W. (2002), Expanding business of licensing, in: (Ed.: R. Goldscheider) Licensing best practices - The LESI guide to strategic issues and contemporary results, New York: John Wiley & Sons, 3-17.

Mansfield, E. (1986), Patents and innovations: An empirical study, in: Management Science, 32 (2), 173-181.

Mansfield, E., Schwartz, M. and Wagner, S. (1981), Imitation costs and patents: An empirical study, in: The Economic Journal, 91 (December), 907-918.

Mard, M. J. (2000), Cost approach to valuing intellectual property, in: Licensing Journal, 20 (7), 27-28.

Mariani, M. and Romanelli, M. (2007), "Stacking" and "picking" inventions: The patenting behavior of European inventors, in: Research Policy, 36 (8), 1128-1142.

Markusen, J. R. (1984), Multinationals, multi-plant economies, and the gains from trade, in: Journal of international economics, 16 (3-4), 205-226.

Marr, R. (1993), Innovationsmanagement, in: (Ed.: W. Wittmann) Enzyklopädie der Betriebswirtschaftslehre Bd. 2 Handwörterbuch der Betriebswirtschaft. Teilband 2. I-Q, Stuttgart: Schäffer Poeschel, 1796-1812.

Martin, X. and Salomon, R. (2003), Tacitness, learning, and international expansion: A study of foreign direct investment in a knowledge-intensive industry, in: Organization Science, 14 (3), 297-311.

Martino, J. P. (1980), Technological forecasting – An overview, in: Management Science, 26 (1), 28-33.

Mayer, R. L. (2003), Das U.S.-Patent - Erwirkung und Durchsetzung unter besonderer Berücksichtigung der Rechtsprechung, Köln: Carl Heymnanns Verlag.

McCarthy, E. (2001), The knowing body, in: (Ed.: G. Csepregi) Sagesse du Corps, Aylmer: Éditions du Scribe, 164-173.

McEvily, S., K., Eisenhardt, K., M. and Prescott, J. E. (2004), The global acquisition, leverage, and protection of technological competencies, in: Strategic Management Journal, 25 (8/9), 713 - 722.

McEvily, S. K. and Chakravarthy, B. (2002), The persistence of knowledge-based advantage: An empirical test for product performance and technological knowledge, in: Strategic Management Journal, 23 (4), 283-305.

Meade, N. and Islam, T. (1998), Technological forecasting – model selection, model stability, and combining models, in: Management Science, 44 (8), 1115-1130.

Menga, P. and Klock, M. (1993), The impact of intangible capital on Tobin's q in the semiconductor industry, in: American Economic Review, 83 (2), 265-269.

Mergers, R. (1992), Uncertainty and the standard of patentability, in: Berkeley Technology Law Journal, 7 (1), 1-70.

Mergers, R. and Nelson, R. R. (1990), On the complex economics of patent scope, in: Columbia Law Review, 90 (4), 839-916.

Merton, R. C. (1973), Theory of rational option pricing, in: Bell Journal of Economics and Management Science, 4 (1), 141-183.

Merwin, M. J. and Warner, C. M. (1996), Techniques for obtaining and analyzing external license agreements, in: (Ed.: R. L. Parr and P. H. Sullivan) Technology licensing – Corporate strategies for maximizing value, New York: John Wiley & Sons, 187-205.

Meurer, M. J. (1989), The settlement of patent litigation, in: Rand Journal of Economics, 20 (1), 77-91.

Meyer, M. (2000), What is special about patent citations? Differences between scientific and patent citations, in: Scientometrics, 49 (1), 93-123.

Michel, J. and Bettels, B. (2001), Patent citation analysis – A closer look at the basic input data from patent search reports, in: Scientometrics, 51 (1), 185-201.

Mindermann, T. (2008), Zur Aktivierung selbst erstellter immaterieller Vermögenswerte nach dem Entwurf des Bilanzrechtsmoderninsierungsgesetzes (BilMoG), in: Die Wirtschaftsprüfung, 07, 273-278.

Minkler, A. P. (1993), Knowledge and internal organization, in: Journal of Economic Behavior & Organization, 21 (1), 17-30.

Moehrle, M. G., Walter, L., Geritz, A. and Müller, S. (2005), Patent-based inventor profiles as a basis for human resource decisions in research and development, in: R&D Management, 35 (5), 513-524.

Møen, J. (2007), R&D spillovers from subsidized firms that fail: Tracing knowledge by following employees across firms, in: Research Policy, 36 (9), 1443-1464.

Monteverde, K. (1995), Technical dialog as an incentive for vertical integration in the semiconductor industry, in: Management Science, 41 (10), 1624-1638.

Monteverde, K. and Teece, D. J. (1982), Supplier switching costs and vertical integration in the automobile industry, in: RAND Journal of Economics, 13 (1), 206-213.

Moran, P. and Ghoshal, S. (1996), Theories of economic organization: The case of realism and balance, in: Academy of Management Review, 21 (1), 58-72.

Moser, U. and Goddar, H. (2007), Grundlagen der Bewertung immaterieller Vermögenswerte am Beispiel patentgeschützter Technologien, in: Finanzbetrieb, 9 (10), 594-609.

Mottner, S. and Johnson, J. P. (2000), Motivations and risks in international licensing: A review and implications for licensing to transitional and emerging economies, in: Journal of World Business, 35 (2), 171-188.

Mudambi, R. and Navarra, P. (2004), Is knowledge power? Knowledge flows, subsidiary power and rent seeking within MNCs, in: Journal of International Business Studies, 35, 385-406.

Muir, I., Brandi-Dohrn, M. and Gruber, S. (2002), European patent law, Oxford: Oxford University Press.

Myers, S. C. (1977), Determinants of corporate borrowing, in: Journal of Financial Economics, 5 (2), 147-175.

Nagaoka, S. and Kwon, U. H. (2006), The incidence of cross-licensing: A theory and new evidence of the firm and contract level determinants, in: Research Policy, 35 (9), 1347-1361.

Nahapiet, J. and Ghoshal, S. (1998), Social capital, intellectual capital, and the organizational advantage, in: Academy of Management Review, 23 (2), 242-266.

Napier, C. and Power, M. (1992), Professional research, lobbying and intangibles: A review essay, in: Accounting and Business Research, 23 (89), 85-95.

Narin, F. (1993), Technology indicators and corporate strategy, in: Review of Business, 14 (3), 19-24.

Narin, F. and Breitzmann, A. (1995), Inventive productivity, in: Research Policy, 24 (1), 50-519.

Narin, F., Hamilton, K. and Dominic, O. (1997), The increasing linkage between U.S. technology and public science, in: Research Policy, 26 (3), 317-330.

Narin, F., Noma, E. and Perry, R. (1987), Patents as indicators of corporate technological strength, in: Research Policy, 16 (2-4), 143-155.

Nawrocki, D. (2001), The problems with Monte Carlo simulation, in: Journal of Financial Planning, 14 (11), 92-106.

Nelson, R., R. (1990), Capitalism as an engine of progress, in: Research Policy, 19, 193-214.

Nelson, R. R. (1959), The simple economics of basic scientific research, in: The Journal of Political Economy, 67 (3), 297-306.

Nelson, R. R. and Winter, S. G. (1982), An evolutionary theory of economic change, Cambridge: The Belknap Press of Harvard University Press.

Nickerson, J. A. (1996), Strategic objectives supported by licensing, in: (Ed.: R. L. Parr and P. H. Sullivan) Technology licensing – Corporate strategies for maximizing value, New York: John Wiley & Sons Inc., 63-82.

Nickerson, J. A. and Zenger, T. R. (2004), A knowledge-based theory of the firm - The problem-solving perspective, in: Organization Science, 15 (6), 617-632.

Nonaka, I. (1991), The knowledge-creating company, in: Harvard Business Review, 69 (6), 96-104.

Nonaka, I. (1994), A dynamic theory of organizational knowledge creation, in: Organization Science, 5 (1), 14-37.

Nonaka, I. and Takeuchi, H. (1995), The knowledge-creating company: How Japanese companies create the dynamics of innovation, New York: Oxford University Press.

OECD (2005), Intellectual property as an economic asset: Key issues in valuation and exploitation – Summary report, Intellectual property as an economic asset: Key issues in valuation and exploitation, Berlin, 1-36.

OECD (2007), Main science and technology indicators, 2007, Paris: Organisation for Economic Cooperation and Development.

Ordover, J. A. (1991), A patent system for both diffusion and exclusion, in: Journal of Economic Perspectives, 5 (1), 43-60.

Osterloh, M., Frost, J. and Frey, B. S. (2002), The dynamics of motivation in new organizational forms, in: International Journal of the Economics of Business, 9 (1), 61-77.

Pakes, A. (1985), On patents, R&D, and the stock market rate of return, in: Journal of Political Economy, 93 (2), 390-409.

Pakes, A. (1986), Patents as options: Some estimates of the value of holding European patent stocks, in: Econometrica, 54 (4), 755-784.

Pakes, A. and Griliches, Z. (1984), Patents and R&D at the firm Level: A first look, in: (Ed.: Z. Griliches) R&D, Patents, and Productivity, Chicago: The University of Chicago Press, 55-72.

Pakes, A. and Schankerman, M. (1984), The rate of obsolescence of patents, research gestation lags, and the private rate of return to research resources, in: (Ed.: Z. Griliches) R&D, Patents, and Productivity, Chicago: The University of Chicago Press, 73-88.

Pakes, A., Simpson, M., Judd, K. and Mansfield, E. (1989), Patent renewal data, in: Brookings Papers on Economic Activity. Microeconomics, 1989, 331-410.

Park, Y. and Park, G. (2004), A new method for technology valuation in monetary value: Procedure and application, in: Technovation, 24 (5), 387-394.

Parr, R. L. (1995), Royalty rates in general and on average, in: The Journal of Technology Transfer, 20 (2), 22-25.

Pavitt, K. (1984), Patent statistics as indicators of innovative activities: Possibilities and problems, in: Scientometrics, 7 (1-2), 77-99.

Penrose, E. T. (1959), The growth of the firm, Oxford: Basil Blackwell.

Perlitz, M. (1980), Compensatory arrangements in international licensing agreements: Effects on market penetration abroad, foreign pricing policy, and conflict areas between licensee and licensor, in: Management International Review, 20 (1), 75-83.

Phillips, D. J. (2002), A genealogical approach to organizational life chances: The parent-progeny transfer among silicon law firms, 1946-1996, in: Administrative Science Quarterly, 47 (3), 474-506.

Pindyck, R. S. (1991), Irreversibility, uncertainty, and investment, in: Journal of Economic Literature, 29 (3), 1110-1148.

Pisano, G. P. (1990), The R&D boundaries of the firm: An empirical analysis, in: Administrative Science Quarterly, 35, 153-176.

Pitkethly, R. H. (2001), Intellectual property strategy in Japanese and UK companies: patent licensing decisions and learning opportunities, in: Research Policy, 30 (3), 425-442.

Plato (1997), Plato complete works, Indianapolis: Hackett Pub. Co. Inc.

Poddar, S. and Sinha, U. B. (2004), On patent licensing in spatial competition, in: The Economic Record, 80 (249), 208-218.

Polanyi, M. (1958), Personal knowledge - Towards a post-critical philosophy, London: Routledge & Kegan Paul.

Polanyi, M. (1966), The tacit dimension, New York: Doubleday & Company.

Poppo, L. and Zenger, T. R. (1998), Testing alternative theories of the firm: Transaction cost, knowledge-based, and measurement explications for make-or-buy decisions in information services, in: Strategic Management Journal, 19 (9), 853-877.

Posner, R. A. (1975), The social costs of monopoly and regulation, in: Journal of Political Economy, 83 (4), 807-827.

Priest, G., L. and Klein, B. (1984), The selection of disputes for litigation, in: The Journal of Legal Studies, 13 (1), 1-55.

Putnam, J. D. (1996), The value of international patent rights, Yale University Press.

Quinn, J. B. (1992), Intelligent Enterprise, New York: The Free Press.

Rabin, M. (1993), Information and the control of productive assets, in: Journal of law, economics and organization, 9 (1), 51-76.

Rafferty, M. (2008), The Bayh-Dole Act and university research and development, in: Research Policy, 37 (1), 29-40.

Rammer, C. (2002), Patente und Marken als Schutzmechanismen für Innovationen, Studien zum deutsche Innovationssystem, Zentrum für Europäische Wirtschaftsforschung, 1-14.

Rampelmann, J. (1996), Classification tools at the EPO, in: World Patent Information, 189 (3), 149-153.

Rampelmann, J. (1999), Classification and the future of the IPC – the EPO view, in: World Patent Information, 21 (3), 149-153.

Ramsay, J. T. (2002), Dreadful drafting: The do's and don'ts of licensing agreements, in: (Ed.: R. Goldscheider) Licensing Best Practices: The LSI Guide to Strategic Issues and Contemporary Realities, New York: John Wiles & Sons, 67-108.

Razgatis, R. (1999), Early-stage technologies – Valuation and pricing, New York: John Wiley and Sons.

Reed, R. and DeFillippi, R. (1990), Causal ambiguity, barriers to imitation, and sustainable competitive advantage, in: Academy of Management Review, 15 (1), 88-102.

Reilly, R. and Schweihs, R. (1998), Valuing intangible assets, New York, Sydney, Toronto: McGraw-Hill.

Reitzig, M. (2004a), Improving patent valuations for management purposes – Validating new indicators by analyzing application rationales, in: Research Policy, 33 (6-7), 939-957.

Reitzig, M. (2004b), The private values of 'thickets' and 'fences': Towards an updated picture of the use of patents across industries, in: Economics of Innovation and New Technology, 13 (5), 457-476.

Reitzig, M., Henkel, J. and Heath, C. (2007), On sharks, trolls, and their patent prey – Unrealistic damage awards and firms' strategies of "being infringed", in: Research Policy, 36 (1), 134-154.

Richter, F. (2001), Simplified discounting rules in binominal models, in: Schmalenbach Business Review, 53 (3), 175-196.

Richter, M. (1990), Die immateriellen Anlagewerte, in: (Ed.: K. v. Wysocki, J.Schulze-Osterloh and J. Hennrichs) Handbuch des Jahresabschlusses in Einzeldarstellungen, 2, Köln: Verlag Dr. Otto Schmidt KG, 3-61.

Rings, R. (2000), Patentbewertung – Methoden und Faktoren zur Wertermittlung technischer Schutzrechte, in: Gewerblicher Rechtsschutz und Urheberrecht (GRUR), 10, 839-848.

Rink, D. R. and Swan, J. E. (1979), Product life cycle research: A literature review, in: Journal of Business Research, 7 (3), 219-242.

Rivette, K., G. and Kline, D. (2000), Discovering new value in intellectual property, in: Harvard Business Review, 78 (1), 54-66.

Roberts, E. B. (2007), Managing invention and innovation, in: Research Technology Management, 50 (1), 35-54.

Robicheck, A. A. and Myers, S. C. (1966), Conceptual problems in the use of risk adjusted discount rates, in: Journal of Finance, 21 (4), 727-730.

Robicheck, A. A. and Myers, S. C. (1968), Valuation under uncertainty: Comment, in: Journal of Financial & Quantitative Analysis, 3 (4), 479-483.

Rockett, K. E. (1990), Choosing the competition and patent licensing, in: RAND Journal of Economics, 21 (1), 161-171.

Rogers, E. M. (1983), Diffusion of innovations, New York: Free Press.

Rosenkopf, L. and Almeida, P. (2003), Overcoming local search through alliances and mobility, in: Management Science, 49 (6), 751-766.

Rost, K., Hölzle, K. and Gemünden, H.-G. (2007), Promotors or champions? Pros and cons of role specialisation for economic process, in: Schmalenbach Business Review, 59, 340-363.

Rostoker, M. D. (1983), A survey of corporate licensing, in: The Journal of Law and Technology, 24 (4), 59-92.

Rubinfeld, D. L. and Maness, R. (2005), The strategic use of patents: Implications for antitrust, in: (Ed.: F. Lévêque and H. Shelanski) Antitrust, Patents and Copyright – EU und U.S. Perspectives, Cheltenham, UK: Edward Elgar, 85-102.

Ryle, G. (1949), The concept of mind, Chicago: University of Chicago Press.

Sanders, B. S., Rossman, J. and Harris, L. J. (1958), The economic impact of patents, in: Patent, Trademark and Copyright Journal of Research and Education, 2 (3), 340-362.

Yli-Renko, H., Autio, E. and Sapienza, H. J. (2001), Social capital, knowledge acquisition, and knowledge exploitation in young technology based firms, in: Strategic Management Journal, 587-613.

Zack, M. H. (1999), Developing a knowledge strategy, in: California Management Review, 41 (3), 125-145.

Zaltman, G., Duncan, R. and Holbeck, J. (1984), Innovations and organizations, Malabar, Florida: Robert E. Krieger.

Zander, U. (1991), Exploiting a technological edge – voluntary and unvoluntary dissemination of technology, Institute of International Business, Stockholm School of Economics, Stockholm.

List of legal documents

University and Small Business Patent Procedures Act (Bayh-Dole Act), 35 U.S.C. § 200-212.

United States Code Title 35 - Patents, enacted by act July 19, 1952, ch. 950, § 1, 66 Stat. 792.

Gesetz über Arbeitnehmererfindungen, (ArbNErfG) vom 25. Juli 1957 zuletzt geändert durch Art. 1 ArbeitnehmererfindungsÄndG vom 18. 1. 2002, BGBl. I, 414.

Drug Price Competition and Patent Term Restoration Act (Hatch-Waxman Act), Public Law 98-417.

Council Regulation (EEC) of 18 June 1992 concerning the creation of a supplementary protection certificate for medicinal products, 1768/92.

Regulation (EC) of the European Parliament and of the council of 23 July 1996 concerning the creation of a supplementary protection certificate for plant protection products, 1610/96.

American Inventors Protection Act, enacted November 29, 1999, as Public Law 106-113 and amended by the Intellectual Property and High Technology Technical Amendments Act of 2002 (Public Law 107-273) enacted November 2, 2002.

Patentgesetz (PatG) in der Fassung der Bekanntmachung vom 16. Dezember 1980 zuletzt geändert durch Art. 2 Abs. 7 GeschmacksmusterreformG vom 12. 3. 2004, BGBl. I S. 390.

IDW Standard S1: Grundsätze zur Durchführung von Unternehmensbewertungen, Institut der Wirtschaftsprüfer, 18.10.2005.

Convention on the grant of European Patents (European Patent Convention), 12th edition, April 2006, published by the European Patent Office.

Gesetz zur Änderung des patentrechtlichen Einspruchsverfahrens und des Patenkostengesetzes, BGBl Jg. 2006 Teil I, Nr. 28, 1318-1322.

Referentenentwurf eines Gesetzes zur Modernisierung des Bilanzrechts, (Bilanzrechtsmodernisierungsgesetz - BilMoG).

ARIPA (1982), Protocol on patents and industrial designs within the framework of the African regional intellectual property organization, http://www.aripo.org/Documents/Protocols/harare_agreement.pdf, 17.10.2006.

DRSC (2002), Deutscher Rechnungslegungs Standard Nr. 12: Immaterielle Vermögenswerte des Anlagevermögens, Bundesanzeiger vom 17.08.2002, Jg. 54, Nr. 197a.

EAPO (1994), Eurasian Patent Convention, 09.09.1994.

EPO (2006b), Convention on the grant of European patents (European Patent Convention), 12th Edition.

FASB (1984), Statement of Financial Accounting Concepts No. 5: Recognition and Measurement in Financial Statements of Business Enterprises, http://www.fasb.org/pdf/con5.pdf, 31.07.2006.

FASB (1985), Statement of Financial Accounting Concepts No. 6: Elements of Financial Statements - a replacement of FASB Concepts Statement No. 3 (incorporating an amendment of FASB Concepts Statement No. 2), http://www.fasb.org/pdf/con6.pdf, 31.07.2006.

FASB (2000), Statement of Financial Accounting Concepts No. 7: Using Cash Flow Information and Present Value in Accounting Measurements, http://www.fasb.org/pdf/con7.pdf, 31.07.2006.

FASB (2001a), Statement of Financial Accounting Standards No. 141: Business Combinations, http://www.fasb.org/pdf/fas141.pdf, 31.07.2006.

FASB (2001b), Statement of Financial Accounting Standards No. 142: Goodwill and Other Intangible Assets, http://www.fasb.org/pdf/fas142.pdf, 31.06.2006.

FASB (2001c), Statement of Financial Accounting Standards No. 144: Accounting for the Impairment or Disposal of Long-Lived Assets, http://www fasb org/pdf/fas144.pdf, 31.07.2006.

Handelsgesetzbuch vom 10. Mai 1897 zuletzt geändert durch Art. 6 Wirtschaftsprüfungsexamens-ReformG vom 1. 12. 2003, BGBl. I S. 2446.

IASB (2004a), International Accounting Standards: Impairment of assets, Official Journal of the European Union International L392/121, 83-119.

IASB (2004b), Accounting Standard 38: Intangible assets, Official Journal of the European Union International L392/121, 120-145.

OAPI (1999), Agreement Revising the Bangui Agreement of March 2, 1977, on the Creation of an African Intellectual Property Organization, http://www.oapi.wipo.net/doc/en/bangui_agreement.pdf, 17.10.2006.

WIPO (1883), Paris Convention for the Protection of Industrial Property, 20.05.1883.

WIPO (1970), Patent Cooperation Treaty (PCT), 19.07.1970.

WIPO (1971), Strasbourg Agreement Concerning the International Patent Classification, 24.03.1971.

List of court decisions

III 58/62, BFH, BStBl. 1966 III, 348-349, 04.03.1966.

III R 75/66, BFH, BStBl. 1970 II, 484-487, 20.02.1970.

Diamond v. Chakrabarty, United States Supreme Court, 447 U.S. 303, 206 USPQ 193, 16.06.1980.

Diamond v. Diehr, United States Supreme Court, 450 U.S. 175, 209 USPQ 1, 03.04.1981.

State Street Bank and Trust v. Signature Financial Group, United States Federal Circuit Court of Appeals, 149 F.3d 1368, 23.07.1998.

MIX
Papier aus verantwortungsvollen Quellen
Paper from responsible sources
FSC® C105338

If you have any concerns about our products,
you can contact us on
ProductSafety@springernature.com

In case Publisher is established outside the EU,
the EU authorized representative is:
Springer Nature Customer Service Center GmbH
Europaplatz 3, 69115 Heidelberg, Germany

Printed by Libri Plureos GmbH
in Hamburg, Germany